Memory as Life, Life as Memory:
The Mystery of Memory

William E. Marsh

authorHOUSE®

AuthorHouse™
1663 Liberty Drive
Bloomington, IN 47403
www.authorhouse.com
Phone: 1 (800) 839-8640

Published by AuthorHouse 09/02/2016

ISBN: 978-1-5246-2641-9 (sc)
ISBN: 978-1-5246-2640-2 (e)

Print information available on the last page.

This book is printed on acid-free paper.

CONTENTS

INTRODUCTION: REMEMBERING AS LIFE

Every Christmas Eve when I was growing up, my mom, dad, and three siblings attended a gathering of our extended family, the aunts, uncles, and cousins who were connected to my mother's side of the family. Year after year we gathered at my grandmother and grandfather's home, the same house where my mother and her four sisters grew up. After Grandma died and Grandpa went to live with Mom's youngest sister, single and recently moved back into the area, we began to rotate venues between the homes of the four daughters who still lived on the West Coast.

After we ate dinner (almost always a roast) and dessert (*always* a concoction called "graham cracker roll"), the women cleaned up the kitchen, and Santa Claus (whom, we later learned, was actually Grandpa stepping outside, knocking on the door, and yelling, "Ho, ho, ho") had come, we gathered around Grandpa in the living room. Before him was a large red candle set in a gold stand. As we all laid our hands on another's shoulder, forming an unbroken link from Grandpa to the people on the periphery of the circle,

Grandpa, a lifelong Catholic, did the sign of the cross, and prayed.

"In the name of the Father and of the Son and of the Holy Ghost," he began, "we thank you, Lord, for this year and all its blessings. We think of those who are no longer with us, we think of those yet to come, and we look forward to this time, this fortnight next year, when we will gather again. In the name of the Father and of the Son and of the Holy Ghost, amen."

A simple ceremony, a simple prayer, yet a ceremony and prayer that, for me, my siblings, and our many cousins, overflow with reminiscence and memory. Why did we do this, year after year, year after year of kids being born, kids growing up, kids going off to college, kids getting married, and kids having kids of their own? We did it to remember. We did it to remember who we are, what we have, where we have been, and where we are going. We did it to remind ourselves of the bonds that held us together, the familial hopes we shared, the common dreams we held. And we did it to prepare ourselves for what would come. Although we did not know, on that night, what would happen next, be it the following morning or the following year, we knew that we would go through it together. We knew we would remember each other.

We remembered to affirm the worth and meaning of ourselves and our lives.[1]

---

1 On the other hand, we note that sometimes memories remember the worst of our familial lives, too. See Heidi B. Neumark, *Hidden Inheritance: Family Secrets, Memory, and Faith* (Nashville: Abingdon, 2015).

Memory makes us human. Without memory, we have no starting point, no beginning, no foundation, no end. Without memory, we have no direction forward, nor do we have a way to look back. Without memory, we're trapped in a stasis, an endless and unbridgeable stasis, a limbo that is neither present nor past, a limbo in which future cannot exist. We live in a vast and undifferentiated moment, a space-time experience ironically devoid of both.

In short, without memory, we probably would not know who, or what, we are. Participating in my family's Christmas Eve tradition year after year for over twenty years (we stopped after Grandpa was gone) reminded me of my roots, my traditions, my heritage. It also helped me, usually without me consciously knowing it, cast a vision for my future, to sketch out a framework within which I could consider what I might do with the next phase of my life. It helped me figure how I might engage the options then before me. In a way that I probably did not realize at the time, my memory of Christmas Eve enabled me to come to grips with the unpredictability and contingency of my existence. It gave me a piece, a piece of emotion, a piece of place which I considered unshakably reliable, a point from which I could always move forward.[2]

All of us can point to various memories, good and bad, that have shaped, framed, or molded our lives. For better or worse, our memories make us who we are. Whether

---

2 As we shall see, however, there are some people who, due to accidents or other mishaps, cease to remember, but who nonetheless know, in some way, they exist. See Rodrigo Quian Quiroga, *Borges and Memory* (Cambridge, Massachusetts: MIT, 2012), 54-55.

they bring happiness or wreak havoc and destruction, they leave their mark. Whether we are conscious of it or not, our memories shape us. Even if we do everything we can to forget them, we build, in almost inexorable fashion, our lives upon them. We cannot escape our memory.

This book is about memory, the power of memory, the weight of memory, the presence of memory. It's about how memory works, emotionally, physiologically, and culturally, and it's about how memory moves and influences us, every moment of every day. Most of all, however, it's about how memory points us to some questions that, try as we might, we cannot definitively elude altogether, questions that force us to confront the very essence of existence. Suppose that no one, no one at all, remembered us? What would the world be like if nothing and no one, absolutely no one, remembered it? Can we live in a universe of memory but a universe that, beyond its lifespan, is itself not remembered? How would we see life if we knew that life itself is not remembered?

Most importantly, what about memory and the person, the very *big* person who, though many of us may want to think or suppose otherwise, is always there: God? For whether we love God or hate and despise him, we're hard pressed to separate him and memory.

Why? By its very nature, memory is metaphysical.[3] It speaks of things we cannot always grasp or understand, things that are there but not, things that seem to dance, gossamer like, on the edge of what we can picture, imagine, or know. Memory makes us think about what we cannot see, but things which we believe are there. Twisting itself around

---

[3] When we say metaphysical, we refer to the realm beyond that which we can normally perceive with our five senses.

our heart, burrowing into our soul, and penetrating every fiber of our days, memory stretches us, stretches us into ethereality, forcing us to ponder the purpose of sentience and to think about how complex we, and life, can be. Is there more to us, memory makes us ask, than what we now see? Is there more to life than what we can now know?

It's hard to think about memory without thinking about God. Indeed, in compelling the thought of God, memory takes us to the deepest meaning of real, the precipice of voice, form, and truth. It makes us wonder about the connections and linkages between the things of this life and the things in the life beyond it. Memory makes us think of that massive and impenetrable realm of presence in which, as the apostle Paul (quoting the Greek writer Aratus) once put it, "We live and breathe and have our being" (Acts 17:25), that vast ambit of vexing and unyielding existential uncertainty daily engulfing us all. Or as the Amboy Dukes song describes it, "The What."[4]

Seemingly infinite and otherworldly, yet very much in the present moment, memory makes us contemplate the divine and eternal, the ineffable, beingness and being. Its mysterious and frustrating mix of transience and ubiquity causes us to wonder: if memory and remembering end with this world, what is life really all about?

How we look at memory determines how we look at the deepest questions of human existence.

Let the journey begin.

---

4 Amboy Dukes, "Journey to the Center of the Mind," in *Journey to the Center of the Mind*, Mainstream Records, 1968.

WHY MUST WE REMEMBER?

Memorial Day, 2013. Alone with her two year old son, Jessica Mitford moves quietly through the cemetery. Arlington Cemetery, which at 624 acres is one of America's largest, is a study in valor and pain, a portrait of bravery, solace, and privation, the nation's most revered place for the final earthly repose of those who have served in the five branches of America's military. For many, it is sacred ground, a hallowed site, one on which those who visit it tread with enormous respect and care.

On this Memorial Day of 2013, Ms. Mitford had come to visit the grave of her husband, killed in Afghanistan in 2012. She held up her son, a two year old boy named Evan, and talked to him about his father, the father he will, heartbreakingly, never know. She wanted Evan to know about his father. She wanted him to be aware of who his father was and what his father did. She wanted to tell him that although his father was no longer with them, he would have given anything to be here and watch Evan grow up.

Ms. Mitford wanted Evan to remember his father. She wanted Evan to remember that were it not for his father he would not be here, that who he was today, and who he would become tomorrow are inseparably linked to this man at whose grave they now sit. She wanted Evan to internalize the memory of a person who, though he would never meet him, is the person who would be one of the foundational determinants in creating the man he will one day be. She wanted Evan to know that his memory of his father would be—should be—central to his future existence. Don't forget your father, she told him.[5]

On the one hand, memory is a beginning. It's a starting point, the clarion and herald of something new. Memory announces closure, but it also announces opening and change. Although it seals the doors of what has passed, it also presents possibilities of future to come. Memory pushes doors open, memory creates new windows to look through. Memory tells us that no matter what had filled it in times past, life will continue to move on. Memory reminds us that life's rhythms and patterns will continue to tumble and flow, will continue to ripple across the oceans of our experience. Existence is never over; life's riddles, mysteries, adventures, and intrigues will in no way end. There is more, much more. Memory is the steady rustling of life's promise.

Indeed. On the other hand, memory is an end. It commemorates closing and finality, marks sum and conclusion. It speaks of people, places, events, and things that, although they once dappled a person's life experience, may now do so no longer. Memory represents what is gone, that which, in a peculiarly unique way, will never return or happen in quite the same way again. Though its images

---

[5] Ms. Mitford's photograph appears on the front page of the May 28, 2013, issue of the *New York Times*.

remain, what these images expressed is, in a singularly precise way, gone. It will never again be *exactly* what it was.[6]

Whatever the memory, good, bad, or indifferent, we use it. We use it to step ahead, and we use it to step back. With memory, we create our way forward, define and structure our path. What we remember, in all its fullness, forms our basis for going forth. Our memory guides, centers, and enables our subsequent life trajectory. It tells us what we had and where we have been; it is the ground on which we think about our past while we project our future. Memory is the fulcrum with which we balance all that has passed with all that comes next, the nexus of space and time out of which we form and develop our dreams, aspirations, and visions for the days and years to come. It sets the stage, it shapes the platform.

As actress Reese Witherspoon, playing author Cheryl Strayed in the movie version of Strayed's book, *Wild,* Strayed's moving account of her solo backpacking trip on the Pacific Crest Trail, remarks at one point, "What if all the things I did were what got me here?" Like an advertisement for the British literary magazine *Granta's* 2015 issue about memory, "We Are What We Remember," Witherspoon's observation underscores a central truth about memory: in more ways than we can imagine, memory makes us. Indeed, memory *is* us.[7]

---

6 Henri Bergson, *Matter and Memory* (Mansfield Centre, Connecticut: Martino, 2011), viiiff.

7 See *Wild*, Pacific Standard River Road Entertainment, 2014. Notice of the issue of *Granta* in question appeared in the January 23, 2015, issue of the *London Review of Books.*

So it is. Memory is a tangle, the tangle of days and months and years into which we set our experiences when we move beyond them, when we may no longer want, need, or require them. Memory looks back as much as it looks forward. It describes, and it circumscribes. Memory is the soil, the framework. Memory is destiny, and memory is end. We are always working out of our memory.

Memory creates a "historical sense" of "continuity" in our life. It is a "durationless instant" which enables us to establish our place in the world. It's inevitable. We cannot avoid memory, nor can we dismiss it. Whether we want it to or not, memory happens. We can't live without memory.[8]

Nor, without memory, can we die. As his first wife, Linda Eastman, was taking her final breaths, falling helplessly into the final darkness of terminal cancer, former Beatle Paul McCartney whispered to her, "Think of an Appaloosa stallion, white and strong, galloping over the hills." As Eastman faded away, McCartney gave her an image, an image long embedded in her memory, an image that he hoped would give her a reason to let go, a reason to step into her mortal end without fear or regret.[9]

---

8 Roger Kennedy, "Memory and the Unconscious" in Susannah Radstone and Bill Schwarz, eds., *Memory: Histories, Theories, Debates* (New York: Fordham University, 2010), 197; Augustine, *Confessions* (Middlesex, England: Penguin, 1961), XI. See also *Matter and Memory,* 67ff. In addition, see Plato's *Theaetus,* in which he explores whether perception, the basis of memory, is knowledge (Plato, *The Theaetetus of Plato,* trans. M. J. Levett (Indianapolis: Hackett, 1990).

9 Although a degree of controversy has attended Linda Goodman's death in 1998, the most credible observers believe that she passed away on the McCartney family ranch outside of Tucson,

Memory provides a reason to live, and memory furnishes a reason to die. If we do not have memory of a past, we likely will not have a reason to think about a future. We may not know who we are, why we are here, or where we are supposed to go now. We will live, and we will die, but we may never know why. We may not be able to say, as did Leo Tolstoy's character Ivan Ilych upon his passing, "Death is finished!" Absent a past, we have nothing to end.[10]

If we do not remember, how can we really die?[11]

Some decades ago, researchers of memory identified a person, a person they referred to as, in order to protect his privacy, H.M. In an effort to alleviate H.M.'s severe epileptic seizures, a team of surgeons removed his hippocampus, located in the lower portion of the brain. The operation succeeded: H.M. never had a seizure again. Unfortunately, H.M. would never experience memory again, either. He woke from anesthesia to find that, tragically, he had literally lost his memory. He had no memory, neither short nor long term. He was at, as it were, ground zero. Not knowing what neurosurgeons now know about the role of the hippocampus in memory, H.M.'s surgeons, in removing

---

Arizona, Paul holding her in his arms. See reports in *rollingstone.com, People.com,* and *Ask.com.*

10 Leo Tolstoy, *The Death of Ivan Ilych and Other Stories,* trans. Aylmer Maude and J. D. Duff (New York: New American Library, 1960), 156.

11 It almost goes without saying that this is a question that many relatives of Alzheimer's victims ask routinely. See John Swinton, *Dementia: Living in the Memories of God* (Grand Rapids, Michigan: William B. Eerdmans, 2015), reviewed by Peter Kevern in *Theology Today,* July 2015.

H.M.'s hippocampus, inadvertently took away his memory. Nothing seemed to be left.[12]

As time passed, it seemed that although H.M. began to recall some memories of his life before the surgery, he could not remember any new ones. As he put it, "Every day is by itself." Although various therapists tried to teach him how to do some of the basics of daily living, such as tying his shoe or brushing his teeth, H.M. had great difficulty in remembering how to do them the next day. He also had difficulty in remembering people from day to day. After some years, he appeared to recognize his wife for more than one day at a time, but even this recognition seemed fragile, threatening to vanish any moment.[13]

Unlike the people in rock group Jethro Tull's song *Living in the Past,* people who, while others wail and stew about what might yet come, instead cannot give up what is long

---

[12] So Alison Winter, *Memory: Fragments of a Modern History* (Chicago: University Of Chicago, 2012), 189. Other commentators, however, believe that although H.M. could not retain his old memories, he could form new ones. See Steven Rose, "Memories are Made of This," in *Histories,* 200, 206; and *Borges and Memory,* 36ff. Of note is that today we know H.M. as one Henry Molaison. See Suzanne Corkin, *Permanent Present Tense: The Unforgettable Life of the Amnesic Patient, H.M.* (New York: Basic, 2013). In addition, consider the recently published *Patient H.M.: A Story of Memory, Madness and Family Secrets* by Luke Dittrich (New York: Random House, 2016).

[13] *Borges and Memory,* 51ff.; *Memory: Histories, ibid.* For a poignant novelistic approach to the loss of short term memory, see Yoko Ogawa's *The Housekeeper and the Professor* (New York: Picador, 2009).

past and forever absent, H.M. had no past to remember. His life had vanished, his days gone.[14]

Yet all observations indicated that H.M. was happy and enjoyed being alive. He came to like gardening, as well as sitting on his front porch and greeting his visitors. He appeared to die a satisfied person. (Whether he *knew* he was satisfied is of course another question.) Did being deprived of memory therefore mean that H.M. did not have a life in the sense that the rest of us do? Did his inability to remember his life mean that H.M.'s life was in vain?

It doesn't appear so. Memory or not, H.M. led a life that, for him, seemed to be of intrinsic value. His lack of memory did not seem to undermine his sense of existence. He knew that he was living a life. He knew that he should eat, he knew that he should smile, he knew that he should sleep. Even though he could remember very little in terms of practical function, he was cognizant of his existence. H.M. was not sorry that he had lived. He remembered enough.[15]

And it was these slivers of memory that sustained him.

Sadly, another subject, named P.B., whose hippocampus was also removed, and who, like H.M., was left with no memory, was not so fortunate. Unlike H.M., despite everything researchers did for him to try to undo the

---

14 "Living in the Past," written by Jethro Tull, from the album *Stand Up*, Island Record, 1969.

15 *Memory: Histories, ibid.* In similar fashion, Haruki Murakami's novel, *Kafka on the Shore* (New York: Vintage, 2006), presents the story of the relationship between a bright but spiritually alienated boy, and a man, who, after an unexplainable mystical encounter in his youth, had lost the capacity to read and write. Even if he could remember, he no longer knew *how* to remember. He had memory, but he did not.

damage, including psychoanalysis and barbiturates, P.B. never recovered. He lived in a fog, a seemingly impenetrable miasma of loss and absence. The day he died, researchers wondered whether he even knew that he had.[16]

Is this really possible? Some years ago, my family and I kept a few rabbits as pets. Generally fun and lovable (except for one who, in a case of a name not fitting the one to whom it is attached, we called Angel, for she was anything but angelic!), but rather messy, they carried on for several years in our house, giving us many moments of joy and pleasure. One day, however, one of the males, Joe by name, began to tilt his head to one side. When we realized that he could not do otherwise, we took him to the vet.

The vet told us that Joe had developed an inner ear infection and, sadly, would need to deal with a tilted head for the remainder of his days (which, as it turned out, were mercifully not much longer). He would never again live and hop with a "straight" head.

Yet Joe continued to do what rabbits do. He ate, he slept, he perked up when we approached his cage, he snuggled and, as best he could, he hopped. He knew he was here, he sensed that he should and could do certain things and, we liked to think, he knew, in his own way, there was a world.[17]

---

[16] *Memory, Fragments,* 88-89.

[17] This of course raises numerous issues regarding animal consciousness. While current research seems to indicate that animals do not possess the detached self-awareness which humans enjoy, it is also concluding that many of them, primarily chimpanzees, are on the other hand very much able to formulate plans for the future. They seem to be at least aware of the passage of time and that they are living in a "space." See Frans de Waal, *The Bonobo and the Atheist: In Search of Humanism Among the*

Even though, phylogenetically speaking, Joe was far below human beings, he possessed memory. He remembered he was here, he remembered he wanted to live. Can we say that Joe was simply aware without remembering? Not really: if he had not remembered from day to day that he was here, we might question whether he would have continued to act as though he were. Though self-awareness is of course its own experience, it cannot occur without memory.[18]

So it was for H.M. Even if he did not remember meeting a person seconds after meeting her, he remembered and knew he was alive and "here" (wherever, in his mind, "here" was) in the world, whatever he conceived or perceived this world to be. Ironically, he remembered, but he did not, and tragically, though he was aware, he was not. He was, as one researcher put it, a memory "unattached" to a center.[19]

And so it is for us. Clearly, it doesn't take much memory to live (consider an earthworm), but it does take some.[20] It is here that we must ask: where does memory, that most basic and fundamental dimension of all living things (including, in a funny sort of way, plants[21]), come from? From where

---

Primates (New York: W. W. Norton & Co., 2013); and Stephen Fleming, "Are Chimpanzees Self-Aware?" in *Psychology Today*, November 16, 2012.

18 On this, see *Anne Whitehead,* Memory (London: Routledge, 2009), 51.

19 See *Borges and Memory,* and *Memory: Histories, ibid.*

20 For memory in earthworms, see Tal Shomrat and Michael Levin, "An automated training paradigm reveals long-term memory in planaria and its persistence through head regeneration" in *Journal of Experimental Biology,* July 2013.

21 See Gareth Cook, "Do Plants Think?" in *Scientific American,* June 2012.

does this mechanism of remembering come? And how conscious are living beings of it? Most importantly, outside of building our future upon our past, why do we need our memory?

Let's break this question apart. One, as we have seen, envisioning the physiological need for memory is easy. For instance, if a creature did not remember to eat, it would die. Or if we human beings did not remember how to talk (we refer here to actually forgetting how to talk rather than a physical condition like autism that sometimes prevents a person from learning how to speak), we would have difficulty communicating with our fellow creatures and beings.

Two, it's quite another matter, however, to envision the moral need for memory. Why do we live and die as creatures who remember? Why, beyond physiological necessity, are we creatures of memory?[22]

---

[22] Answers to this question are legion. They range from various religious perspectives that hold that God or some gods made humanity to live and be, to existentialism and its philosophical companions, which proclaim that there is in fact no reason that humans should be here at all. For the former, just to name a few, see the creation accounts in Genesis 1 and 2; the Babylonian story of *Enuma Elish* in Alexander Heidel, *The Babylonian Genesis* (Chicago: University of Chicago, 1942); and the "Akkadian Creation Epic," trans. by E. A. Spiser, in James Pritchard, editor, *Ancient Near Eastern Texts Relating to the Old Testament* (Princeton: Princeton University, 1969). For the latter, see, again, to name a few, the writings of Jean Paul Sartre who, in his *Being and Nothingness* (trans. Hazel E. Barnes (New York: Washington Square, 1966)), claimed that, "Man is a useless passion," and German philosopher Martin Heidegger, who in his *Being and Time*, (trans. Joan Stambaugh (Albany, New York: State University of New York, 1996)), suggested that people are

Vexingly enough, we must realize that if we are to understand ourselves as remembering beings who are remembered, we must conclude that we have purpose. We must acknowledge that there is a reason why we remember, and there is a reason why we are remembered. If we are to view ourselves and our memory as meaningful, we must therefore admit that our origins are those of intention. We are supposed to be here. There is a reason why we exist. And this affirmation of point is not the ostensible inevitability of random oscillations in a quantum field or the warping of gravity, space, and time, but rather the fruit of a nexus of personality, intelligence, and reason. Life, memory, and remembering simply do not "pop" into existence. Life, memory, and remembering must precede them. If we contend that we remember for more than mere survival, and we all do, we must thus realize that we are the products of a being who, in remembering us, proceeded to bring us, in some fashion, into existence. We are the result of a coalescence of memory, purpose, and intentionality of transcendent dimension. We are creatures who have been remembered and, unless whoever remembered us has walked away, in deistic fashion,[23] from his creation, creatures

---

simply "thrown" into the world without plan or explanation. All they can do is live—and wonder why they do.

23 See, among others, Lawrence Krauss, *A Universe from Nothing: Why There is Something Rather than Nothing* (New York: Atria, 2012); Stephen Hawking, *The Grand Design* (New York: Bantam, 2012); and Lisa Randall, *Dark Matter and the Dinosaurs* (New York: HarperCollins, 2015).

who, as long as we live—and die—continue, in a singularly transcendent way, to be remembered.[24]

Hence, if we insist that no one is remembering us, we bump into grave contradiction. On the one hand, we contend that we are personal beings who remember. On the other hand, we hold that the cosmos has no meaning and that there is no reason why we are here. This means that we really should have no moral need to remember. What would be the point? Yet we all have and inhabit this moral need to remember. We all want to remember and be remembered in turn. Implicitly or not, we believe we have purpose and a point.[25]

But how we can claim this in a meaningless world?

We cannot not. If we insist that we are mnemonic beings, and we all do, we must admit that we are the result of intentional creation. Memory thus affirms our essential worth. It establishes the fact of moral sensibility in the universe.[26]

---

[24] Deism holds that God created the world and then walked away from it. He never looked at or thought about it again.

[25] In addition, as Christian Smith points out in his *Moral Believing Animals* (Oxford: Oxford University, 2003), p. 40-61, we are moral and "believing" creatures as well.

[26] A clever take on this question is found in the 2015 play "D Deb Debbie Deborah." Focused on who she is and why she is here, the lead actor at one point asks, suppose that, "somebody just dreamed me up, and that one day they'll wake up and I'll be gone like they just imagined me?" See *D Deb Debbie Deborah* by Jerry Lieblich, 2015. For yet another view, see the 2010 movie *Inception,* an intriguing look at how people construct their perceptions of their worlds, leaving the viewer unsure as to which world is real and which is a dream (Warner Brothers).

In the autumn of 1969, the British band rock Pink Floyd, who built its musical reputation by producing innovative, what some might say *avant-garde*, and highly surreal music, released an album, *Ummagumma.* Its cover presented the band's members lined up in various poses: the one in front was seated in a chair; the next one was sitting on the grass; the next one was standing up, gazing at the sky; the fourth was doing a partial headstand. Behind the seated band member was another photograph. It was arranged exactly like the first, but the band members had changed places. The one once seated in a chair is now doing a partial headstand; the one once sitting on the grass is now sitting on the chair, and so on. Photograph followed photograph, each one smaller than its predecessor, each fading ever more deeply into the mirrored chasm of what appeared to be an endless series of photographs. Yet anyone could see that this endlessness had a starting point, that being the very front of the album. We had explanation as to why the photos were there. We knew how this apparent endlessness had begun.[27]

Without memory, however, endlessness or not, we do not know anything. We're simply there—and what is "there"?

So we return to the question embedded in the title of this chapter. Why memory? Why must we remember? Perhaps the best answer to this question is, why not? Not only do we need memory to live, we need it to die. We need memory to define we who we are as moral beings, who we are as conscious and choice making beings today, tomorrow, and every day thereafter. Memory affirms us as personal beings; it underscores our humanness and our

---

[27] Pink Floyd, *Ummagumma* (Capitol Records, 1969).

human limits. It speaks to us of our station and place, reminds us of the truth of our tiny, helpless, yet profoundly worthwhile presence in a vast and opaque cosmos. It tells us of beginning, it talks to us of end. In a universe whose thresholds continually confound our own, memory insists that we cannot exist apart from transcendent omniscience and the absolutely metaphysical.

Embodying existence, winnowing and communicating earthly love and divine transcendence, memory reflects and expresses the activity and presence of the grace essential to the life of the most distant stretches of the universe. Memory enables form, memory establishes shape, meaning, settlement, and presence. We cannot do without it.

Now that we know, in part, why we need memory, it's time to answer a more practical question. And that question is this: what is memory?

WHAT IS THIS THING WE CALL MEMORY?

So what's memory? The easy answer is of course to say that it is remembering. Yet this of course begs another question: what's remembering? And what does it mean to "remember" a memory? And what does it mean to "remember" that we "remember" this memory? And to "remember" that we "remember" that we "remember" remembering it? It seems without end. Consider this first: memory is more than mere recall. We may remember something today, but not tomorrow; or we may remember something from years ago and not remember what we ate for breakfast this morning. As quiz shows like the perennially popular "Jeopardy" remind us, most of us cannot readily "know" what we remember unless we're challenged to "remember" and recall it. Rarely do we "know," in a conscious sense, all that we "remember." Memory is not just what we think we know at any given time. It encompasses things we think and "know" we know as well as things that we do not know we know. It is the known *and* the unknown.

Consider Hillary Clinton, former U.S. Secretary of State, as she is giving a news conference. Before the conference, her handlers advise Mrs. Clinton on what to expect, the questions she might need to answer, and the information she would need at her disposal. Yet when Mrs. Clinton steps up to the podium, it is doubtful that she is at that precise moment fully conscious of everything she had been told. Yet when she is asked a question, she comes up with an answer congruent with what she "knew." She didn't "know" the answer, but she did.

On the flip side of this equation, we realize that there are occasions when even the most ambitious and ostensibly well versed of us fail to remember. Perhaps one of the most salient examples of this is the recent public debacle of one-time presidential candidate Rick Perry. When asked, during the 2012 presidential campaign, which three federal departments he would eliminate if he were elected to the presidency, Perry could not remember all three. To his great embarrassment, he could only say two. Yet it is very likely that were Perry asked this question at another time, he would be able to cite all three. Unfortunately for him, although he "knew" and remembered the information, it appeared that, at the point, he did not.[28]

That's why memory is so complicated. Like singer Adele's characterization of a friend's past as "a movie," something

---

[28] See the video on You Tube: www.youtube.com/watch?v=kTNjhcyx7dM. In addition, consider the Riken-MIT Center for Neural Circuit Genetics at the Massachusetts Institute of Technology's research finding that, given proper circumstances, a scientist can create a "false memory," that is, a memory of something that never really happened. See the *New York Times,* July 26, 2013.

he experienced when they were both young, something that is here in mind only, so is memory. It's here, but not; there, but not.[29] Although we remember in images, be they of thoughts, words, people, events, and deeds, we do not "see" them as we do a butterfly in a garden. We do not physically witness our memories. Yet we have them. And we know we do (at least some of them). Even those who have been given remarkable gifts of synesthesia (the ability to set out and categorize and recall, in systematic fashion, all that one remembers about a given thing), do not "see" their memories outside of themselves. They, too, "see" them only in their minds. But like all of us, they know, in some way, they have them.[30]

As neurologists see it, although memory is recall—of all kinds—it is vastly more than perfunctory recollection and retrieval. Memory is object, and memory is experience. It involves the totality of the human person. Memory takes many and varied parts of our mind and physicality and weaves them together into an organic system, a highly flexible and malleable organic system that remembers as much as it forgets, that stores as much as it releases, a system whose output we can rarely assess or predict accurately. Memory is all of us, our outer compass and inner treasure,

---

[29] See "When We Were Young," written by Adele Adkins and Tobias Jesso, Jr., on *25* (Columbia Records, 2015).

[30] See *Borges and Memory,* 42-44, 108-109; Jonathan K. Foster, *Memory: A Very Short Introduction* (New York: Oxford University: 2009); and Arnold H. Modell, *Imagination and the Meaningful Brain* (Cambridge, Massachusetts: MIT, 2006). For an entertaining look at synesthesia and its practical outworking, see the third episode of the made for television series *Sherlock* (PBS, 2010).

a phenomenon, expression, and experience that seems as frighteningly and usefully present as it seems achingly and painfully distant. It tantalizes and teases; surfaces and vanishes; hops, dances, and lilts. It's here and there, yet it's nowhere, too. Rarely, however, is it everywhere.[31]

We can break memory into six broad parts. These include knowledge memory; sensory memory; explicit memory; implicit memory; short term memory; and long term memory.

First, knowledge memory. Knowledge memory is the knowledge, the information and facts, long or short term, that we remember and, significantly, can recall.[32] Broadly speaking, we can call all memory "knowledge" memory. This means that every memory, whether welcomed and appreciated or not, becomes part of our "knowledge," information on which we, consciously or not, base our lives. Knowledge memory is comprehensive and complete. It is all the stored and, sometimes, recollected information we have about our experiences in the world. We do not always know all of it that we have, but we also cannot live without it. As H.M.'s story reminds us, we need our knowledge memory to live.[33]

"Knowledge" memory includes episodic memory and semantic memory (which together are called "declarative

---

[31] I use this phrasing with thanks to the Beatles for their song "Here, There, and Everywhere" from *Revolver*, Capital Records, 1966.

[32] Yet we also understand that, as we have seen and shall see more in turn, not being able to recall a memory does not mean that this memory has vanished altogether.

[33] On the distinction between mind and brain, see John R. Searle, *Mind: A Brief Introduction* (New York: Oxford University, 2004).

memory"); flashbulb memory; cultural memory; body memory; pure memory; and involuntary memory.[34] All of these "memories" indicate some ability on the part of the one who is remembering to recall a type or level of knowledge. Except for involuntary memory (understood in a physiological or systemic sense[35]), they represent the "rememberer's" successful effort to store and recollect a piece of information. Importantly, more often than not, the rememberer remembers this piece of information in relationship to or on the basis of other information which she already possesses. No one begins with British philosopher John Locke's "blank slate."[36]

We will describe these memory types in detail later. Let's now consider the second broad category of memory: sensory memory. All memory begins with sensory memory. Sensory memory represents the immediate information we derive from our senses, that which we take in through hearing, seeing, tasting, touching, or smelling, almost without consciously doing so, in the course of our day. In many ways, sensory memory "is" memory. It is the memory from which knowledge memory comes. Yet not all knowledge memory

---

34 See *Memory: Introduction; Memory, op cit.*; and John Sutton, Celia B. Harris, and Amanda J. Barnier "Memory and Cognition" in *Memory: Histories,* 211. Also, *Imagination and the Meaningful Brain, op cit.*; Mark Rowland, *The New Science of Mind* (Cambridge, Massachusetts: MIT, 2010); and *Mind, op cit.*

35 We distinguish here between the involuntary memory of the heart or lung, memory over which we have little control, and things a person seems to unexpectedly "remember" in the course of her everyday activity.

36 See John Locke, *An Essay Concerning Human Understanding* (New York: Barnes and Noble, 2004), Vol I, Book I, I-II.

becomes sensory. Although we may "sense" a sensation, we do not always turn it into knowledge memory. We do not always remember it.

We turn now to the third broad memory type, explicit memory. Explicit memory is precisely what it implies: things that a person consciously knows she is remembering. This could include the way that a commuter knows that she knows the best route to work, or the way a person knows that she knows how to fix a particular meal. She is acutely aware that she knows how to reach her workplace, she is innately cognizant that she knows how to prepare the meal.

The fourth broad memory type is implicit memory. Implicit memory is what a person does not necessarily know she is remembering but which, unbeknownst to her, daily affects and influences her. This could be the contents of a belief system which a child hears from the day she is born and which, even if she subsequently decides she no longer believes it, nonetheless, whether she knows it or not, continues to shape her. Or it could be a long suppressed memory of a childhood trauma which, whether the one who experienced it knows or not, still influences her.[37]

---

[37] On the former, see T. M. Luhrman, *When God Talks Back* (New York: Knopf, 2012); Colin McGinn, *Inborn Knowledge* (Cambridge, Massachusetts: MIT, 2016); Dan Wakefield, *Returning: A Spiritual Journey* (Boston: Beacon, 1997); and Proverbs 22:4, which reads, "Train up a child in the way she should go and when she is old she will not depart from it." On the latter, see, seminally, Sigmund Freud, *General Psychological Theory* (New York: Macmillan, 1963); *The Interpretation of Dreams,* trans. James Strachey (New York: Basic, 2010); and *Introductory Lectures on Psychoanalysis* (New York: Liverwright, 1989).

Although explicit and implicit memory differ greatly from each other, we need both to live and make sense of our world. Our full flourishing requires our buried past as much as it demands our overt present.

How can we understand the fifth broad type of memory, short term memory? Short term memory is exactly what the word says, memory that only lasts for a short time. Short term memory is a memory that our brain does not retain for significantly longer than it takes for us to experience it. For a fleeting moment, short term memory remembers something. Yet just as quickly, it will never know or remember this something again. It's a memory that is gone forever. Once we experience it, we never experience it again. We "know" it, then we do not. The memory vanishes and, try as we might, we cannot retrieve it. Short term memory can be likened to a "stream of consciousness, our perception of the present," and nothing beyond it. In a way, we do not "even store it [our short term memory] in our brains." It's a "pulse," a "pulse reverberating around closed chains of neurons," as much "here" as it is definitively gone.[38] Dynamic, yet without form or motion, short term memory captures aptly the limits of who we are.[39]

Yet short term memory is more than simple absent mindedness or, as one of my former neighbors put it, "senior moments." Short term memory is something we once remembered distinctly, but now, inexplicably, it seems,

---

38 Marvin Minsky, *Computation: Finite and Infinite Machines* (Englewood Cliffs, New Jersey: Prentice Hall, 1967), cited in Robert C. Berwick and Noam Chomsky, *Why Only Us: Language and Evolution* (Cambridge, Massachusetts: MIT, 2016), 51.

39 *Memory: Introduction,* 27; *Borges and Memory*, 68-69.

do not. For instance, we may read or hear something one day and think, "Ah, how interesting!" then a few moments or days later be unable to recall it. Sometimes these lapses deal with very mundane things (can you remember what you had for dinner three nights ago?), and other times with more significant matters (have you ever forgotten the flight number of a person whom you were supposed to pick up at the airport?).[40]

I suspect that most of us would like for our short term memory to become long term memory. But not always. Many years ago, just after I had obtained my driver's license, I drove myself and some friends to a local drive-in theatre (a rare sight in most parts of the country these days!) to see a movie. This was not an ordinary movie. It was a movie about vampires. And it was frightening. I don't remember the name (no long term memory!), but I still remember the final scene. The movie told the story of a man and woman who found themselves in a world populated with vampires and who, through a great deal of effort, succeeded in eradicating them. As the movie drew to a close and they prepared to step into a house which they deemed totally free of vampires, the

---

[40] For an amusing example of absent mindedness, consider an incident from the life of the great scientist Isaac Newton. According to one of his biographers, Newton was one day riding his horse home, pondering a mathematical puzzle. He eventually decided to dismount and walk, thinking that this might improve his concentration. It did. In fact, it improved Newton's concentration so much that he literally forgot he even had a horse next to him. The horse shook off its bridle and bolted ahead of him to its barn. Newton never knew the horse was gone. See Frank Manuel, *A Portrait of Isaac Newton* (Cambridge, Massachusetts: Harvard, 1968).

man, without looking at the woman, said, "Well, they're all gone. We're safe. Let's go in."

When he turned towards his woman friend, however, the man was not greeted with a normal smile, but with a mouthful of fangs. The woman had secretly been a vampire all along. The movie's final scene is her sinister face, poised to sink huge teeth into the man's neck. It is a scene I remember to this day. I wish I didn't. I wish this scene had registered in my short term memory. But it did not.

We often have no control as to whether we remember something for the short or long term. Our brain shifts and changes rapidly and, despite what some worldviews and religions contend, we cannot direct and superintend everything in it. In addition, what we remember, short or long term, depends on what we already have in our brains. And this, as we shall soon see, is something we cannot always determine.[41]

Now let's look at the sixth broad memory type, long term memory. Long term memory is what it says it is: memories we retain for a long time. Whenever I hear singer Judi Collins sing Joni Mitchell's "Both Sides Now," I cannot help but think back to a time many decades ago when I heard this song, not for the first time, in the days immediately before my college graduation. As my parents and I strolled through the campus one evening, we came

---

41 We think here of a phenomenon such as Scientology. In his *Dianetics* and other writings, L. Ron Hubbard argues that, properly administered, Scientology's programs will enhance intelligence and improve mental clarity, including memory. See L. Ron Hubbard, *Dianetics* (New York: Bridge, 2007); originally published in 1950. See also *Memory: Introduction,* 26ff.

upon a group of my friends arrayed around a boombox, playing this song. Without me trying to, I imprinted this momentary sensory memory into my long term sensory memory. Unconsciously, I made it a memory, a memory now decades old, that impacts me even today. It is a memory that always surfaces when I hear this song.

Similarly, whenever I hear Crosby, Stills, Nash, and Young's song, "Helpless," I cannot help but remember the room, the living room of one of my best friends in high school, where I heard it for the first time. And I remember exactly what I was doing, too. I don't even need to try to summon the memory. It simply irrupts into my consciousness.[42]

A couple of years ago, I listened to a person recount her time at a Beatles concert. So powerful was this experience, so deeply embedded her memory of it that, she said, every time she hears "I Wanna Hold Your Hand," she cannot help but remember her time at the concert. It is forever embedded in her memory, forever sparked, loudly and unbidden, by her hearing of this song. It's a long term memory that will be with her until the day she dies.

---

[42] We should note that we can also call long term memory "involuntary" memory. Here we are not talking about the involuntary memories of human physiology, the memory that keeps our lungs breathing, our hearts beating, and our stomachs digesting. We are rather talking about, to draw a page from Marcel Proust, whose remarkable *In Search of Lost Time* we will examine in more detail later, a memory that somehow comes to us as we live our lives. We do not always know we have it, we do not always know we will experience it. But it comes to us. See Marcel Proust, *In Search of Lost Time,* trans. C. K. Scott Moncrieff (New York: Random House, 1934).

On a more serious note, I think of Stanley Kubrick's *Clockwork Orange.* A difficult movie to watch (and challenging novel to read), *Clockwork Orange* tells the story of a gang of hoodlums who go on a rampage in London and its environs. At one point, they break into a home in the countryside and rape its female occupant while her husband is forced to watch. As they do, they play a song, a silly and nonsensical song about singing in the rain. Later in the movie, as things progress, the husband inadvertently hears the same song. Without wanting or meaning to, he remembers the incident. He remembers the pain, he remembers the anguish. He weeps all over again.[43]

Several years before my father unexpectedly passed away in the autumn of 1983, I played for him pianist Dinu Lipatti's performance of Bach's "Jesus, Joy of Man's Desire." The instant Dad heard the first note, he knew exactly it was. "That's Bach," he exclaimed. So it is that to this day every time I play that particular rendering of Bach's piece, I remember, without trying to, Dad and that time with him. I feel the joy, I feel the pain. I feel my life all over again.

Whether I want to or not, I live the past once more.[44]

Or when I look at a bank of clouds for more than a few seconds, I inevitably flash back to a childhood memory in which I am riding in the backseat of my family's car, looking up at the clouds and wondering what God is doing at this moment in heaven. I cannot help but remember, I cannot help but recall. It is a memory that will be with me forever.

---

43 *A Clockwork Orange,* Warner Bros, 1971. Based on Anthony Burgess's book of the same name (New York: W.W. Norton & Co., 1965).

44 Again, see *Lost Time.*

Even long term memory, however, can be lost. Some of this has to do with years and age; some, unfortunately, has to do with darkness and disease. Consider afflictions such as amnesia, dementia or Alzheimer's disease (recall the case of poor P.B. or H.M.). In these cases, whether they try to or not, people cannot remember the most rudimentary knowledge about themselves or their lives. They appear to have forgotten everything. A friend of ours experienced this rather painfully a number of years ago when her mother, fading away with Alzheimer's, one day told her, "I'm sorry, but I don't think I know who you are." Her mother had forgotten her own daughter.[45]

The other side of this is that mnemonic capacity varies widely. Some of us have photographic memory, but most of us do not. Additionally, as we mentioned at the outset, we never really "know" all that we remember.[46]

---

45 For a recent and particularly heartbreaking look at this type of experience, see Jonathan Kozol, *The Theft of Memory* (New York: Crown, 2015).

46 The writer C. S. Lewis, among others, is reputed to have had a photographic memory. See the biography about him by Alister McGrath (Carol Stream, Illinois: Tyndale, 2012). So is, allegedly, the media and tycoon maven David Geffen. Also, consider people like Kim Peek. Peek had an extraordinary memory. He read dozens of books every day and could recall everything he had read. And he never forgot it. The scope of his mnemonic ability is almost unfathomable. See the *Rain Man,* starring Dustin Hoffman and Tom Cruise, a movie based on Peek's life. People like Peek and another savant, A. R. Luria, have perfected the art of synesthesia, a phenomenon we discussed earlier, the ability to consciously "store" memories in systematic (creating something like a "memory theater," a concept which we will discuss in the

As we noted in regard to explicit and implicit memory, we observe that we need short term and long term memory to live holistically. Although we may wish we remembered everything, we in truth do not. Similarly, we definitely wish for our most memorable moments to remain with us for all of our days.[47]

Now that we have briefly surveyed the six broad categories of memory, let's turn our attention to the specific memory types that we earlier noted comprise knowledge memory. First, episodic memory. We can define episodic memory as the "memory for the [major] events" a person experiences in her life. Episodic memory is the memory of significant moments. It is wide ranging, spanning the breadth of one's years, from the first day of school to the first day of work, from a wedding day to a baby's birth, from the loss of a parent to retirement, and everything in between.[48]

Two, semantic memory. Semantic memory is the memory of facts and concepts. It might be the name of a state capital, the formula for a Euclidean triangle, the altitude of Mount Evans in Colorado, or the workings of mitochondria.[49]

---

next chapter) fashion for later recollection and recall. See *Borges and Memory,* 103-107.

47 On this, consider Jill Price, who could not forget anything, even the worst things that had happened to her. She remembered these things constantly; everything she had experienced, she remembered, literally, all the time. While some may envy this level of memory, Price called it a "burden." *Borges and Memory,* 119-122.

48 *Memory: Introduction*, 36ff.

49 *Ibid.*

Three, flashbulb memory. What's flashbulb memory? A flashbulb memory is the memory of an extraordinarily vivid event which has been indelibly engraved in the rememberer's imagination. We might call flashbulb memory an extraordinary episodic memory. Usually, although not always, this is a memory of a particularly traumatic experience. For those who lived through it, flashbulb memory could be the ambush attack on Pearl Harbor that drew America into World War II. For those who were born later, it might be the assassination of John Fitzgerald Kennedy in November of 1963. For those who were born later still, a flashbulb memory would be the tragedy of September 11, 2001. Another instance of flashbulb memory is the experience of a childhood friend of mine who, when he was nine years old, watched his father come to the breakfast table one Saturday morning, sit down, then drop dead of a heart attack. Yet another is the recollections of mountaineer Jim Wickwire as he watched a fellow mountaineer pass out of this life:

> "After asking me to relay messages to his family and closest friends, Chris [fatally injured] entreated me to help him die with dignity. However, I could think of no way to ease his suffering or speed his death. I asked him whether he wanted his body left in the crevasse or brought out. He said his father could decide. At about nine-thirty, six hours after we fell into the crevasse, Chris conceded, "There's nothing more you can do, Wick. You should go up."

> I told him I loved him and said a tearful good-bye. As I began my ascent, Chris said simply, 'Take care of yourself, Jim.'
>
> "Back on the surface, physically spent, emotionally exhausted, and racked with guilt, I pulled on a parka and collapsed into my half-sleeping-bag and bivouac sack. Lying at the edge of the crevasse, I listened to my friend grow delirious from the searing cold. He talked to himself, moaned, and, at around eleven, sang what sounded like a school song. At 2:00 a.m. I heard him for the last time. Chris Kerrebrock was twenty-five. I was forty."

Wickwire will carry this flashbulb memory for the rest of his life.[50]

Although some researchers believe that in some instances the way people remember flashbulb memories may not always represent precisely what happened, all agree that they are memories that are engraved permanently on an individual psyche. Like Wickwire's poignant recounting and remembrance, they never go away.[51]

Four, body memory. Body memory is what our body "remembers" about how we can best live our lives. For instance, if we are a committed athlete, we train our bodies to respond favorably to whatever challenge we subject it. We train it to "remember" how to perform well. A hurdler's body

---

50 See Wickwire's *Addicted to Danger* (New York: Atria, 1999), 5ff.

51 Felicity Callard and Constantina Papoulias "Affect and Embodiment" in *Memory: Histories,* 253.

"knows" to leap over each oncoming hurdle; a cyclist's legs "knows" how to pump harder when the cyclist is going up a hill; a tennis player's arms "knows" how to use a backhand if a ball comes approaches from her "weak side." In every case, the body "remembers" how to respond in the best way possible.

Body memory is also a reminder of how the body experienced a past memory. To use an example from Marcel Proust (1871-1922), whose name we cited in a previous footnote,

> "Or perhaps, while I was asleep I had returned without the least effort to an earlier stage in my life, now for ever outgrown; and had come under the thrall of one of my childish terrors."[52]

As Proust sees it, sleeping reminds him of the eventful bodily experiences of his past.[53]

More recently, body memory has figured in a number of child abuse cases in which those who had been abused seemed to "feel" past events with no sense of "hindsight or perspective." With additional therapy, however, they were able to connect what their body had felt with what their mind had suppressed for many years. They "remembered" their experience of abuse. Their minds came to recall, vividly, what their bodies had long been remembering.[54]

---

[52] *Lost Time,* "Overture," 4.

[53] *Memory,* 107; *Matter and Memory, op cit.*

[54] Alison Winter, *Memory: Fragments of a Modern History* (Chicago: University Of Chicago, 2012), 189.

Five, cultural memory. Cultural memory is the memory of cultural traditions and beliefs. It is that which people use to bind themselves in nationalistic unity; remind themselves of that out of which they have come; pass on their convictions to their children; or to corporately recall a shared experience. [55] Moreover, as the work of Svetlana Alexievich, recipient of the 2015 Nobel Prize for Literature, indicates, cultural memory is most evident and sustained in people most vulnerable to the events on which it based. It is in the dispossessed that cultural memory remains the most acute and present.[56]

For the Armenians, this would be the memory of the Turkish genocide of 1915. For Jews, it is the memory of the Exodus and Holocaust.[57] For the Native American Lakota,

---

55 *Memory,* 132. In addition to the events listed here, consider the lengthy and oppressive reign of Francisco Franco in Spain during the middle of the twentieth century and the many cultural memories it bequeathed, for better or worse, to that country's people. See *Franco's Crypt: Spanish Culture and Memory since 1936* (New York: Farrar, Straus and Giroux, 2014). Another example, though on a smaller scale, might be, for those who lived through it, the shootings deaths of four unarmed college students on the campus of Kent State University on May 4, 1970. For one account, see http://dept.kent.edu/sociology/lewis/lewihen.htm

56 See Alexievich's recently translated *Secondhand Time: the last of the Soviets,* trans. Bela Shayevich (New York: Random House: 2016), 10, in which one of her interviewees speaks of a "collective memory" of living in Soviet Russia; and her 1997 *Voices from Chernobyl* (Ostozhye).

57 On the Holocaust, see, in particular, the work of writer Primo Levi, whose meditations on his experience of the concentration camp at Auschwitz have done much to sustain the global memory of this horrific event. On this, consult *The Complete Works of*

it is the memory of the Sun Dance. For people who serve in a military force, it is the memory of what they and they comrades accomplished in a particular mission. The list goes on and on.[58]

Is not cultural memory also flashbulb memory? Would not, say, my childhood friend's flashbulb memory of seeing his dad collapse of a heart attack be a cultural memory as well? It would not. Cultural memory points to events of broadly significant form and impact, such as the moments of September 11, 2001, not traumatic events specific to an individual human being and only that human being. Cultural memory's lens casts a much wider span of effect.[59]

Primo Levi, ed. Ann Goldstein (New York: Liveright, 2015), as well as Levi's memoir, *If This is a Man,* trans. Stuart Woolf (New York, Orion, 1947). Consider also the Jewish memory embedded in the feast of the Passover (Exodus 11ff) and International Holocaust Day, commemorated on January 27 of each year.

58 In regard to the Armenian genocide, although to this day the Turkish government insists that it didn't happen, every reputable historian agrees that it did. See Ronald Grigor, *They Can Live in the Desert and Nowhere Else: a History of the Armenian Genocide* (Princeton, New Jersey: Princeton, 2015); and Meline Toumani, *There Was and There Was Not: A Journey Through Hate and Possibility in Turkey, Armenia, and Beyond* (New York: Metropolitan, 2014). On the Sun Dance, see William Stolzman, *The Pipe and Christ* (Chamberlain, South Dakota: Tipi, 1995), and Ron Zeilinger, *Sacred Ground* (Chamberlain, South Dakota: Tipi, 1986).

59 Of course, we could argue in turn that, for instance, Josef Stalin's bitter childhood memories of his father helped create in him the inclinations that led him to become a totalitarian dictator whose actions would result in the deaths of fifty million people. While this may well be true, we should not push such correlations

Six, "pure" memory. Here we return to Bergson. For Bergson, as we observed, memory is inevitable. Regardless of what we do, memory will happen. Memory is therefore "pure." It is a thoroughly natural and essential component of human experience, one that is intrinsic to the human being. Memory is as pure and unaffected and necessary an experience as any a person may have. Memory is "pure" because although it is specific to and reflective of each individual person, it is an experience universal to all. Whoever we are, memory will happen in us. Nothing we do can diminish or halt memory's necessity and inexorable movement in us and our lives.

Memory is thoroughly and wonderfully human.[60]

Seven, procedural memory. What's procedural memory? Think of a child learning to tie her shoelaces, someone learning how to floss her teeth, a person learning the proper way to set utensils around a plate on a table, or a young boy learning to ride a bike for the first time. Often termed non-declarative memory, sometimes called working memory, procedural memory is the memory of tasks and activities which we learn and master to be, in any society, a respectable and reasonable human being. Procedural memory is what we do to live. It is practical and, at times, necessary recall. Whereas we will continue to live if we fail to recall the chemical content of salt ($NaCl_2$), we may not if we forget how to eat or drink. Similarly, although we will certainly go on living if we fail to remember the anniversary of Canada's

---

too far, lest we encounter a host of unresolvable psychological puzzles.

60 Keith Ansell-Pearson, "Bergson on Memory" in *Memory: Histories,* 63; *Memory,* 126-127.

founding (July 1), if we forget how to tie our shoes, we may subject ourselves to embarrassment when we trip over our shoelaces. Procedural memory enables us to live in an orderly (and what this looks like will of course vary from culture to culture) way.[61]

On the other hand, with apologies to *Dear Abby, Ann Landers, Miss Manners,* and the like, we do not need procedural memory to formulate a vision for our lives. We do not need to know how to tie our shoes (the most famous example of someone who either didn't wish to or didn't know how to do this being of course Albert Einstein[62]) in order to decide what we want to do with our time on this planet, or even what to do the next morning. Regardless of whether we put our fork on the left or right of our plate, we will still be able to ponder the direction and meaning of our lives. We will still be able to contemplate deeper things. We will still find ourselves thinking about life's meaning.[63]

---

61 See James M. Henslin, *Sociology: A Down to Earth Approach* (New York: Pearson, 2011), for a discussion of the notion of civilization and its definitional elasticity.

62 See Walter Isaacson, *Einstein: His Life and Universe* (New York: Simon & Schuster, 2008).

63 For a particularly incisive look at this, see Viktor Frankl, *Man's Search for Meaning* (Boston: Beacon, (2006). In addition, consider Josiah Royce's *Philosophy of Loyalty* (New York: Macmillan, 1908), which observes that all people "live for a purpose," and that all people care about "what happens after death" (126-127). For insight into how difficult finding purpose can actually be, see Langdon Gilkey, *Shantung Compound* (New York: Harper and Row, 1966), his account of his time in a Japanese prison camp during World War II.

Yet clearly we benefit from having procedural memory. We profit from knowing how to brush our teeth, get dressed, use an eating utensil, or apply the brakes on a car. A society in which no one had procedural memory would be a society of chaos (indeed, we might wonder whether in the absence of procedural memory a society, classically defined, could even exist at all).

Yet procedural memory consists of more than tasks we learn to function socially. It also encompasses skills that we learn, be they for sports, vocation, or recreation. For instance, learning how to throw a baseball, shoot a basketball, or kick a soccer ball all represent instances of procedural memory.[64] More often than not, these become lifelong skills, abilities which a person remembers for the rest of her life (for as any U.S. president who has thrown professional baseball's opening day pitch knows, although he may not throw the ball accurately, he nonetheless knows how to throw it[65]).

Other examples of procedural memory include the abilities of skilled craftsmen, people like carpenters, electricians, or plumbers, people who know how to perform various specialized operations and procedures required to accomplish a given task. Another is a surgeon who, after years of training, becomes sufficiently proficient in the "tools" of her trade so as to perform a given operation or surgical procedure successfully.

---

64 Of course, as anybody who is not an American knows, most of the world calls soccer "futbol."

65 On this, consider the comedy *Dave,* in which the "president" not only throws the ball, but does so with surprising speed and accuracy. See *Dave,* Warner Bros., 1993.

You may be thinking at this point, however, that procedural memory is coming very close to knowledge memory and body memory. And you'd be correct. Whether it is learning how to fix a faucet in response to a late night emergency call or studying Confucius' *Analects* as prelude to determining one's life destiny, it is still memory. What's the difference?

In truth, procedural, knowledge, and body memory work together. The picture of a mountaineer, trained and ready for the rigors of the altitude, making her way up a peak, moving to what she hopes will be a glorious and memorable vista without any knowledge of how to use ropes, carabineers, or ice axe comes to mind. Regardless of how conditioned or knowledgeable she is, unless she can get to the top safely, she will not be able to enjoy the vista and the scenic wonder it may bequeath her. As climber John Roskelley notes repeatedly in his poignant *Nanda Devi, The Tragic Mountain,* enthusiasm is no substitute for knowledge of climbing if one is to scale a Himalayan peak successfully.[66]

Or consider that although one who studies to become a teacher must learn the knowledge inherent to her field, she must also learn the fundamentals of pedagogy. She must learn how to communicate her knowledge in a meaningful and understandable way. As study after study

[66] John Roskelley, *Nanda Devi, The Tragic Expedition* (Seattle: Mountaineer, 2000). Roskelley tells the heartbreaking story of a group of climbers who set out to scale the peak Nandi Devi in the Himalayas but soon found themselves woefully unprepared for the challenge. One young woman, named Nanda Devi by her father Willie in honor of his deep affection for the mountain, eventually succumbed to the effects of the altitude and, before her father's horrified eyes, died.

has demonstrated, knowledge alone does not make a good teacher. Good communicative technique is essential. One of my teachers in graduate school was incredibly knowledgeable about his subject area, the Hittites. But he didn't know how to communicate it. Three days a week, he stood before us, spewing out from behind his massive beard information without illustration, break, form, or category. He had knowledge memory, he had body memory. But he had absolutely no procedural memory. His lessons were streams of consciousness. We learned nothing.[67]

Similarly, as a friend of mine who is a cardiac surgeon once told me, referring to his medical school experience, "All day, they beat technique into me. It was painful. Then every night I had to go home and memorize pages and pages of information about the way the heart worked. It was a nightmare: one burden to another, day after day, year after year.

"But I suppose I wouldn't be able to do what I'm doing now if I had not gone through all that."

So true. My friend needed knowledge memory on which to base his procedural memory. And he needed procedural memory to give form and practicality to his body memory. We can be thankful that those who teach or who operate on us have been schooled in the "why" as well as the "how," in knowledge as well as procedure, and that in many often indiscernible ways, procedural memory, body memory, and knowledge memory blend together.

---

[67] See, just to name one such study, Parker J. Palmer, *The Courage to Teach* (New York: Jossey-Bass, 2007). In point of information, I note that the Hittites ruled an empire that dominated what is present day Turkey from 1800 to 1200 B.C.

The adventures of a certain cat named Holly bear this out in a near incredible way. A few years ago, Holly and her owners, who lived together in West Palm Beach, Florida, went on vacation in Daytona Beach, several hundred miles away. At some point during their stay in Daytona, Holly slipped away to explore, we are to assume, her version of the wild unknown. Try as they might before they left, her owners could not find her.

Subsequently, deciding that they would never see Holly again, her owners returned to West Palm Beach. Two months and 200 miles later, Holly appeared in a backyard in West Palm Beach, about a mile from her owners' house. She was bedraggled and emaciated, but otherwise in sound health. Today, Holly is fully recovered, safe in the hands of her original owners, who are delighted to have her back. She remembered her procedural memory, how to sniff, hunt, and eat; she remembered her knowledge memory, the warm and fuzzy feeling she had when she was at home with her owners; and she remembered her body memory. Her knowledge memory motivated her to return home, and her body and procedural memory enabled her to get there.

(How, you may ask, did her owners know it was Holly? Happily, some years before, Holly's owners had a microchip implanted in her to aid in identification should she ever "misplace" herself. When the veterinarian to whom Holly's finders took her found the implanted chip, the rest was easy.)

How did Holly do it? Behavioral scientists have no ready explanation. As one put it, "I have no data for this." Nonetheless, speculation has been rampant, most of it centering on a cat's ability to detect scents over long distances, its innate gyroscopes, or its, dare we say, memory for familiar places, a memory so powerful that it "draws" the cat as it proceeds towards its destination.[68]

The bigger point here is that whether memory is knowledge, body, or procedural, it is in the end the combined weight and effects of all three that create the formative memories we have, hold, and use as a basis for living. Like Holly, a human knows, whether by being taught or through observation, to do certain things, a particular set of fundamental functions, to survive. Also like Holly, a human will in turn fold these "procedural" understandings into her body and knowledge memory so that as she continues on her way, she will be able to grapple with life successfully.[69]

As we move forward, we must keep all of this in mind. Memories rise out of experience, yes, but we "experience" and interpret experience on the basis of what we have learned about life to that point. We do so by using, as one writer puts it, "inferences borne of perception" to understand our reality.[70]

Furthermore, as we observed earlier, knowing how to operate a vacuum cleaner will probably not change our lives in the way that will a discerning book, memorable adventure, or exceptional piece of art or music. As the case of H.M. demonstrates so aptly, we need knowledge memory, deep, broad, and rich knowledge memory, to explore and

---

68 See Katherine Schulten, "The Mystery of the 200 Mile Cat Journey" *New York Times,* January 23, 2013.

69 This of course raises the issue of feral children, those who are not necessarily raised by human beings, and how some, when they are brought to "civilization," learn to become relatively human once more. Though this is beyond the scope of our meditation, see, again, *Sociology, op cit.*

70 *Imagination and the Meaningful Brain, op cit.*

grasp the nature of our beingness and existence most fully. Memory's most significant dimension is the way it enables us to grasp the fundamental meaning of our times and the delicate orb of physical and metaphysical that surrounds them. Memory shows us how to live each day with joy, purpose, and meaning. And although we need procedural and body memory to do this most successfully, we need knowledge memory first.

This is why this book will focus on knowledge memory. What we know, our knowledge memory, becomes the basis for *how* we know, how we conduct and understand ourselves in this reality. It is as much a start as it is an end. Knowledge memory (which we will henceforth call simply "memory"), grounds and frames everything.

However, we should note that although memory (knowledge memory) changes, it in fact remains the same. Many years ago, I watched a friend of mine named Kate talk to a group of high school students who were on a work trip in an Indian reservation in South Dakota. Enjoy this time, she encouraged, but take time to find its larger meaning. Take time to see what else God has for you, what reason(s) he might have for bringing you here to contribute to the well being of one of the most impoverished regions of the country. "Stake out a place, and make a time," she said, "a place and time in which you can say that, 'yes, I've found something from God here, something that I intend to carry into the life to which I will return next week.'"

"Make this a place," she added, that "you will remember."

Then Kate shared her own starting point, her own physical place of meditative beginning, a place that she remembered even to that day. It was deep in the mountains of Wyoming, a nameless meadow, a meadow with running stream and abundant wildflowers, sparkling endlessly in the mountain sun, a meadow that, in her mind, is set apart. It is to this meadow that, when she can, Kate goes, because it is in this meadow that she finds the insights that enlighten and sustain her. Her memory of this place keeps her whole. Having once been a seminal point of meaning for her, it has now become for her a lasting point of meaning, a continuing memory of a formative memory. Her memory has become that which generated a particularly incisive dimension of her existential vision, a sort of "flashbulb" memory in reverse. Not only was it *what* she knew and remembered, it became the basis for *how* she remembered as well.[71]

On the other hand, Kate's memory of this meadow will change constantly. As she goes on with her life, taking in new experiences and stepping into new events, she will develop new memories. These memories will then blend and build upon her existing memories to create new ones in turn. Though she will still treasure the meadow, she will likely remember it differently as she ages. She will see it differently,

---

[71] This brings up another dimension of memory, that of the relationship of memory to place. Though we will discuss this idea more throughout the book, consider, for now, the work of sociologist T. M. Luhrmann (whose work we mentioned earlier), particularly her article "The Zone of Social Abandonment in Cultural Geography: On the Streets in the United States, inside the family in India," in *Culture, Medicine and Psychiatry,* 36: 493-513 (with Jocelyn Marrow). See also John R. Stilgoe, *Outside Lies Magic: Regaining Awareness in Everyday Places* (New York: Bloomsbury, 2009), and *What is Landscape?* (Cambridge, Massachusetts: MIT, 2015).

she will approach it differently. But she will still remember it. Memory never stands still, but it always remains.

The Native American tribes of the Southwest tell the story of an Indian boy who grew up not wanting to pursue the things of his compatriots. He was not interested in hunting, fighting, and councils. All he wanted to do was paint. And what a painter he was. The tribe grew to love his paintings, to appreciate deeply the color and imagination that he brought into their lives.

Eventually, as did every young man in the tribe, the boy went on his vision quest, that essential and solitary journey on which young Indian men embark to find their life calling and destiny. The boy traveled to the mountains beyond his tribe's encampment to spend two, three, or more nights (the young braves never knew how long it would take) so as to seek out the life vision the Great Spirit had for him. The boy already knew, however, that he had been gifted and called to paint. What more could he learn?

The boy never returned from his quest. Some days later, a group of men journeyed to the mountains to look for him. They didn't find him. In fact, they could not find a trace of him, not a hint of evidence that he had even moved across the land. He had vanished. What the men did find, however, was this: a vast field covered with a type of flower they had never seen before. We know it today as Indian Paintbrush.[72]

---

[72] We find Indian Paintbrushes all over the mountains of the American West. They consist of bright orange and red petals on a one to two foot stalk. They're strikingly pretty and well worth any trek one makes to see them. A good place to see a profusion of them is a canyon in Wyoming's Grand Teton National Park named, aptly enough, Paintbrush Canyon.

The boy, they concluded, had found his vision. And he had left, they realized, the legacy it had bequeathed him. He had left a memory of himself. But it was not a memory of the physical person he was. It was a memory of what he created. Going forward, although the tribe would remember the boy for his remarkable artistic talents, they would remember him even more for the flowers that his talent, in the hands of the Great Spirit, had spawned. It was a new memory, yet it was a new memory grounded intimately in the old. Though the memory had changed, it in fact remained essentially the same.

In future years, each time members of the tribe saw an Indian Paintbrush, they remembered the boy. They recalled the gift he had made to the tribe. As the boy's contemporaries passed on, and as the people of the next generation came to life, lived, and died, and the generation following it did the same, they all would continue to remember the boy. He would never be forgotten. His name, his deeds, his gift—his memory—would endure, always new, yet always, significantly, old, forever gestating and blooming anew in the hearts and minds of his tribe.[73]

Musician Warren Zevon, perhaps most famous for his composition *Werewolves of London,* a rollicking tale of a werewolf on the loose in the streets of that English city, learned, in 2002, that he had peritoneal mesothelioma, an

---

73 We will save for later discussion and connection the rather depressing words of Ecclesiastes 9:5, which observe that the memory of the dead is soon forgotten, as well as the related contention of C. S. Lewis in his *Weight of Glory* that it is possible for people to be forgotten even by God (C. S. Lewis, *Weight of Glory* (New York: HarperOne, 2015).

incurable form of lung cancer. His doctors predicted he would last three months. Zevon then chose to do the thing he knew best: make music. Gathering a host of musical friends, including Jackson Browne and Bruce Springsteen, and working as long as he had energy to do so, he produced an album, *Wind*, that was released shortly before he died in September of 2003 (contrary to the doctor's predictions, Zevon lived for nearly a year after the diagnosis). It was certified gold in December of that year.

One of the songs on *Wind* is particularly heartbreaking. It is "Think of Me." While you're going about your day, he asks, be it doing your housework, walking to the park, or looking at the sky, please take time to think of me. Whatever you do and wherever you go, he pleads to his listeners, do not forget about him. Those who knew Zevon understood exactly what he was saying. He wanted to be remembered, to not die unforgotten, to have some assurance that even after he had long been gone, he would be recalled and talked about, always, it is fair to say, with fondness.[74]

Yet as Zevon's closest friends, particularly those who helped him make the record, came to think of him, although they would remember him as he was, they would also, each time they reflected on him, remember him in a different way. Their memory of him would change even as it remained the same. He would be Warren Zevon, but he would also *become* Warren Zevon. He would always be present, stirring feelings and sparking tears, yet he, or the remembrance of him, would, from one recollection to the

---

[74] See Zevon's album *Wind,* Artemis Records, 2003.

next, never be the same. Though the memory of him will not stand still, it will always remain.[75]

Have you ever listened to people reminisce about their children? Recalling long ago memories about a child's antics or behavior, they will, usually laughing, share their recollection of the experience. Although their memory of the experience may remain fairly intact, each time they retell the story about that child, they tell it slightly differently. Why? Each time they tell it, they are different. They may be older, they may be in a different place or state of mind, they may be doing different things, they may have a different relationship with that child, or something else. Our present circumstances shape how we remember our past circumstances. Memory changes, but it remains.

This is also why, depending on their age and station in life, children find the retelling of such stories progressively more or less embarrassing, poignant, or otherwise significant. For instance, I enjoy remembering the story of how my daughter, now nearly thirty, but then in the midst of her potty training, one day came to me and announced, "I'm going to stand next to you and go poop."

I always laugh when I remember the incident. Predictably, when she was a teenager, my daughter never laughed when I recounted it: too embarrassing. Now that she is older, however, she does. She understands that because so much time has passed since the incident, it does not represent the person she is today. Again, the memory has

---

75 We will address later the issues that this conclusion raises about the difficulty of deciding how we *experience* memory. Do we perceive it? Do we sense it? Which is it?

not changed, but it has. My daughter and I have changed, and so has the memory. Yet it remains. Just like our lives.

Moreover, a memory never stands alone. As we noted at the outset of this chapter, memories are remembering, and memories are remembering our remembering—and remembering our remembering our remembering. They're contingent, interdependent, and impermanent. Memory is life, memory is death; memory is what we are and it is who we are. It's everywhere and yet, oddly enough, it's nowhere.

Let's review. One, we observed that there are six broad types of memory: knowledge memory (facts and information, categorized as episodic memory; flashbulb memory; cultural memory; body memory; pure memory; and involuntary memory); sensory memory (immediate sensation); explicit memory (memory we know we have); implicit memory (memory we do not always know we have); short term memory (here today, gone tomorrow, if not sooner); and long term memory (forever in our brain).

We also noted that although these six broad based categories of memory are distinct, they ultimately work together in the life of a remembering being. We need all of them to function and live sensibly, meaningfully, and rightly. We need flashbulb memory as much as we need involuntary memory; we need short term memory as much as we need long term memory; we need procedural memory as much as we need body memory, and so on. We function best when our memory types are working in meaningful concert with each other.

Two, we saw that memory, though it is "here" and "there," it is in fact neither. We cannot visibly see it, we cannot palpably touch it. It's always old, yet always new;

always changing, yet always remaining the same. Memory shapes as much as it loosens, affects as much as it effects. It's a thoroughly multi-faceted and elusive thing.

What's next? One, we will try to determine, from a physiological standpoint, how memory works. How do we remember? Two, we will take a journey through the history of memory. How have people through the ages viewed memory? How do people view it today? Although this question seems straightforward—have not people always looked at memory as, well, memory?—we shall see that the answer is far more complex. We shall see that the way we view memory today, as it did for our predecessors in their day, expresses and reflects how we view ourselves and our world. We shall see that because we moderns have a very different view of the self than did our ancient predecessors, our picture of memory is different, too. Three, what is the spirituality of memory? What does memory have to do with God? Finally, we will explore the idea of forgetting. Sometimes we must forget in order to remember. If we can remember everything, what, really, are we actually remembering? What happens to memory when we forget? Moreover, what happens to God's memory if he forgets? Or can God forget?

HOW DO WE REMEMBER?

When we think about how memory works, we should note that it involves three interrelated processes: perception, storage, and retrieval. How is this? One, we cannot have a memory without perceiving something. We must have an experience of the world that we can remember. Two, we cannot remember what we perceive unless our brain stores it. We may perceive something, but unless the brain stores it, we will not really "remember" it. Otherwise, when we next go to look for it, we will not find it. It will be gone. Three, we must be able to retrieve the memory. We must be able to pull the memory out of the storehouses of our brain in order to call it a "viable" memory. Oddly, we must be able to remember in order to "remember."[76]

---

[76] "Viable," however, is a loaded term. As we observed earlier, we frequently do not "know" we have a memory until we attempt to retrieve it. Hence, we may have many more "viable" memories than we think.

[73] Of course it goes without saying that as we shall soon see, whichever definition of reality we choose, we make it frightfully dependent on our perception, and our perception may not always,

What's perception? Perception is two things. One, perception is how we see, hear, smell, taste, and touch in the world in which we live and move. Perception is our experience, our sensory experience of that which we physically encounter. Two, perception is what our brain does with what we see, hear, smell, taste, and touch in the world. It is the way that our mind processes the information it perceives. Perception is,

> "A meeting between two words, inner and outer: on the one hand, we have the self-generated impression, and on the other, the external material object. In perception, the object serves to elicit what has its origin elsewhere; it does not create what it elicits."[77]

---

at a given moment, accurately assess the state of the world around us. Yet we must trust our perception. What else do we have to determine the shape of what we experience? Yes, some of us will perceive a multi-layered reality, and some of us will not. Does this mean that one of our perceptual mechanisms is faulty? Of course not: it merely means that some of us have chosen to conclude and believe that, on the basis of the evidence available to all of us, we perceive things that others do not. Yet our perception does not create reality; reality would exist regardless of whether and how we perceive it. Our perception simply determines how we view and experience reality. Hence, some people will believe in the transcendent because they believe they have experienced it, whereas others will reject such belief because they do not believe they can or will experience it.

77 Colin McGinn, *Inborn Knowledge: The Mystery Within* (Cambridge, Massachusetts: MIT, 2015), 71.

Or as another writer put it, perception is, "What your brain believes is there." With perception, the information we take in through our senses, we define reality and, subsequently, create our world.[78]

Hanging on the wall of the Metropolitan Museum in New York is a painting by the French artist Nicolas Poussin (1594-1665) called *Blind Orion Searching for the Rising Sun.* It shows Orion, the mighty hunter of Greek mythology, the hunter who, according to some versions of the story, was a lover of the moon goddess Artemis. Orion roamed the earth almost at will, slaying many fierce and formidable animals along the way. Now, however, he is blinded (for, we are told, walking over the ocean (he was a son of Poseidon, the god of sea) to the island of Chios and attacking Merope, daughter of Oenopion[79]), and is looking for the sun whose rays he believes will restore his sight.

Like all of us, Orion is looking for light. He is looking for a way to perceive, to see, physically, with his eyes. He is trying to create a world.[80]

As do we. We wander through the landscapes of our lives, constantly seeking, constantly perceiving, processing,

---

78 *Memory: Histories, op cit.*

79 See Robert Graves, *Greek Myths: The Complete and Definitive Edition* (New York: Penguin, 2011).

80 The happy ending of the story is that after Orion died (stung, many versions, note by a scorpion on the orders of Artemis), Zeus, recognizing Orion's greatness, set him, along with Scorpion and his two dogs, Canis Major and Canis Minor (the constellations we know today as the Big Dipper and Little Dipper), into the sky. There Orion would roam, pursuing, some say, Leto the hare, for all eternity. His glory would endure forever. See also William E. Marsh and David Traynor, "Journey," original art, 2015.

and creating, then recreating our world. Or as David Hume put it, we are continuously receiving "impressions," sensations on which we base our understanding of reality and, consequently, our picture of our world.[81] As we live out our lives, our brain continually processes and senses, making links, triggering thoughts, and establishing connections between all that we experience. Its neurons and synapses are constantly communicating with the neurons of the senses (for the ear, the hammer and anvil; for the eye, the cones and rods; for the skin, the layers of the epidermis; for the tongue, its taste buds) to "decide" how to respond to the information and impressions they are bringing in. Then, depending on the type of information, our brain remembers it, be it for a moment or a lifetime. Subsequently, this memory, however long we may have it, becomes knowledge.[82]

---

[81] David Hume, *An Inquiry Concerning Human Understanding,* ed. Charles W. Hendel (New York: Bobbs Merrill, 1955).

[82] On the other hand, consider the argument of Christopher Chabris and Daniel Simons in their *The Invisi ble Gorilla: How Our Intuitions Deceive Us* (New York: Potter/TenSpeed/Harmony (Crown), 2010), that even if we *think* we recall what we have heard, we may not have necessarily done so. Our memories, they claim, deceive us. Although we may ordinarily dismiss this as unimportant, a lapse of being human, it becomes critical in the case of an "eyewitness" testifying in court. Does this person *really* remember what she purports to? See also *Imagination and the Meaningful Brain, ibid.* In addition, consider the idea of knowledge. Briefly, knowledge is what we know. Although this seems circular, it is true: what we know is our knowledge. What do we know? On the one hand, what we know is the cumulative and continuing result of the brain's summarizing, connecting, inferring, and categorizing the contents of our perception and experience that have come to us via our senses. On the other

This means that perception is foremost a work of the neurons in our brain. Everything that we "perceive" we do so because of the neural patterns of our brain. Every perception induces a certain level of neural activity which in turn alters and physically changes and reshapes the neuronal structures of the brain. As one writer puts it, our brains possess a "plasticity" which enables the brain to respond and, subsequently, morph and adjust according to the external stimuli that we call sensory experience. For instance, suppose you "see" a deer. Why do you "see" it? You see it because your eyes, the face of the visual system, are sending, through its rods, cones, ganglion cells, and axons, signals to your brain's neurons for processing. Based on the information it already possesses, the neurons then affirm that you see a deer. In so doing, the neurons shift and alter, and so do, quite imperceptibly, you. The brain is ready for a new perception.

So it is that,

> "We use this [sensory] information to extract signs, and we create concepts and form internal representations that are the basis of our thought; we then form memories."[83]

---

hand, however, what we know, really, is only what we consciously remember of the information our senses transmit to us. If we do not remember something, we cannot really say that we know it. See also Howard Caygill, "Physiological Memory Systems" in *Memory: Histories*, 227ff.

83 *Borges and Memory*, 144.

In perceiving *and* remembering, our brain creates our world.[84]

Significantly, however, the world our perception creates is not necessarily the world as it is. *The Teachings of Don Juan: A Yaqui Way of Knowledge,* Carlos Casteneda's memoir about his experiences with peyote in the American Southwest, speaks candidly about this point. Repeatedly, Casteneda says that although he decided that what he perceived under peyote's hallucinogenic effects was reality, he was well aware that it was in fact not a reality that existed outside of his mind. While his perception was indeed reality, his experience of where he was at a given moment, it was not what reality most is. It was only what he thought—or wanted—it to be. It was only a semblance of what is factual and true.[85]

In addition, perception is selective. We perceive according to what is in our brains. That is, we only see that for which our brain has categories to see, that for which our brain has patterns to grasp. For instance, a person with a deep knowledge of the thinking of Pablo Picasso will perceive things in his paintings that a person without this knowledge will not. Or a person who has limited knowledge about Russia will perceive it differently than one who possesses a great deal of knowledge about it.

---

84 For more on this, see Alan Jacobs, "Coleridge and the Maker," in *Books and Culture,* May/June 2015. We should also note that this equation changes when we talk about religious belief. Those who believe in a metaphysical being do not so much create what they believe but rather believe that this being has created. They believe in things they cannot construct on their own.

85 See Carlos Casteneda, *The Teachings of Don Juan: A Yaqui Way of Knowledge* (New York: Washington Square Press, 1985).

When I take people backpacking, be it the Grand Canyon or the volcanoes of Hawaii, I know that because I have been to those places many times, I will "see" and understand them differently than the others, those who are going for the first time. Similarly, when a friend of mine leads a trip to the Kluane Mountains of the Yukon, he will perceive them very differently than the others in the party. He's seen and experienced them many times before.

Many years ago, a friend of mine named Tim received a painting from his girlfriend Gina. It pictured a climber poised on the edge of a jagged peak, looking into the rising sun and saying, "Do you have to cross the world to see the other side?" When I asked Tim what this meant, he replied, "I don't need to go overseas; I can get there by thinking about it."

Perhaps he can. Yet if Tim has never been overseas, he will certainly not perceive it in the way that will someone who actually leaves her country and travels to another land. It's impossible. We perceive according to what we already know.[86]

---

[86] This process is not confined to Christianity only. Anyone who has been raised according to a particular religion or religious worldview will tend to see the world through the eyes of that worldview. One example is the continuing conflict between the Sunni and Shia Muslims. Both have been raised to view Islam in a particular way and tend to see the world and everything that happens in it through those eyes. Yet the process holds true outside religion, too. Consider the wilderness experience organization Outward Bound's trips for inner city youth. Having known little but asphalt and concrete for all their lives, these youths do not always see, at least right away, everything that the mountains can offer them. They do not yet have the "eyes"

To offer another take on this idea, I return to a book, *When God Talks,* which I mentioned in an earlier footnote. In it, sociologist T. M. Luhrman presents the results of her observations about how evangelical Christians interact (or believe that they interact) with God. After conducting numerous interviews and observing several evangelical churches, even joining one for a year and a half, Luhrman concludes that the answer lies in the extent to which these evangelicals have, in a largely unconscious way, "trained" their minds to make them amendable, receptive, or capable of grasping information which they believe to be from God. Over many months and years of thought, study, and prayer, she notes, these evangelicals have, again, not always in a conscious or deliberate way, shaped their minds so as to be able to discern when God, as they see it, is talking to them. It is the time they spend in bible study, community worship, and prayer that makes them ready to embrace and accept what they hear or see, metaphorically speaking, in their mind and heart as words from God. Months and years of mental shift and change, driven, as always, by perception, storage, and memory, have produced a brain that understands, in the eyes of its possessor, how to deal with what it believes and perceives to be words from God.

Not only is perception a function of who we are in the moment, perception makes us who we will be in the next.[87]

---

to do so. After two weeks in the wilderness, however, they do. Similarly, a person who has been raised in a family that hunts regularly will, more often than not, view and perceive wildlife differently than a person who has been brought up in a family that does not believe in the utility or worth of hunting.

87 See *When God Talks, op cit.* To this, we may add the insights of Woodrow Shew, a professor at the University of Arkansas, who

Clearly, we do not have complete control over what and how we perceive. Perception is a function of movements and forces not all of which we are aware, and not all of which we may desire, want, or request. We often perceive without even knowing it. We cannot control everything that we take in. All we know are "appearances," and not, as Immanuel Kant observed long ago, "things in themselves." All we know is what we think we do.[88]

Nonetheless, we understand that we perceive in a world that is, as Ludwig Wittgenstein said, a "given," "knowable as well as unknowable."[89] It's tangible, sensible, and real, a "separateness" that is not us but rather a separateness into which we have been "thrown"[90] and subsequently live and function. We live and perceive in a world that is as thoroughly real as it is independent of any of our efforts to establish its reality and presence.[91]

---

believes that "intense visual input forces the brain into a brief moment of chaos," out of which the "visual cortex spontaneously" returns the brain to normal function. What we perceive is always shaping us. Moreover, regardless of the content of the perception, it shapes the brain in ways of which we are not always aware. See *Arkansas,* the magazine of the Arkansas Alumni Association, Fall 2015, 4.

88 Immanuel Kant, *Critique of Pure Reason*, trans. Norman Kemp Smith (Boston: New Bedford, 1929).

89 In an updated exposition of this idea, see Marilynne Robinson's *The Givenness of Things* (New York: Farrar, Straus & Giroux, 2015), 90. In addition, see Ludwig Wittgenstein, *Philosophical Investigations,* ed. Meredith Williams (New York: Rowman and Littlefield, 2007).

90 *Being and Time, op cit.*

91 See René Descartes, *Meditations on First Philosophy,* trans. Laurence J. Lafleur (New York: Bobbs Merrill, 1960); David

Similarly, we remember in a real world. Whether we remember a work of our imagination or a fully material event, we do so in an autonomous world of form, substance, and sense. Whatever our brains apprehend, ingest, and remember, physically real or not, they do so in palpable and tangible existential and sovereign point and presence.

In sum, without perception, perception in a real world, memory, memory that is real as it is effectual, never begins.

This brings us to storage. To begin, we should note that perception and storage occur almost simultaneously. It is not easy to delineate between them precisely. For instance, in perceiving a stimulus, the brain "creates" a memory. Yet the brain cannot perceive the stimulus without filtering it through its mnemonic storehouses, its many vaults of recollections and existing memories. It always looks for a neural context in which to understand and categorize the perception it experiences. In other words, the brain must remember in order to perceive. It must etch a new memory on the basis of its various tangles of old ones. On the other

---

Miller, ed., *Popper Selections* (Princeton, New Jersey: Princeton, 1985); Benedict de Spinoza, *On the Improvement of the Understanding,* trans. R. H. M. Elwes (New York: Dover, 1955); and Ludwig Wittgenstein, *Tractatus Logico-Philosophicus,* trans. C. K. Ogden (New York: Dover, 1999). On the other hand, note that Hinduism holds that all things are essentially Brahman, that all things are each other, and that everything is therefore, from an ontological standpoint, the same. Everything is everything: there is no separation. See Dominic Goodall, trans., *Hindu Scriptures* (London: Phoenix, 1996). For one more view on the issue of perception and reality, see the movie, *The Matrix,* Warner Bros., 1999, which portrays a world run by cognitive machines. In this world, humans are merely cogs in the machines' minds.

hand, the brain must perceive, must pick up and process sensory intimation, in order to even spark a remembering. What we can therefore conclude is whether the memory thus remembered is short term or long term, it is always born in perception, then given life, however brief, in storage. In addition, without storage, this memory will never be. Perception and storage work together, constantly creating and storing, storing and creating, then creating and storing and storing and creating once more, over and over and over again. Thus intertwined they live, and thus intertwined they die.[92]

How does the brain create and store memories? Inside a part of the hippocampus (which we identified previously as being prime, though not totally encompassing, to memory),[93] is a structure called the subgranular zone. Within the subgranular zone, various networks of tightly packed neural stem cells will, if stimulated by sense perceptions, generate new neurons to process them. As these neurons subsequently integrate themselves into existing neural circuits, they "create" memory, guiding and enabling the brain in developing new remembrances and recollections in response to the sense perceptions it has received. It is these neural stem cells that allow us to continue to take in and remember new data about our world. As we perceive, they respond, engendering new structures—new mnemonic structures—on the basis of the "old" structures they have

---

[92] *Memory: Introduction,* 27.

[93] Note, however, *Permanent Present Tense, op. cit.,* in which author Suzanne Corkin points out that without the hippocampus, the "narrative richness" of the memory is gone. Its "story" is lost.

previously created. It is these neural cells that define, constitute, and "store" our memories.[94]

How do these neural stem cells do this? Deep in these cells lie molecules that contain a substance called "cyclic AMP." When neural stem cells in the subgranular zone encounter new sensory data, their AMP levels rise. This rise in AMP levels activates a certain set of the cells' genes. This genetic activation spurs the creation or synthesis of new proteins. These proteins then establish additional synaptic connections among the cells, synaptic connections which in turn "create" memory.[95] A memory is therefore a new layer of protein, a new protein that in turn powers a new synaptic connection, a new mnemonic linkage in the brain. Reduced to its physiological essence, a memory is a new wrinkle in the brain, a fresh and unique twist or fold in the neuronal tissue. In short, when an organism remembers, its neuronal capacities and connections, embodied in protein, actually multiply and physically change. Protein is generated, new synapses find form, and new connections come into existence. As a result, the brain is not the same brain as it was before. In contour as well as content, it has changed.[96]

---

94 See "Neurons and Anxiety," Mazen A. Kheirek and René Hen, *Scientific American,* July 2014. Check also *Memory: From Mind to Molecules,* Larry R. Squire and Eric R. Kandel (Greenwood Village, Connecticut: Roberts and Company, 2014). See also *Imagination and the Meaningful Brain,* 110-122; and *Memory: Introduction,* 45, 57.

95 *Ibid.;* Eric R. Kandel, *In Search of Memory* (New York: Norton, 2006).

96 Steven Rose, "Memories Are Made of This" in *Memory: Histories,* 202ff.

Moreover, thanks to the ability of researchers to identify, in part, these new folds, we can actually "see" genuine organic "trace" of memory.[97]

Where does the brain store memories? Although the hippocampus plays a significant role in "printing" or impressing new memory into the brain, a memory owes its final storage place and, therefore, its temporal identity, to the cerebral (or visual[98]) cortex.[99]

What's the cerebral cortex? A membrane that surrounds the brain like a silk envelope, the cerebral cortex is a network of billions of nerve cells and synapses which are constantly moving and changing and storing information. These cells and their attendant synapses are always altering, transforming and, in some instances, storing, the stimuli they receive. Therefore, when we perceive, when we experience a stimulus and "make" a memory, short or long term, although it is the neural cells of the subgranular zone that are generating the synapses and proteins to enable us to do so, it is our cerebral

---

97 *Ibid.; Memory: Philosophical Study,* 134-5. See also a famous series of experiments with rats (what would we do without rats!) and, believe it or not, a certain species of snail called *Aplysia californica,* in which researchers have discovered that when an organism "remembers" or "learns," the "electrical properties and biochemistry" of certain neuronal synapses actually changes. They grow visibly and "structurally" larger. Moreover, the "efficacy" of their neurotransmitters improves. The synapses therefore become better equipped to do their job of apprehending, processing, storing, and transmitting stimuli and information. We might say that remembering strengthens the brain. It enhances the brain's ability to do its job.

98 *Memory: Histories,* 255; *Memory: Fragments,* 85-86.

99 *Memory: Introduction,* 85.

cortex that is, like a producer who oversees all aspects of the making of a movie, ultimately guiding and embedding the memory in its storage place. When the cerebral cortex stores this memory, this newly created concoction of synapse and correlation, be it temporarily or permanently, it becomes memory. While the neural cells of the subgranular zone do the initial work of creating memory, it is the cerebral cortex that finishes and completes the brain's mnemonic enterprise. In the big picture, we owe our memories to the activity of the cerebral cortex.

And it is in the cerebral cortex's dynamic, the constancy of its activity, that we see physiological explanation for why our memories are always changing. Memories move and dance and change amidst the neuronal folds of the brain precisely because the cerebral cortex is continually moving and changing them. It changes them the first time it stores and remembers them, it changes them the second time it stores and remembers them, and it changes them the third time it stores and remembers them. And so on. Furthermore, as the cerebral cortex is processing, enabling, and storing new memory, it is also remembering and processing and storing and changing an old one. Because the cerebral cortex is constantly connecting new memory with old memory, continually changing the brain's storehouse of stimuli and impressions, there is, as we observed, never really an old memory. Thanks to the cerebral cortex, when new memories are made, though old memories remain, they do not remain in their original state. Nor do they remain in the same "place," either. They are still "there," but not where they were before. We will never retrieve or remember them in quite the same way again.[100]

We might therefore say that memories are everywhere but nowhere. There is not a particular place in the brain where a given memory will be stored for all time, nor is there a particular way the brain stores it. Nothing about a memory, be it the categories housing it, the neurons, proteins, and synapses processing it, or the impression it makes on its holder, stands still or remains the same. Although a memory may be "new," it is in fact no more new than it is old; as soon as it forms, another memory arrives to take its place. There is no permanently "old" or "new" in memory.

Hence, regardless of where the cerebral cortex is storing a memory at a particular point in time, we have no way to predict, at least not yet, *precisely* where it will store this memory going forward. We have no way to know how the cortex will reshape and use existing neuronal proteins, connections, and categories to make new proteins and connections and, as a result, create a memory in the future. We have no way to know how the cortex will work in the next moment. The memories it has today, it will not have tomorrow, and the categories it is using today it will more than likely discard or redo come morning. For this reason, even if we knew how to look for a memory, even if we could step into the cortex's filing system and retrieve it, the instant we did so we would lose it. As one writer put it, memory is localized as well as nonlocalized. It's here, but it's also

100 *Borges and Memory,* 71-73.

there, woven together with other recollections, thoughts, and intimations even as it separates itself from them.[101]

In addition, as much research points out, the brain is not a storage cabinet with neat and tidy drawers out of which it pulls, on cue, various bits of information for us to use in understanding and connecting with new perceptions. We cannot access the brain as we can a flash drive; its precise storage methods and categories elude us. All we know is that the brain remembers.[102]

Moreover, although we may, from an experimental standpoint, "see" a memory in the guise of new synapses, neurons, and proteins in a brain, we still do not really see it as it is. We cannot look at the memory as we would a motion picture. We can only view it as a structure in a brain. Again: memory is there, but it is not.[103]

And given the brain's complexity—over 85 billion cells with 10,000 connections apiece[104]—we perhaps will never see memory in full.[105]

---

101 See, as previously cited, *Memory: Histories; Memory; Memory: Introduction;* and *Borges and Memory.* In addition, see the already mentioned "Neurons and Anxiety" in *Scientific American.*

102 On this, see Wassily Kandinsky, *Concerning the Spiritual in Art,* trans. M. T. H. Sadler (New York: Dover, 1977).

103 See *Memory: Fragments,* 257ff.; and "Physiological Memory Systems" in *Memory: Histories,* 231-232.

104 See, to mention one, *An Introduction to Brain and Behavior,* Brian Kolb and Ian Q, Whishaw (New York: Worth (Macmillan), 2012), as well as "All Circuits Are Busy," an interview with neuroscientist H. Sebastian Seung, in the May 27, 2014, edition of *The New York Times.*

105 *Ibid.*

Moreover, the *way* we remember changes all the time.[106] As Daniel Boorstin points out in his magisterial *The Creators: A History of Heroes of the Imagination*, those who create must, like the brain, constantly break boundaries and step outside of what their society considers to be reasonable and safe to develop anything of uniquely meaningful value. As the brain unpacks and unfolds, constantly reworking its past and present, so the creator steadfastly tears down the present and acceptable, continually altering, revising, and reimaging the way she thinks, conceives, and imagines to identify a new way for humans to move forward.[107]

In sum, storage, though it is nearly simultaneous with perception, is the product of the brain's ability to digest, grow, and change in response to perception, the steady flow of sensory information and stimuli which a person encounters. Storage creates memory, and storage renders *a* memory. For at least an instant, even if it is no more than a nanosecond, storage makes a memory present and active

---

[106] The way our brain processes memory reflects how the brain works. Our brain is always reworking, reassembling, and reconstituting the way it responds to sensory input and the categories it uses to do so. It's constantly growing and changing. It never stands still. If it did, we'd be dead. For this reason, we can have new memories; for this reason, we can remember even as we do not; for this reason we can reimage and reposition our past as we move forward through present and future to come. And for this reason we see that even though nothing remains the same, everything really does remain the same. We see that although what was once "there" is now not there, it is still "there." For an intriguing novelistic approach to this dichotomy, see Hermann Hesse's *Siddhartha,* trans. Hilda Rosner (New York: Bantam, 1981).

[107] Daniel J. Boorstin, *The Creators: A History of Heroes of the Imagination* (New York: Vintage, 1992).

and manifest in the brain. Moreover, as it does, storage reshapes the brain, adding, in ways large and small, to its singularly complex web of proteins, synapses, and neurons. In addition, in changing the brain, storage changes, in ways we often cannot grasp, us as well. We cannot generate new memory and remain exactly the same.

Yet storage is elusive. We do not know, from moment to moment, where it places a memory. While the constancy of perception ensures that storage constantly happens, the dynamics of storage guarantee that what it does with perception never stands still. What is "here" in the brain one day may not be "here" in quite the same place the next. Storage is never static, and it's never alone. It's an ever shifting process, a process that carries a phenomenality all its own. Storage is the necessary end and, ironically, beginning, of perception.

Perceiving and storing a memory, however, are not enough. We need to be able to retrieve it. Unless we can retrieve a memory, unless we can recall what we have committed to memory, it will not be of any immediate use to us. When we remember, we retrieve. We call out a memory, a perception we have grasped, processed, and put into mnemonic storage, for our present use. We "tell" our brain to produce what we think (or hope) we know.

This could be something as simple and automatic as remembering that two plus two equals four, or something as complicated and painstaking as remembering the fundamentals of stoichiometric equations. We believe (or if we are a student taking a test on stoichiometric equations, we perhaps hope!) that we can bring forth the memory. We believe, or at least we would like to believe, that because we perceived the information, we have stored it, and that we therefore can retrieve it.

We should note that when we say that we "ask" our brain to recall a memory, what we are really doing is asking *ourselves* to recall the memory. That is, we believe that we have a given memory stored in our brain, and that, if we try, we can remember it.[108]

Hence, when we recall or retrieve a memory, we are in fact "remembering" it, seemingly for the first time. Yet it's not our first time. At some point in the past, we had remembered it. We are simply "remembering" it again. Moreover, in remembering it "again," we create a new memory. We create a memory of remembering it. Remembering creates a memory. And when next we remember this memory, we create another new memory in turn. And so on. Nonetheless, as we noted in the last chapter, we still retain, in some form, the original memory, for it is only because of it that we can have these other memories.

In practice, however, the process is much quicker than how we are describing it here. Be it recalling that the sun rises in the east or that we are to stop driving when we come to a red light, we do so nearly instantaneously. We rarely think about it. Although in the case of the meanings of the symbols of the *I Ching* or the intricacies of quantum theory

---

[108] See Berkencker, Sven, *Memory: A Philosophical Study* (New York: Oxford University, 2010), 128ff. Also, in regard to the relationship of this to the relationship of the mind, body, brain, and identity, consult the works we cited earlier. In addition, as this meditation has already made clear, note that a person is more than her materiality and that, for this reason, the notion of mind, *with* memory, points us to the metaphysical.

we may take longer to recall (or reconstruct) our memory of them, the net effect is the same: it doesn't take long.

Either way, however, when we retrieve a memory, we and our brains are working together, working together as a seamless and holistically connected entity to find it. Weaving the totality of our volitional and mental processes together, we construct a tapestry of neuronal and existential commingling that enables us to connect the patterns of our inner deliberations with the fact of our outward encounters. Though we are not our brains, in retrieval we almost seem as if we are: "we" and our brain work with each other to locate and ferret out the memory we seek. Moreover, although we may not always understand the full picture of how we and our brain connect with each other, we live and act on the basis of the momentary mnemonic clarity it provides us. As we remember, so we retrieve; and as we retrieve, so we remember.[109]

Retrieval is therefore fraught with ambiguity. We know it happens, yet we do not know *where* it happens, that is, the place in the brain from which it brings forth a memory. In addition, we do not know, precisely, how we are able to come up with this particular memory. We may "see" or sense the memory, and we may know that we can use it, but we do not always understand, unless we have photographic memory,

---

[109] See, for instance, *Imagination and the Meaningful Brain,* 171-172; 194-195. As I noted earlier, however, it is the instantaneous nature of the mnemonic process that makes us feel as if we are "working" with our brain, when in fact our brain is an integral part of who we are. This is why the exchange seems virtually seamless.

why we do. Why this memory, this precise memory, and not another?

Complicating this picture even more, we must note that retrieval calls out all kinds of memory, be it sensory memory, working memory, short term memory, or long term memory, then mixes them together in what often seems to be one general act of memory. It is sometimes difficult to tell which is which. Although each of these memory types seems to stand in a class of its own, each also seems to reflect, to a point, the other. They are deeply interconnected. Yet we (our brains) are somehow able to bring them forth as what each one, in its purest essence, is.

For instance, how many times have you noticed that many people, when reminded of a particular fact they could not seem to recall in the present moment, respond, "I knew that!" At one time, they certainly did. A minute ago, it seemed that they did not. But now they do. Does this mean that this memory was a short term memory that somehow became long term memory and then a short term memory again? Was it working memory? Or has it always been, in some shape or form, "living" in the cerebral cortex, "secretly" influencing, shaping, or otherwise creating memories anew? Did it suddenly pop into existence? And what had the brain been doing with it until now?[110]

Although we understand that we can retrieve our memories, we also understand that we do so in an immensely intricate nexus of neuronal activity. As we sometimes seem to perceive and store simultaneously, so we also seem to retrieve even as we store and perceive. The process is marvelously complex. Though perception, storage, and retrieval are

[110] *Borges and Memory, ibid.*

dependent on the other, they are not; while they may build on each other, they may also not. Either way, we rarely know exactly what is going on. All we know is that we remember. All we know is that, empowered with sensory abilities and choice making capacities, we perceive, store, and retrieve what we daily experience in the world.

And as anyone who has watched a quiz show like "Jeopardy" or observed a wildlife expert tracking the path of a particular animal knows, some people seem to be able to do this more effectively than others. Like storage, retrieval is variable and elusive.[111]

What can we now say about how memory works? One, we see that memory is the result of three interrelated neuronal processes. The first is perception. We encounter the world, we take in information. The second is storage. We "remember" what we encounter. A memory is a stored perception. The third is retrieval. We call out the stored memory; we bring forth our perception. We "remember" the memory.

If this memory was a short term memory, we of course do not "remember" it. Try as we might, we cannot retrieve it. If it is a long term memory, however, we do. We "find" it in our storehouses of remembrance.

Two, memory always forms and develops on the basis of the memories already in the brain. Memory is the coming together of the brain's response to the stimuli it encounters with the brain's knowledge of what is already

---

[111] See "Jeopardy" (https://www.jeopardy.com/); and, to name just one, a "tracking school" established by famous animal tracker Tom Brown to train people in the art of tracking animals in the wild (https://www.**trackers**chool.com/)

there. The brain creates a memory according to how it weds past remembrance with present perception to create a meaningful picture of what has happened. It cannot create new memories apart from old ones. Memory is the assembling and manufacture of knowledge upon knowledge, and information upon information. It is new, but it is old. Either way, however, it is always fresh.

Three, memory is always changing. It's never static. Whenever we remember anything, then remember that we remember it, we remember it in a new way. To remember anything is to remember it differently from when we initially remembered it.

Four, memory's *place* is never static. Its location is always changing. We know our memories are in our brain, yet most of the time we do not know exactly where in the brain they are. In addition, the instant that we try to find or think of a memory, it moves to a new place. Although we "know" it's there, we do not know "where" it's "there." In a way, it is nowhere. Memory and remembering constitute a massively complicated blur between old and new, here and there, and in and out, and much more. Again, all we know is that, somehow and some way, we remember. And that, either way, a memory is "there."

Memory is therefore the creation, from the day one is born to the day one dies, of knowledge in response to perception. Memory is what the brain stores and retrieves about how it perceives the world. Memory is teacher, guide, and sustainer, a path of insight, growth, and enlightenment. It makes us who we are.

Yet memory is a mystery. We know we experience it, yet we still do not know where it is. Memory is like a wild cat, always on the prowl, shifting, fudging, and changing with each fresh set of stimuli, ever distant yet ever present, always there but never here. Though we perceive, store, and retrieve, we cannot always say to what end we do so. But we remember. We can do nothing else.

Many questions remain, but we will move on. Our next task will be to examine, briefly, the history of memory. We will look at the way that people have pictured or understood memory, scientifically and philosophically, through the ages. As they have moved from the jungles of Africa and the deserts of Mesopotamia and grown into the beings—you and me—who inhabit the highly complex urban civilizations that dominate much of the planet today, how have humans thought about their ability to remember? [112]

---

[112] Clearly, this is a very brief summary of the history of the human species. What we most wish to ask is, given how humans have moved and grown across the planet and its history, how have they remembered?

MEMORY AS HISTORY, HISTORY AS MEMORY[113]

When we think about the history of memory, we should of course realize that humans have been remembering for as long as they have been human beings. As we noted, to be human is to remember. Given the ubiquity and necessity of memory for all sentient beings, we may infer that present humanity's various ancestors and precursors were remembering beings, too. The mental processes that our brains employ today were surely in place, in some way, the moment that hominids emerged on the planet. Although later in this book we will consider how this eventuality came to be, for now we will focus on how people have viewed

[113] Given what we have seen to this point, using the term "history" in regard to memory seems almost a misnomer. In many ways, memory *is* history. However, as we shall see, how people have thought about memory as history has evolved in significant ways during the course of humanity's time on this planet.

this thing that they have come to call memory. How have humans dealt with their ability to remember?[114]

We will consider prehistory first. For this, we will look at the Neolithic period. With the Neolithic (a word which means "new stone"), roughly 10,000 B.C. to 3,000 BCE, we see solid evidence of the human species engaged in systematic reflection and mnemonic preservation. People built permanent settlements, domesticated animals, and began to farm. They lived in organized societies with specific rituals and cultural practices. While some people remained nomads, most derived their subsistence largely in one place.[115]

Evidence of the Neolithic exists throughout the planet. From Asia to Africa (the continent from which most researchers believe humanity emerged[116]) to Europe to

---

[114] From an evolutionary perspective, we use the word "emerge" carefully. In terms of memory, we must note that when a being is emerging and therefore coming into apprehension of memory, it is already a being who is living in a past, present, and future. To begin to remember is not to begin to exist but rather to be aware of the fact of existence. It is to build upon and blend with the old even as it is to separate and differentiate into the new. See, most recently, Robert C. Berwick and Noam Chomsky, *Why Only Us: Language and Evolution* (Cambridge, Massachusetts: MIT, 2016).

[115] See, among others, *The Cambridge Ancient History* (Cambridge: Cambridge University, 1970.)

[116] See the five volume set, *Olduvai Gorge,* edited by George Leakey and authored by Louis and Mary Leakey, published by Cambridge University Press in 2009. On the relationship of this theory to the religious view of the Garden of Eden, see, among others, Geoffrey Parker, ed., *Random House Compact Atlas of Human History* (New York: Random House, 1997);

North and South America, archaeologists have identified countless artifacts from culture after culture after culture, all dating from this time period. In addition, it seems that the oldest Neolithic settlements were located in the ancient near east (called today the Middle East). From here, the data seems to indicate, human settlement spread out, eventually penetrating into every corner of the planet. This movement occurred via land and sea, as some people moved from the Middle East into Africa and Europe; others migrated northeast, eventually settling in the Americas; and still others left the jungles of Southeast Asia for the beaches of Polynesia and Australia.[117]

Language appears to have developed in similar fashion. Much research has established that the major languages of the world can all be traced to a small set of linguistic roots which appear to have originated in the Middle East or Central Asia. From here, it seems that languages diverged and multiplied as humanity moved to different locations and geographic challenges.[118]

All this is to say that when we explore memory among our prehistoric ancestors, we are safe to conclude that we

---

Carl G. Rasmussen, *Zondervan Atlas of the Bible* (Grand Rapids: Zondervan, 2010); and Colin Tudge, *Neanderthals, Bandits & Farmers* (New Haven, Connecticut: Yale University, 1998).

[117] *Cambridge Ancient History, op cit.*

[118] See, to name a few, *ibid.;* Noam Chomsky, *On Language* (New York: W.W. Norton, 1998), and *What Kind of Creatures Are We?* (Cambridge, Massachusetts: MIT 2015); and Christopher Fynsk, *Language and Relation* (Stanford, California: Stanford University, 1996).

will see a relative uniformity of mnemonic expression among them and their remains.[119]

What is our evidence of Neolithic memory? It is extensive. From structures to ritual appurtenances to tools and kitchen wares to weapons to paintings and figurines, we see clearly that the people of the Neolithic, though they wrote nothing down, actively remembered.[120]

It is the artifacts associated with burial, funerary ritual, and deities on which we wish to focus most, for these represent direct attempts to preserve or commemorate a memory of people after death. When people, regardless of where they lived on the planet, laid a comrade or loved one to rest, they established a means to remember them. In building a tomb for a deceased person and setting into it remembrances of the life this person had lived, be they household articles, court retinues (in the case of a ruler), weapons, or agricultural implements, this person's survivors sought to create a memory. They sought to create a memory for themselves, and they sought to create a memory for the deceased. Not only did they wish to preserve a remembrance of the life that has ended, they strove to develop a picture how it might, ideally, continue.

If we think back to what we observed about the construction of memory, we can conclude that as time passed in the aftermath of the burial and the commemorations

---

[119] For more, see Jared Diamond, *Guns, Germs, and Steel: The Fates of Human Societies* (New York: W. W. Norton & Company, 1997).

[120] *Cambridge Ancient History, op cit.* Also, see Mircea Eliade, *A History of Religious Ideas,* trans. Willard R. Trask (Chicago: University of Chicago, 1978), Vol I., and Marija Gimbutas, *The Language of the Goddess* (London: Thames and Hudson, 2001).

attached to it, the survivors' memory of the deceased changed. The memory remained, of course, but each time a survivor visited the burial site or remembered the deceased in her home, she thought of him a little differently, remembered him in a slightly different way. As the survivor went on and came into new experiences, regardless of whether these were directly connected with the deceased, she developed a new memory of him. With every new perception, the cerebral cortex continued to change, reconstructing and reconstituting the memories that coursed constantly through it.

We can make a similar case with the many Neolithic commemorative figurines we have found. Every time a person looked anew at a figurine, her perception and therefore whatever she remembered or believed about this figurine changed as well. As this person's memory changed, her brain changed as well, steadfastly creating new proteins and synapses and, therefore, memories on the basis of what was already present in it. Memory remained, but it did not, for it constantly took on new shapes and forms. The dynamics of memory ensured that this person's experience and memory of the figurine would never be the same.

In sum, in terms of memory, the people of the Neolithic did everything that we do today. With memory, they celebrated festivals and commemorated the dead; shared the art of the building of their wares and infrastructures; passed on cultural, familial, and religious traditions to their children and brethren; and transmitted new methods and approaches for coping with life challenges. In innumerable ways, they used memory to sustain themselves and their picture of life.

The dawn of civilization and the emergence of written language, however, changed everything about memory. Though people of course continued to commemorate and remember, they did so in markedly different ways. They now went beyond using symbols to remember. They used words, written words, to record their memories, words that we can read, in translation, today. As a result, we have palpable linguistic evidence of memory, troves of written attestations of people using their memories to preserve remembrances of their beliefs; fellow members of their communities; techniques of agriculture, cooking, and warfare; and ways of dealing with the puzzles of existence. We see memory become "visible" in a way that it had not before, that, from one standpoint, language "is" memory.[121]

Nowhere is this more pronounced than in the ancient near east (again, what we call the Middle East today). The ancient near east included the civilizations of Egypt, Sumer, Assyria, Babylon, Persia, Hattusa (the Hittites), and Israel. It also encompassed the Nubians of Africa; the Urartians in eastern Anatolia; the Phoenicians, the global traders who have been credited with developing history's first alphabet and who served as a channel for cultural exchange throughout the Mediterranean region; the great port state of Ugarit; and the desert civilization of Aram, never a significant military power but a state that developed Aramaic, the language that would eventually become the *lingua franca* of the ancient world, to name just a few more. We will focus, however, on memory in the dominant cultures of the region: Egyptian,

---

121 Isabel Fonseca, *Bury Me Standing: The Gypsies and Their Journey* (New York: Vintage, 1995), 93.

Sumerian, Assyrian, Babylonian, Hittite, Persian, and Israelite.[122]

Almost all of us have seen photos of the pyramids and monuments of ancient Egypt.[123] These impressively massive structures, built with the labor of thousands upon thousands of workers, stand as ample testimony to the Egyptians' efforts to preserve memory. Though enormously valuable to the health of the Egyptian economy and sense of national unity, the pyramids' primary focus had to do with memory. Those who had pyramids built for themselves (the pharaohs) wished to be remembered. They wished to be remembered by one, the gods; and two, the people—their subjects—they left behind.[124]

Foremost, however, the pharaohs sought the memory of the gods. In building the pyramids and having them stocked

---

[122] Indeed, Jesus himself spoke Aramaic. Justice demands that we also mention the civilizations of ancient India, the cultures of the Indus Valley, for they had extensive trade contact with the nations of the ancient near east and left many artifacts for us to examine and ponder. For the sake of brevity, however, and because out of the peoples of the ancient near east came Judaism and Christianity (and later, Islam), religions which have proven to be so vastly influential in the flow of world history, we will focus on the cultures of the ancient near east and how they used memory to make sense of their lives. See, again, *Cambridge Ancient History;* Enrico Ascalone, *Mesopotamia,* trans. Rosanna M. Giammanco Frongia (Berkeley: University of California, 2005); and George Roux, *Ancient Iraq* (New York: Penguin, 1993).

[123] Indeed, the pyramid of Giza was considered to be one of the seven wonders of the ancient world.

[124] B. G. Trigger, B. J. Kemp, D. O'Connor, A. B. Lloyd, *Egypt, a Social History* (Cambridge: Cambridge University, 1983).

with all that they believed they would need in the next life, then arranging for the recitation of various funerary prayers upon their death, the pharaohs aimed to position themselves to enjoy the full benefits of the memory of the gods. They wanted the gods, principally Amon-Ra, the sun god, and Osiris, god of the dead, to remember them, to remember them upon their earthly passing and grant them a place in heaven, a seat at the throne of the celestial deities.[125]

As one tomb inscription puts it, "Now that he is a god [the ancient Egyptians believed that the pharaoh was, in life, a god, and that, upon death, he would step into the fullness of his divinity] living forever, magnified in the West [most of the ancients believed that the afterlife began in the West[126]] may he become a remembrance for the future, for all who come to pass by." Or as a portion of the *Book of the Dead* indicates, upon his death, the pharaoh will tell the gods that he has done everything he ought to have done, that he has satisfied every requirement of righteous and just living, and that for these reasons he wishes to "be announced" to the pantheon and be ushered into eternal life. He wishes for the gods to remember him as a just person.[127]

---

125 *The Egyptian Book of the Dead,* trans. E. A. Wallis Budge (New York: Dover, 1967), chapter 125.

126 The ancients were not alone in this. J. R. R. Tolkien's perennially popular *Lord of the Rings* (New York: Ballentine, 1965), which draws heavily from Icelandic and Norse mythology, and C. S. Lewis's equally popular *Chronicles of* Narnia (New York: Macmillan, 1950), which reflects his background in medieval literature, also present the place of the afterlife as being in the West.

127 *Book of the Dead, ibid.* See also *Ancient Near Eastern Texts Relating to the Old Testament,* 32-34. Note, however, that not

We see similar pleas in other cultures, too. For instance, in his prayer to the Sun God (Shamash), the Assyrian king Ashurbanipal (reputedly the builder of history's first formal library) prayed, "Judge his [the king's] case; turn his fat to prosperity [in the ancient world, being fat was considered a sign of good fortune and blessing, as it indicated that a person was hale and well fed]. Keep him in splendor; daily let him walk safely; forever may he rule." In other words, for all his military prowess and renown (the Assyrians were legendary for their military might and, unfortunately, attendant cruelty), in the end Ashurbanipal wished for Shamash to, out of all the other people and nations of the earth, think about and consider him, to recognize and remember him as he passed out of the present life. He wanted Shamash to allow him to "dwell in joy" in the world to come.[128]

Memory, however, encompassed more than the emotions of death and dying. In one of the most passionate prayers of the ancient near east, the Hittite king Mursilis I requested of the gods, on behalf of his people, to deliver the nation from a plague that was sweeping through his land, the land of Hatti (modern day Turkey). "Take pity," he says, "let the plague abate in the Hatti land. Hearken to me, Hattian Storm-God [the chief god of the Hittites], and save my life. This is of what I have to remind you: the bird takes refuge in its nest, and the nest saves its life. Again: if anything

---

all of the pharaohs were men. The most notable exception was Hatshepsut, a woman who reigned from 1478 to 1458, B.C.

[128] *Ancient Near Eastern Texts; Mesopotamia, op cit. Iraq, op cit.*

becomes too much for a servant, he appeals to his lord. His lord hears him and takes pity on him."[129]

Mursilis wished for the Storm God to hear him, to think of him, to be reminded to him, to, in other words, remember him and, in so doing, his people as well. The king longed for his god to remember him and his people when he looked upon the mountain regions in which they lived, and to attend to them, to give them relief from the pain sweeping through their lives. For Mursilis, as he reminded his god, "has confessed his guilt . . . and his father's sin": he deserves a hearing. He deserves, he believes, to be remembered.[130]

By far the most poignant reflections on memory in the ancient near east come from the Hebrews, who lived in what we today call Israel. Enshrined in the Hebrew and Aramaic texts of the Hebrew Bible (the *Tanakah,* known to most of us as the Old Testament), these reflections are rooted in the Hebrews' belief and memory that God (whom they called Yahweh) had called them into a covenantal relationship (expressed in the Hebrew word *hesed*), an eternal commitment to shepherd them to spiritual and geographic greatness. Time and time again, the Hebrews asked Yahweh to affirm his memory of the covenant (*ber'ith*), to remember and help them as he guides and directs the course of human affairs.[131]

---

[129] *Ibid.* See also O. R. Gurney, *The Hittites* (New York: Penguin, 1952), 134-166.

[130] *Ibid.* Most ancients believed that illness was the result of transgression against the gods.

[131] Clearly, though many will take issue with the worth of this assertion today (consider the ongoing conflict between Palestine and Israel today), we will here focus solely on what the biblical

Yahweh first disclosed this covenant to the Hebrew patriarch Abraham. As the text states,

> "Now the Lord [Yahweh] said to Abram [Abraham's birth name, a word meaning "father of a multitude"; only later did God change it to Abraham, which means "father of a great multitude"], 'Go forth from your country, and from your relatives and from your father's house, to the land which I will show you; and I will make you a great nation, and I will bless you and make your name great; and so you shall be a blessing; and I will bless those who bless you, and the one who curses you I will curse. And in you all the families of the earth will be blessed.'" (Genesis 12:1-3) [132]

If we set aside (for space does not permit us to elucidate it fully here) the enormous weight that this covenant has put upon all subsequent human history, we see that, for the Hebrews, God's memory for them encompasses and describes the very essence of life and being. Everything about existence, past, present, and future, is wrapped in memory, God's memory for them. Memory carries and sustains it all.

---

text says about the nature and history of the covenant between God and Israel.

[132] Unless otherwise noted, all scripture references are drawn from the *New American Standard Bible* (Grand Rapids, Michigan: Zondervan, 2000).

Moreover, for those who believed in God before Abraham was born, memory, God's memory of them, was central as well. Almost immediately after the Fall, almost immediately after Adam and Eve made the fateful decision to violate the dictums of the structures in which God had set them, God promised remedy. He offered them a vision of redemption. He invited them to remember, to remember with hope that, going forward, he still cared for them. He would not forget them (Genesis 3:15).[133]

Similarly, during the Flood, when all the earth was inundated by water, the text tells us, God "remembered" Noah and his family. He kept him safe, kept him whole, and ensured that, as he had promised, he would use Noah to restore the human population of the earth (Genesis 9:15).

So it was that when Yahweh tells the Hebrews that he would deliver them from slavery in Egypt (an event which Jews celebrate today in the feast of Passover), he reminds them that he is doing so because he "remembers" his covenant with them, the covenant which he had established with their father Abraham many centuries before. He reminds them that he has not forgotten his commitment to them. He hears them, he remembers them, and he will therefore act on their behalf. In promising to deliver the Hebrews (Abraham's "seed") from the pharaoh of Egypt, Yahweh is affirming the enduring truth and sustaining power of his memory for his chosen people (Exodus 1-15).

---

[133] As countless commentators have observed, even as God fumed over Adam and Eve's actions, he sowed clothing for them. Despite what they had done, God continued to view them with compassion (Genesis 3:21).

Many Hebrew psalms have to do with Yahweh remembering his people. Consider Psalm 98:3, which reminds its readers that "God remembered his loving kindness to his people." In similar fashion, Psalm 111:5 tells the people that Yahweh will "remember" his covenant forever. Alternately, some psalms depict the people reminding Yahweh of his covenant with them, a point we will explore further later (Ps 25:6; Ps 106:4). In every instance, memory, God's loving and empowering memory, is the basis of the Hebrews' relationship with him.

Yet it is in the writings of the prophets (*devim)* that we see the force of God's memory most clearly. Time after time after time, Yahweh reminds the people that despite everything they have done to trouble and anger him, he will nonetheless remember his covenant with them. One day, he promises, the nation will see the fruit of the promise he made to Abraham. One day, God vows, he will return to Earth and establish for all time the kingdom he has promised his people. One day, one glorious day, Messiah will come. And on that day, God promises, all the people of the world will see him (Isaiah 65:17-18; Jeremiah 33:14-18; Amos 9:11-15).

Hence, be it the Egyptians, Assyrians, Hittites, or Hebrews, we see that the people of the ancient near east saw memory as crucial for their communications with each other and the gods (or in the case of the Hebrews, God). Memory was their way to live lives favored by the gods, the way to approach their deities for grace and blessing, the means by which they could live this life well. It was also the pathway for living well in the life beyond this earthly one. Like us today, the people of the ancient near east could not live without memory. Memory was essential to their existence.

Generally speaking, however, aside from perhaps the Hebrews, we do not see any effort on the part of ancient near eastern people to understand memory as a uniquely human activity. We do not see them attempt to ponder memory as a particular aspect or unique facet of their experience. For them, memory was simply another dimension, albeit an important one, of their lives. They did not consider it an object of independent reflection.

The Greeks changed this. For the Greeks, memory was an object and experience worthy of extensive consideration and study. Because the literature on this is vast, we will restrict ourselves to looking at two philosophers who studied memory in detail: Plato (428-348 B.C.) and Aristotle (384-322 B.C.). First, Plato. Plato saw memory as a process of deliberate inscription, a deliberate inscription of a perception on, metaphorically speaking, a wax tablet. When someone tries to remember something, when a person tries to store a perception that becomes, as all perceptions eventually do, knowledge, she "imprints" the perception into her mind, the metaphorical wax tablet.[134]

Once the perception is imprinted, it stays. Like an ancient ruler's signet ring seal on an important document, it cannot be ignored or lost. It's permanent. The perception thus becomes a memory that becomes knowledge, an

[134] *Memory,* 19; Plato, *Meno,* trans. W. K. C. Guthrie (New York: Penguin, 1956), £ 81-82.

inviolate and thoroughly embedded mental record of a sensory experience.[135]

Of note is that Plato distinguished between perceptions and knowledge that a person is consciously trying to remember, and perceptions and knowledge into which a person comes simply by walking through the world. Put another way, it seems that Plato differentiated between what we call sensory memory, raw, fundamental, and often short term memory, and long term memory. He valued the input of the senses as much as he revered the brain's ability to retain it.

In addition, it is worth mentioning that for Plato, knowledge is multi-dimensional. As he presents it in the *Republic,* the knowledge that we acquire through perception is ultimately derived from what he calls the "Forms." Set apart from Earth in an "ideal" world, the Forms represent the "blueprint" for every object in the physical reality. Every object that we see in our physical reality has a counterpart, a foundational counterpart in the world of Forms without which it could not exist or be understood and named. For instance, for every variety of horse on this planet, there exists one ideal "form" of a horse from which all varieties are derived. If an ideal form for a horse did not exist, we would not have horses, nor would we know how to describe one if we saw it. When we see and remember, we are actually seeing and remembering, through our soul (*psyche*), the particular form for this memory. When we remember a black horse, we are able to do so because our soul is remembering the

---

[135] *Ibid.*, and Paul Ricoeur, *Memory, History, Forgetting*, trans. Kathleen Blarney and David Pellauer (Chicago: University of Chicago, 2004).

ideal form of a horse and is enabling us to associate it with the animal standing before us. Hence, although we imprint (remember) a perception on our wax tablet of a mind, we are actually doing so because our soul is remembering the ideal forms of the objects that make up this perception and, as a result, transforming them into knowledge. Just as we might consider them doing so today, Plato envisioned that sensory and long term memory will eventually become one.[136]

Moreover, for Plato, memory is "dialectical." It's an art, an art that is developed through a process of oral question and exchange about remembering and recollection.[137] As Plato saw it, by engaging in a systematic procedure of collection, response, and recall, a person comes to remember and, furthermore, demonstrate that she does. Memory is a work in constant progress. In this, Plato emphasized oral recall over writing, highlighting what he called "living memory," what people remember on the basis of oral recitation, as the preferred picture of remembering and recall. Living memory is what people remember when they apprehend and imprint and, most important, recollect the Forms. Living memory is knowledge which people use to deal with the practicalities of their lives, including the challenges of death and dying.[138]

Hence, for Plato, memory is a two stage process. First, it is what a person perceives and embeds in a metaphorical wax tablet in response to what her soul "remembers" about

---

136 Plato, *The Republic,* trans. Francis MacDonald Cornford (New York: Oxford University, 1970), XIX.

137 Otherwise known as the Socratic Method, still used in classrooms today. The Socratic Method encourages people to examine an issue or position by repeatedly questioning and picking apart the assumptions behind it until one arrives at its core meaning.

138 *Memory,* 23ff.

the Forms as she walks through the world. Second, it is how a person recalls what she has embedded in her wax tablet, her picture of the world.

Now, Aristotle. In contrast to Plato, Aristotle believed that true knowledge is to be found within the world. He did not subscribe to Plato's theory of Forms. Knowledge is solely a work of the senses. For Aristotle, memory therefore consists of perceptions that the mind, which Aristotle (like Plato) saw as a wax tablet, metaphorically speaking, imprints onto itself. Memory is the fruit of perception that has become true knowledge. It has nothing to do with what is outside the world á la Plato's Forms, but is solely the result of processes within this world. As Aristotle sees it, memory is not about the soul "remembering" an ideal form in an ideal world, but about the brain apprehending and processing what it encounters in the present and visible world.

Memory is therefore a thing "of the past" which the mind holds physically in the present, an object of perception which the holder is then able to recall as knowledge. It is a copy, an imprinted copy of what a person has perceived and come to know, a copy of sense experience and knowledge that a person lays down in the "wax" of her mind. It comes from this world, and it is to be used in this world.[139]

We might compare Aristotle's idea of memory and knowledge to that of the scientific method, developed

---

[139] Aristotle, "On Memory," in *The Complete Works of Aristotle,* ed. Jonathan Barnes (Princeton, New Jersey: Princeton University, 1984), Vol I. It is also worth noting that despite his seemingly "earthbound" view of knowledge, Aristotle in fact believed strongly in the notion of eternity. See Richard Sorabji, *Time, creation, and the continuum* (Chicago: University of Chicago, 1983).

by Francis Bacon during Western Europe's sixteenth and seventeenth century Scientific Revolution. According this method, when a scientist sets out to investigate an empirical phenomenon, he (during this time, all scientists were men!) must first develop a hypothesis about what he expects to find. Subsequently, he devises and performs an experiment to confirm or deny the hypothesis's validity. In so doing, the scientist relies solely on the physical evidence he gathers in the course of his investigation to formulate his conclusions. He does not make a decision about anything except on the basis of what he observes, and he does not look to anything beyond the physical evidence to test and evaluate his hypothesis. The scientist does not therefore assume that there is a larger truth or meaning to be found. He's interested only in analyzing and understanding the physical phenomenon that the experiment presents to him.

What he sees determines what he believes.[140]

For Aristotle, as for Plato, recollection is a learned process, one at which some people are better than others. Recollection is a matter of habit and judgment, an activity which a person masters by engaging in it regularly and systematically. Through practiced recollection, a person recalls what her mind holds, what is embedded in the wax tablets of her brain. Recollection brings up a memory that has been stored as a copy of a perception (that has become knowledge), an image, not of imagination, but of tangible connection with what has happened. As a person learns to recollect with greater ability and skill, she is able to able to more adroitly recall and integrate her memories into her

---

[140] Francis Bacon, *Novum Organum,* trans. and ed. Peter Urbach and John Gibson (Chicago: Carus, 1994).

ongoing perception of and reflection on her immediate experience.

Also, like Plato, Aristotle emphasized that writing was of minimal importance in memory. For him, memories were best explored and recalled through oral challenge and exchange. Engaging and responding to her memory orally best enabled a person to recollect and recall the imprints of knowledge that she had gathered through her perception.[141]

To sum up, we observe that Plato and Aristotle both believed that what perception takes in through the senses comes to be imprinted on the brain, somewhat like an imprint on a wax tablet. In addition, both men recognized that a person will not "imprint" everything she takes in, that some perceptions may not, as they understood the term, become knowledge. On the other hand, they agree that, properly trained, a person can recollect the genuinely important information that she has imprinted in her mind. Recollection is an art, a technique at which a person grows steadily more competent as she engages in careful and considered practice of it.

Hence, we see that for the Greeks, unlike the peoples of the ancient near east, memory is a distinctive activity deserving of study and contemplation. It is an art, an art of perceiving, imprinting, and recollecting. To remember is to consciously engage in recollection and recall, and to think about memory is to deliberately think about the past in the present moment. To remember is to increase one's knowledge of her immediate experience. In contrast to the ancient near eastern vision of memory as central to a meaningful life

[141] *Memory,* 25.

vision, the Greeks viewed memory as a means to an end and not necessarily a totality or end in itself.

Before we move onto the Middle Ages, let us note, for the record, that the Romans, who eventually supplanted the Greeks as the intellectual leaders (although they in fact copied much from the Greeks) of the Western world, viewed memory in much the same way. It was an art, a habit, a practice to be mastered, a process in which a person strives and endeavors to recall, on cue, what has been "impressed" on her mind.[142]

With the collapse of the Western Roman Empire in 476, the political landscape of Europe irrecoverably changed. Memory, however, did not. Let's consider the ever profound Augustine (354-430). For Augustine, the African prelate and bishop of Hippo, memory consisted of what he described as "images," a series of nonphysical pictures that a person has lined up in systematic fashion in her mind and which she could recall later. Today we might call this synesthesia, the term that, as we noted, describes the practice by which people with extraordinarily retentive memories bring their memories to light.[143]

Yet Augustine wrestled with how to distinguish between the memory of a "thing," for instance, a horse, and the memory of a "notion" such as health or forgetfulness. He also wondered about the "vast spaces" between the images that were apparently in his mind. If, he reasoned, he has

---

[142] See Marcus Tullius Cicero, *On the Good Life*, trans. Michael Grant (New York: Penguin, 1971).

[143] See Gary Willis, *St. Augustine: A Life* (New York: Penguin, 2005). Consult as well Simon Critichley, *Memory Theatre* (London: Fitzcarraldo, 2014).

memories of oceans, stars, and mountains, then he must also have a memory of the spaces between them, the planes of dimension that separate them in the world. Yet if his mind only stored images of objects, how would he therefore remember a "space?" How does one have an image of a "space?"[144]

Each of these questions is worth a lifetime of study. For the time being, however, we will restrict ourselves to noting that for Augustine, memory is a function of the *memoria* (the Latin word from which we get the English word "memory"). Center and processor of all thought, the *memoria* is essential to a human's ability to remember. When a person perceives, her *memoria* analyzes and processes it. Through her *memoria,* this person acquires and learns, and through the *memoria* she comes to store what she has learned. And it is through the *memoria* that a person recalls what she has stored. Augustine thus saw the *memoria* in much the same fashion that Plato saw the soul. Both soul and *memoria* process, both soul and *memoria* remember, and both soul and *memoria* teach and enlighten. Given the extent to which Augustine folded Plato's thinking into his Christian theology, this is not surprising.[145]

Moreover, in a way not unlike Plato and his idea that the soul remembered eternal realities or truths, Augustine thought about the relationship of memory and God. Observing that memory contains "logical, grammatical truths" which his own mind "recognized" as true, he went on to say that the knowledge of God is something that

---

[144] Augustine, *Confessions,* trans. R. S. Pine Coffin (New York: Penguin, 1961), XI-XII

[145] *Memory,* 42-43; *Confessions,* XI-XII.

a person learns and subsequently stores in her memory as a "communion" with the eternal. Memory is therefore the starting point of human exchange with the divine (a conclusion for which we have already contended). It is the seat and enabler of how humans come to know God. As Plato's soul connects people with the eternal Forms, so does memory (*memoria*) function as the conduit for ascertaining and imbibing the eternal truths rippling through time, space, and reality.[146]

On the other hand, as did his Greek and Roman predecessors, Augustine saw memory as an art. Memory is a process in which a person learns, by traveling through a complex and intricate series of places and structures in her *memoria*, to recall what she has stored in her mind. He viewed the acts of storage and recollection as abilities which a person could either use and subsequently improve or, intentionally or otherwise, ignore and delete. For Augustine, although everyone remembers some things, it is the person who is able to remember and recall these in a systematic and comprehensive way who has perfected the mnemonic art to its fullest extent.

Subsequent European thinkers continued in this vein. Although memory remained an art, it took on new form. As the Middle Ages faded and the Renaissance took hold in Italy and eventually the whole of Europe, people came to view memory through they termed "memory theaters." They believed they could "store" memory in the seats, aisles, and scaffoldings of a mental theater, then access it at will. Across Europe, from Guilio Camillo (1480-1544) and Robert Fludd's (1574-1637) constructions of memory in imaginary

146 *Ibid.*

theatrical playhouses to Dante's (1265-1321) *Divine Comedy* and its carefully layered complexities of Purgatory, Heaven, and Hell, people set about to "institutionalize" memory in the folds of their minds. For them, memory involved one, a collecting of perceptions; two, a storing of perceptions in the theaters of their minds; and three, the process by which, level by level, they found in these theaters what, at a given time, they needed to know. Memory was decidedly an art, a voluntary and self-sustaining process to recall knowledge that a person had intentionally stored and now needed to use in the present moment. In harbingers of the modern notion of synesthesia, people viewed memory as a matter of consciously recollecting what had been consciously put in the "theaters" of the brain.[147]

To this point, what we have seen is that aside from the inhabitants of the ancient near east, people viewed memory as not so much an experience but as a task, an art, a challenge. Memory was something in which a person ought to engage, something a person needed to do to function with reason and purpose in civil society, an activity at which a person must be adept in order to understand herself and her place in the world. Memory was a deliberate choice and decision.

Moreover, memory could be found. Quite apart from the person remembering it, memory had a life of its own.

The Enlightenment turned this upside down. One of the pivotal shifts in Western history, the Enlightenment marked the end of people using God to find truth. It insisted

---

[147] See Dante Alighieri's *Divine Comedy* (New York: Holt, Rinehart and Winston, 1968); Francis A. Yates, *The Art of Memory* (Chicago: University of Chicago, 1966), and *Confessions, op cit.*

that people could find truth with their own reason, and their own reason only.[148]

Memory did not emerge from this shift unscathed. Let's look at John Locke. Today, John Locke is most famous in the West for his assertion that all humans have the right to "life, liberty, and property." We see this declamation, in slightly modified form, in America's *Declaration of Independence,* which affirms the right to "life, liberty, and the [somewhat Benthamian] pursuit of happiness."[149] But Locke was also known for his work on knowledge and its relationship to memory, and it is to this that we now turn.[150]

Fundamental to Locke's view of memory are his ideas about the human being and how the human being knows things. For Locke, human identity is established on the basis of consciousness, a consciousness that can be "extended backwards to any past action or thought; so far reaches the identity of the person, it is the same *self* now it was then." It is a person's consciousness of herself that marks her as a genuinely sentient being.[151]

Hence, to remember is to experience one's self, to experience the fact of one's existence. Memory begins and ends with the self. In contrast to Augustine, Locke, though

---

148 Although the literature is voluminous, see Peter Gay, *The Enlightenment: The Rise of Modern Paganism* (New York: W. W. Norton, 1996); and Anthony Pagden, *The Enlightenment: Why It Still Matters* (New York: Random House, 2013).

149 So did Jeremy Bentham, the classic utilitarian, say that we ought to seek the greatest happiness for the greatest number of people. All else is ancillary. For more, see the Internet Encyclopedia of Philosophy (www.iep.utm.edu/**bentham**/).

150 *Essay Concerning Human Understanding, op cit.*

151 *Essay Concerning Human Understanding,* II, XXVII

he believed firmly in God, believed that the transcendent (think of Plato's notion of Forms or Augustine's idea of an eternal Father) has nothing to do with memory.[152]

With Locke, memory is no longer an art or skill, but rather the experiential narrative of a human being, the story which describes and contains the happenings of a particular person's life. Memory is the meaning of a life, the "continuity" and experience of time and space in which a person constructs her sense of self. It constitutes the ideas and knowledge that populate a person's life, a "repository" and constantly changing record of her apprehensions of and reflections on her experience. It's never static, it's never constant. In a way, it doesn't really exist.[153]

With this, we leave the medieval picture of memory far behind. No longer is memory a theater in which a person systematically stores her perceptions for later recall. No longer is it an art, no longer is it a practice. Now memory is simply an experience, the subjective experience of what would eventually become, as we shall see, subjective knowledge.

Picking up the pieces Locke left of the Western imagination, David Hume (1711-1776), the Scottish philosopher whom we have mentioned previously, proposed some influential juxtapositions between memory and imagination. In so doing, Hume, most famous, or depending

---

[152] *Ibid.*, II, X. Throughout this meditation, we will use transcendent to describe that which exists but which is not a physical part of this material reality. For instance, God is transcendent, meaning that he is "trans" (translated in many Indo-European languages as "beyond") normative sentience.

[153] *Ibid.*

on one's perspective, infamous for his observations on the agnostic character of knowledge and the impossibility of proving a miracle to be true, Hume deepened Locke's idea of the self as arbiter of reality and, by extension, memory. His thoughts would shape not only how the Enlightenment viewed memory but the Romantics' view as well. Indeed, Hume's observations would continue to transform the Western view of memory well into the twentieth century.

We will touch on only a few elements of Hume's thought to make our point. One, we should note that for Hume, the human being is, as he put it, is "nothing but a bundle of perceptions, which succeed each other with an inconceivable rapidity, and are in personal flux and movement." Put another way, as Locke viewed the human being as a movement of conscious experience, so did Hume see the human as an amalgam of process and perception. We are our perceptions—and our perceptions are always changing.[154]

Two, memory, Hume asserted, cannot be distinguished from the imagination. What we really have in memory is "belief," the sense of the "immediacy" of an idea in the mind. Memory is therefore as much present as much as it is absent, and imagination is as real as it is unreal. Highly fluid, memory is always changing, a product of each passing moment, the fruit of a continuous experience of consciousness. We cannot necessarily find it, nor can we necessarily know it. All we can do is perceive, consciously or not, each passing moment, and construct ourselves and our memory exactly as these perceptions demand, no more, no

---

[154] *An Inquiry Concerning Human Understanding,* Section II.

less. Nothing is permanent, and nothing can be definitively known.[155]

We are therefore conscious selves who are consciously experiencing the world, yet we do not know, permanently or indubitably, anything in it. Our memory is there, but it is not. We are selves, but we are not; selves who remember, but who really do not.

In coming to this conclusion, Hume effectively demolished the notion that memory could ever be anything other than a subjective experience. As Hume saw it, we are nothing more than disconnected selves in a scattered, random, and unknowable world. Experience, and even *it* is shaky, is all we have.

In short, how could memory possibly be an art if it is merely an event we simply, by dint of our humanness, experience?

In Hume's trenchant observations, we see the beginnings of a way of viewing the human being that soon exceeded the Scot's wildest imagination, a human being who is defined by nothing more than where, emotionally as well as geographically, she is at a given point in time. As the Enlightenment's ethos continued to penetrate every corner of Europe, Hume's vision of memory would carry the day: it is only life, the present and subjective experience of being, that matters.

Perhaps. But what, in truth, is life?

With this, we turn to the Romantics. We will cast a wide net here, touching not just on those who have come to be associated with the Romantic movement of the early nineteenth century, but those who followed in its wake,

---

[155] *Ibid.*, Book II-III.

people like Marcel Proust, Henri Bergson (whose name we have seen before), Sigmund Freud, and others. We will see how the Romantics took Locke and Hume's notion of the self as the center of memory and memory as the experience of consciousness at the center of existence to make memory that which drives and centers everything we do. In addition, we will illustrate how this in turn set the stage for, in the wake of the immense carnage and hopelessness that permeated the early and mid-twentieth century, memory's evolution into a vehicle of collective trauma and corporate remembrance.

We begin with the French philosopher and voyeur Jean Jacques Rousseau (1712-1778). Although Rousseau did not write during the early nineteenth century, the period generally acknowledged as the "official" Romantic era, he nonetheless wrote in a highly romantic vein. Nowhere is this most true than in his *Confessions.* Though much could be said about the *Confessions,* Rousseau's poignant and incisive account of his early life and learning, and how it created an autobiographical style so radically different from that of Augustine's *Confessions*, we will restrict ourselves to a few points which are pertinent to our present journey.

Prime among these is that in nearly polar contrast to Augustine, Rousseau presented his "confessions" as an experience influenced solely by earthly circumstance and caprice. Whereas Augustine pondered everything in his account through the lens of divine love and faithfulness, Rousseau told of a life lived entirely apart from transcendence (although he did make an occasional reference to "Providence"). He wrote as a self in a closed world, a self shaped by that closed world, and a self that is conscious only of that world. Rousseau's is a highly subjective account of a peculiarly insular process of personal growth. It is an account in which memory, his recollections of his childhood and his recounting of his numerous adult encounters with a number of mistresses becomes, significantly, the means to finding truth. Rousseau makes memory the way in which he comes to know what is most real, his personal key to dealing with the uninvited and unintended life circumstances in which he finds himself. It's not an art, nor is it a practice. It's a path and road, a path and road that have become the permanent yet dissembled consciousness of existential experience. As he writes,

> "I promised to depict myself as I am; and to know me in my latter years it is necessary to have known me well in my youth. As objects generally make less impression on me than does the memory of them, and as all my ideas take pictorial form, the first features to engrave themselves on my mind have remained there, and such as have subsequently imprinted themselves have combined with these rather than obliterated them."[156]

And later on, he adds,

> "The further I go in my story, the less order and sequence I can put into it. The disturbances of my later life have not

---

[156] Jean Jacques Rousseau, *The Confessions,* trans. J. M. Cohen (Baltimore: Penguin, 1954), Books Four, Five.

> left events time to fall into shape in my head. They have been too numerous, too confused, too unpleasant to be capable of straightforward narration."[157]

Memory therefore has very little independent force or meaning. Even if memory leads one to the truth, this truth will not be *the* Truth, the truth of metaphysical absolutes that drove the Hebrews and Augustine to call upon God. It will be a truth that is specific to Rousseau, a deeply and uniquely personal insight that enables him, and only him, to make sense of himself and his world. Rousseau's is a thoroughly postmodern account of existence: truth is relative to each individual and her journey, and absolute truth does not exist. As truth becomes the self, so does the self become the truth.

Truth is what we make it to be.

In Rousseau's wake, memory became, more than ever, that which held together very disparate lives in a very disparate reality. It became the fulcrum of the human effort to establish an absolute sense of existence, an existence of definable purpose yet an existence afloat in a sea of highly scattered and seemingly meaningless particulars. Remembering is the point, indeed, the only point of existence.

Let's look at the British poet Samuel Taylor Coleridge (1772-1834). One of Coleridge's most famous poems is *Kubla Khan: or, a Vision in a Dream.*[158] In it, the author, by

---

157 *Ibid.*, Book Twelve.

158 For the historians among us, yes, the name of this Mongolian ruler is usually spelled "Kublai".

his account, having left the city to retreat to a small house in northern England, one day falls into a deep sleep. In this sleep, he experiences a profoundly moving dream. When he awakes, he sets out to record it. His recollections describe a world filled with the glory of the Mongolian ruler Kublai Khan (grandson of the better known Genghis Khan). As Coleridge pens out what he remembers, he realizes that the dream has changed his life. He feels revived, having "within" him a vision of a "damsel with a dulcimer" whose song causes him such deep delight that it "'twould win me, that with music loud and long [and], I would build that dome [Kublai Khan's palace] in air." His memory of his dream inspires Coleridge to build and live in a new world, a new reality of pondering and imagination. His life can never be the same. Memory has individuated and redefined everything about his sense of self and what is real. He will never know anything in the same way again.[159]

The aptly named William Wordsworth (1770-1850) continues in this fashion. In his *Lines Composed a Few Miles above Tintern Abbey,* Wordsworth writes eloquently of the power of memory to shape him in the present moment. As he returns to wander on the banks of the River Wye, he remembers,

> "'These beauteous forms,'" that "'through a long absence, have not been to me as is a landscape to a blind man's eye; but oft, in lonely rooms, and 'mid the din of towns and cities, I have owed to them in hours

---

159 Samuel Taylor Coleridge, "Kubla Khan" in W. H. Auden, ed., *Poets of the English Language* (New York: Viking, 1950), Vol IV.

> of weariness, sensations sweet, felt in the blood, and felt along the heart.'"[160]

Wordsworth's memory of the "beauteous" forms moves him deeply, stirring his innermost heart. He remembers who he was before this memory, and he thinks about who, on its other side, he has become. He realizes how this memory has stirred and moved him as few things have before. In remembering this memory, Wordsworth sees a "new" present. He knows he will never be the same.

Wordsworth also comes to see that memory is a reminder of the fleetingness of existence. Memory is as much about remembering as it is about forgetting. Toward the end of the poem, he writes,

> "If solitude, or fear, or pain, or grief, should be thy portion, with what healing thoughts of tender joy wilt thou remember me, and these my exhortation! Nor, perchance—if I should be where I no more can hear thy voice, or catch from thy wild eyes these gleams of past existence—wilt thou then forget that on the banks of this delightful stream we stood together[!]"[161]

Not only does memory create a new present, it conjures a new future as well. In highly poignant words, Wordsworth captures the subjective heart of memory: the human

---

[160] William Wordsworth, "Lines Composed a Few Miles Above Tintern Abbey" in *Poets, op cit.*

[161] *Ibid.*

longing to be remembered. Will you, Dorothy, he asks, remember me? Will you connect what has passed with what is now present? Will you reflect on what is now gone so as to fold it into what has now come? Wordsworth makes memory the creator of self, its narrative of beginning and, significantly, the hope of its end. He links memory to self, self to community, and community to the world. Memory is everything.

We next turn to the colorful and dashing Lord Byron (1788-1824). In language reminiscent of Warren Zevon, whose heartbreaking words we looked at earlier in this book, Byron writes in *Fare Thee Well,*

> "Still thine own its life retaineth, still must mine, though bleeding, eat; and the undying thought which paineth is—that we no more may meet. These are words of deeper sorrows than the wail above the dead; both shall live, but every morrow wake us from a widow'd bed."[162]

Byron understands all too well the nature of human existence. He wants to be remembered, but he knows that even if he is, he will never again meet this person to whom he is making this request. She is gone forever. The self he is, and the self she is will never again be united together as selves, except in memory. It is memory that holds their lives together, and it is memory that will keep them, once together but now forever apart, as one. For Byron, memory connects his present known with a future unknown even as,

---

[162] George Gordon, Lord Byron, "Fare Thee Well," in *Poets, op cit.*

ironically, that future leaves him. So does he write toward the end of the poem, "Sear'd in heart, and lone, and blighted." Memory is all he has to establish his sense of self, now, at the end and, he perhaps hopes, beyond it.[163]

Yet for all this, memory, as Bryon realized, will not preserve him. It is only itself, and one day, as he well knew, it will vanish completely. It is not genuine hope.[164]

Before we move on, let's remind ourselves that for the Romantics memory is the definer of a self that is disconnected from any larger picture of reality or truth. Alone in a vast and exciting world, the self has only memory to hold its sense of individuality, community, and cosmos together. Memory is the glue, memory is the divide. It connects the self with its life, and it also separates the self from its life. Hence, as the Western world continued to move away from belief in a personal God and the framework of transcendental purpose it provided, memory was left as the only thing from which people could find meaning. Absolutely free yet deeply enchained by its own despair, Western humanity looked to memory as its only hope.[165]

We now look at Marcel Proust, whose astonishingly lengthy recounting of his life, *A La Recherche du Temps Perdu* (*In Search of Lost Time*), is universally acknowledged as one of humanity's richest meditations on the power of the past.[166] Our interests are twofold. One is look more fully at

---

163 *Ibid.*

164 On Bryon, consider, for one, John Galt's *The Life of Lord Byron* (New York: Sagwan, 2015).

165 For additional reading on this topic, see Charles Taylor, *A Secular Age* (Cambridge, Massachusetts: Harvard University, 2007).

166 *Lost Time, op cit.* It is worth noting that Karl Ove Knausgard's, *My Struggle,* trans. Don Barlett (New York: Farrar, Straus and

what researchers have termed Proust's use of "involuntary memory." The second is to consider Proust's view of time, time as passage, and time as the flow of memory, and how these two visions of passage fuse together to define and describe the fullness, in memory, of human existence.

As we observed earlier, involuntary memory is a memory that a person experiences (remembers), but one that this person does not consciously try to retrieve or produce. As Proust sees it, involuntary memories are driven by sensations, scents, music, or other things that, without a person really trying to get them to do so, invoke memories that are associated with them. They are memories we didn't ask or try to have, but are rather memories that are stirred by what we, without really thinking about it, presently experience.

In "Overture" (the opening chapter of *In Search of Lost Time*), Proust, thinking about a "madeleine" (a small sponge cake made in the Lorraine region of France) and how eating it stirred memories of his aunt Léonie, remarks that, "The sight of the little madeleine had recalled nothing to my mind before I tasted it." Proust had not been trying to remember his aunt when he saw the madeleine. Tasting it, however, sparked, without him insisting it do so, an "involuntary" memory of her.[167]

Elsewhere in *Search of Lost Time,* Proust writes,

Giroux, 2009-2013), an even lengthier recollection than Proust's, has garnered numerous awards around the world. Accounts of memory and recollection, it seems, remain as popular in our day as that of Proust's.

[167] *Lost Time,* Vol I, 36

> "And as in the game wherein the Japanese amuse themselves by filling a porcelain bowl with water and steeping in it little pieces of paper which until then are without character or form, but, the moment they become wet, stretch and twist and take on color and distinctive shape, become flowers or houses or people solid and recognizable, so in that moment all the flowers in our garden and in M. Swann's park, and the water-lilies on the Vivonne and the good folk of the village and their little dwellings and the parish church and the whole of Combray and its surroundings, taking shape and solidity, sprang into being, towns and gardens alike, from my cup of tea."[168]

Without him even trying to make it do so, Proust's one cup of tea triggers a profusion of memory, a flood of recollection and recall that speaks vividly of what he has unconsciously buried in his brain. Not only is memory an experience, it is an experience over which we do not always have conscious control. It forms and shapes us without us even asking it to do so. Like the Romantics who lived earlier in the century in which he was born, Proust renders memory the center of existential encounter.

To our second point, Proust's picture of time and memory, we cite the following meditation, one that appears in the closing lines of his masterpiece:

[168] *Ibid.*, 54.

> "I would therein describe men—even should that give them the semblance of monstrous creatures—as occupying in Time a place far more considerable than the so restricted one allotted them in space, a place, on the contrary, extending boundlessly since, giant-like, reaching far back into the years, they touch simultaneously epochs of their lives—with countless intervening days between—so widely separated from one another in Time."[169]

People, Proust seems to be saying, stretch beyond what we remember. Their lives are like vast amoebas, spreading and bubbling across all the events and epochs of their time and, as a result, extending almost indefinitely the boundaries of the small and finite space they occupied in the course of their lives. Their memories of the past become memories of the present that in turn become memories of the future. Space craters, time is undone, recall becomes endless: memory has tamed them all.[170]

In another instance, Proust observes,

> "It is because I used to think of certain things, of certain people, while I was

---

[169] *Ibid.*, Vol II, 1124

[170] Ironically, Proust's conception of time ran counter to that of Henri Bergson, whose metaphysical view of memory we noted earlier. For Bergson, time was immensely present and real, and memory therefore as presently real as that which was not. See Jimena Canales, *The Physicist and the Philosopher* (Princeton, New Jersey, Princeton University, 2016).

> roaming along them, that the things, the people which they taught me to know, and these alone, I still take seriously, still give me joy. Whether it be that the faith which creates has ceased to exist in me, or that reality will take shape in the memory alone, the flowers that people show me nowadays for the first time never seem to me to be true flowers."[171]

Because he uses memory to create it, Proust cannot always see the present as real and true. What is, has become what is not. Once again, time has collapsed into itself and space has vanished. Only memory remains, memory as start and end, memory as bedrock and framework, all at once yet for no reason. Nothing is true.

As he considers his affections for a lady named Albertine, Proust remarks,

> "And I ought really to have discovered sooner that one day I should no longer be in love with Albertine. When I had realized, from the difference that existed between what the importance of her person and of her actions was to me and what it was to other people, that my love was not so much a love for her as a love in myself, I might have deduced various consequences from this subjective nature of my love and that, being a mental state, it might easily long survive the prison,

---

171 *Ibid.*, Vol I, 141.

> it must, like every mental state, even the most permanent, find itself one day obsolete, be 'replaced,' and that when that day came everything that seemed to attach me so pleasantly, indissolubly, to the memory of Albertine would no longer exist for me."[172]

Though wondrous and true, whether for years or an instant, memory is nonetheless fleeting, a hazy and fading picture of a past that is no longer here. It is present as much as it is absent, trapped by time even as it shapes it. Either way, however, memory cannot overcome the fact of time. It is in time that memory is born, and it is in time that memory dies. Whereas time comes and goes yet never really disappears completely, memory is eventually lost altogether. Memory is the synthesizer, but time is the ground. And even it is vacuous and fleeting.

As Proust further notes,

> "There was, then, embedded in my friend Bloch a father Bloch who lagged forty years behind his son, told impossible stories and laughed as loudly at them from the heart of my friend as did the separate, visible, and authentic father Bloch, since to the laugh which the latter emitted, not without several times repeating the last word so that his public might taste the full flavor of the story."[173]

---

[172] *Ibid.*, Vol II, 773.

[173] *Ibid.*, Vol I, 581.

Though we suspect the son knew full well from whom he acquired his story telling skills, we also suspect that he probably did not always know where his father's influence left off and his own creativity began. Memory influences even as it retreats, colors even as it goes black. So does the dust settle: only time remains.

In another observation, this one made as he watched a group of young women, Proust states,

> "The individual is a part of something that is more generally diffused than himself. By this reckoning, our parents furnish us not only with those habitual gestures which are the outlines of our face and voice, but also with certain mannerisms in speech, certain favorite expressions, which, almost as unconscious as an intonation, almost as profound, indicate likewise a definite point of view towards life."[174]

As he did in his earlier conclusion about father and son Bloch, Proust notes that we become our memories, and our memories become us. Entangled in the passage of time, we walk as memory making beings who are constantly making memories of the memories we make, even as the memories we make render us consistently timeless beings. To live is to carry memories, memories of our parents, our grandparents, and more, to recall what time has sown, yet never to quite know what it means. Time enables all, yet fractures all, too. Remembrance is never fixed, recall is never fully known.

---

[174] *Ibid.,*681.

Memory is no more than a nuance of time. It's nothing.

It seems, then, that in every way Proust has captured much of the way that we see memory today. His thoughts on the role of memory in the human experience; his observations on the relationship of memory to time; his notion of involuntary memory; and his idea of how a memory influences, in some way, every generation that follows it all coincide with what we have noted, to this point, about the workings and processes of memory. With Proust, we see the beginning of memory in our time. Building on the ethereality of the Romantics and the Western European rejection of the conventional notion of God, Proust developed a picture of memory in which we invest even today.[175]

Now let us look, briefly, at the work of Sigmund Freud (1856-1939). Universally acknowledged as the father of modern psychoanalysis, Freud exercised an influence which, although it has waned in recent years, was, at its peak, vast. This includes his work on memory.

For Freud, memory is the root of the many neuroses which he believed plague every human being. Many of the psychological problems with which people deal, he insisted, are the result of neuroses, unconscious responses to various experiences of childhood trauma, usually of a sexual nature, which people unwittingly embed in their memories. Memory, be it conscious or unconscious, is therefore seminal in creating who people are. It is only as they deal with and overcome the negative impact of their memories that people

---

[175] For more, see Friedrich Nietzsche, *The Gay Science,* translated by Walter Kaufmann. (New York: Random House, 1974), Book Four, §125.

can become whom they are most destined to be. Memory is the key to a fulfilling life, the door to a meaningful existence.

Just as we do today, Freud suggested that we do not "remember" a memory but rather the memory of a memory. When a patient remembers her memories, she does not remember it in the way that it actually happened. Her memory changes even as she remembers. And she doesn't always know how it does. Hence, even if this person manages to eviscerate this memory and construct a new view of herself, she will never be able to shake off the old completely. She will carry it until the day she dies. Total eradication is nearly impossible. Good or bad, positive or negative, this person's memory, for better or worse, will always make her who she is. She is a product and creation of her memory.[176]

Like Proust, Freud presented memory in a thoroughly modern way. He made memory the constructor of the self, the formative determinant of a person's felt and expressed humanness. Complex and multi-faceted, memory is the starting and ending point of what a human being is, and will be.

Proust and Freud's conclusions mirrored and deepened those that had come before them, hardening the edges and limits of physical possibility. Writing in the long shadow that the Enlightenment and the Romantics cast over Western Europe, they used memory to arrive at a radically new way of viewing and understanding the self. Their deft phrases and measured insights about the self and its experience of recall

---

176 Sigmund Freud, *A General Introduction to Psychoanalysis,* trans. Joan Riviere (New York: Washington Square, 1924), Part III; *Interpretation of Dreams, op cit.*

pushed memory completely away from the metaphysical, catapulting it into the birth of another seminal movement in Western thought: modernity.

What's modernity? A late nineteenth century product of the Enlightenment and Industrial Revolution, modernity posited that the only way for people to find meaning was for them to take everything that they had once found to be meaningful completely apart. Shoving God far to the margins, if not beyond them, of probability, modernity was the Western world's effort to detach itself, with finality, from any and all visions of transcendence as a way to find hope and meaning. It supplanted the idea of a divinely given narrative with a narrative of human individuation. Modernity made humanity the only driver of its history, rendering history and all that it comprised a work of this world and this world only.[177]

As the German philosopher Friedrich Nietzsche, speaking in the guise of a madman, famously put it at the time, "God is dead." And, he added, "We have all killed him." How right he was. Having in the past two centuries steadfastly done everything they could to jettison God from their vision of truth, the people of Western Europe really had "killed" him. They had made him inutile for any reasonable interpretation of existence. For them, God was as useless as he was unreal. In every way, God, Europe's onetime anchor of personality and truth, is over and gone.

With this, human beings now viewed themselves as free, completely and absolutely free to become whomever

---

177 See, to name just a few, Philipp Blom, *Fracture: Life and Culture in the West, 1918-1938* (New York: Basic, 2015); and Peter Gay, *Modernism: The Lure of Heresy* (New York: W. W. Norton, 2010).

and whatever they wished to be. They could go anywhere and explore anything they chose. Nothing was off limits, nothing was sacrosanct. Individual experience, regardless of its origin or outcome, was the only definer of meaning. Subjectivity was prime.[178]

Modernity shifted humanity's view of the self from one embedded in God to one embedded in the human being. Definitively rejecting the medieval view of the human being as a creation in the image of God, people came to construct their sense of self solely upon their perception of themselves in the world. They made their experience and interpretation of the world the unchallengeable basis of reality. The beginning and end of all that is real, the human being therefore became the only arbiter of what was true. Whatever and whoever they were, people were so because of themselves, and themselves alone. How they, and they alone, experienced and responded to the world became the sole adjudicator of possibility and truth.[179]

Significantly, although this insight set people, in a thoroughly existential sense, free, it also left them very lonely. It made them brave yet enormously pitiful beings, orphaned clumps of material sensibility caught in a maw of life, aspiration, and memory with no way out. God was gone, but they were, too. Edvard Munch's *Scream,* his unsettling painting of an anonymous and nameless human being trapped in a web of profound personal ennui, portrays

---

178 *The Gay Science, op cit.*

179 See, among others, Charles Taylor, *Sources of the Self: the Making of the Modern Identity* (Cambridge, Massachusetts: Harvard University, 1992); and Peter Watson, *Ideas: A History of Thought and Invention* (New York: Harper Perennial, 2006).

this aptly. And a line from Henrik Ibsen's *Peer Gynt* drives this home:

> "Was I ever myself? Where, whole, and true? Myself, with God's seal stamped on my brow?"[180]

No one knows who she is. All people have is their memory. And even it, grand as it is, is ultimately nowhere to be found.

With this, Western humanity made memory, more than ever, a defining experience of subjectivity, and nothing more. No longer was it a structure, level, or place; no longer was it a practice or art. No longer was it even oneself, for an absolute "self" had vanished. Memory was nothing more than a state of beingness, an intimation and awareness that encompassed and circumscribed, but not really, who a person was. Once a theater, once the truth, memory was now a nameless ocean, a vast and endless ocean of unfathomable space and time, a limitless and groundless narrative of the individual self, the disconnected and directionless story of every human being. Its shores had eroded, its waves untamed and subsumed: why, countless people asked, remember at all?[181]

So did memory end. Divorced from the past and banished from the present, it lost any relevance or point. Because experience, shorn of its transcendent epistemological anchor and bereft of permanent form or value, had become

---

[180] "Peer Gynt" in *Ibsen's Selected Plays,* ed. Brian Johnston (New York: W. W. Norton, 2004). For additional thoughts on Munch's painting, see http://marshytruth.blogspot.com/search?q=munch

[181] *Memory, op cit.*

relative, memory fell to pieces, torn apart by humanity's new openness to the immanent (not transcendent) possibilities of existence. If nothing has permanent form or foundation, then how can we possibly remember anything that matters or, much less, is true? And even if we could, what would be the point? The past was as uninviting as the present, for both were no more than evanescent expressions of temporal and fleeting beings. Who needs either one?[182]

Modernity left memory a waif, an erstwhile fountain of consciousness that was never really there. Caught in modernity's grip, memory became an outlier, an accessory, nothing more than the ever shifting and decisively shaky recollections of an indefinable and, in large part useless and unnecessary, past. It had uttered its last gasp.

Or as George Orwell portrayed it in his *1984,* "The past was erased, the erasure was forgotten, the lie became truth." Even what had been erased had been forgotten: only a lie, a fabrication of what was probably never there, remained.[183]

Contradiction and emptiness had come full circle.

History, which humanity had to this point viewed as a necessary record of human adventure, challenge, and insight, and the essential preserver and purveyor of form and tradition, came to an end, too. No longer did people believe they needed a comprehensive picture of what had taken place, for now they saw it as little more than a tangle of indecipherable and meaningless individual lives. There

---

[182] This comes across rather acutely in Samuel Beckett's plays *Endgame* and *Waiting for Godot,* works in which there seems to be no reason to remember, for there is nothing worth remembering. Who cares? After all, life is a joke.

[183] George Orwell, *1984* (New York: Signet, 1950), 64.

was nothing to be remembered. Present experience, present and bottomless experience and what it was becoming were far more important. Wholeness vanished. All significance was encapsulated in the individual human being, and only the individual human being who, ironically, remained unfathomable, meaningless, and beyond definition. Humanity wallowed in a happy nothingness, a happy nothingness of past, present, and future tumbling together into a bottomless abyss.[184]

In "Wish You Were Here," its decidedly bleak but fully realistic picture of this new world, the rock band Pink Floyd, whose *Ummagumma* album we mentioned some pages ago, captures this nothingness well. We are, the song opines, no more than fish, random and unexplainable fish swimming aimlessly and endlessly in a bowl, moving through life, living month after month, and year after year, yet finding nothing, nothing at all.[185]

With this, history and memory collapsed on themselves, each falling into the other. History was now memory, and memory was now history. But neither meant anything. There is no longer an old, there is no longer a new. Everything is immediate, but everything is immediately gone. History occurs, but history fades. Memory happens, but memory disappears. Pleasant or traumatic, joyous or heartbreaking, it doesn't matter: either way, life means nothing.[186]

---

[184] William E. Marsh, *Nothingness, Metanarrative, and Possibility* (Indianapolis: Author House, 2007).

[185] Pink Floyd, "Wish You Were Here," EMI Harvest Records, 1975.

[186] Jacob Burkhardt, *Force and Freedom: Reflections on History,* ed. James Hastings Nichols (New York: Median, 1965); and Eviatar Zerubavel, *Time Maps* (Chicago: University of Chicago, 2003).

No one, however, could really live this way. Speaking through the character Aloysha in his *Brothers Karamazov,* the Russian writer Fyodor Dostoyevsky (1821-1881), observed that,

> "For the mystery of human life is not only in living, but in knowing why one lives. Without a clear idea of what to live for man will not consent to live and will rather destroy himself than remain on the earth, though he were surrounded by loaves of bread . . . there is nothing more alluring to man than his freedom of conscience, but there is nothing more tormenting, either."

Later in the story, speaking of what would happen if every restraint, physical as well as metaphysical were loosed, Dostoyevsky observes, again via Aloysha, in words that have proven frightfully prophetic,

> "But,' I asked, 'how will man be after that? Without God and the future life? It means everything is permitted now, one can do anything?' 'Didn't you know?' he said. And he laughed"

If there is no past, if there is no tradition, and if there is no purpose, then there is no point. Nor is there any meaning.

Today is all, but how could it matter if the past means nothing? When God dies, everything else does, too.[187]

Ironically, and tragically, somehow, some way, however, memory must remain.

World War I, or the Great War (for never before had the world seen conflict on such a widespread and horrific scale), drove this point home. As the Lisbon earthquake of 1755 decimated Enlightenment optimism, so did the Great War and its unspeakable toll of destruction and suffering shatter modernity's hope of a better world without God. Angst gripped the Western imagination, breeding a sense of profound helplessness and despair. Meaninglessness reigned.

Out of this miasma, however, a once past vision of life resurfaced. A consensus emerged, a consensus that perhaps humanity had not found a way to create its own destiny after all. Perhaps life is not as good and grand and hopeful as people thought. Maybe history is important after all. Maybe memory has a genuine point.[188]

And memory returned. People began to see memory for what it had always been: a way to remember. They made memory a way to deal with pain and loss. They used memory to build a better future, a future acutely conscious of the lessons of the past. Memory became a way to remind people of who they had been, moral ugliness and all, so as to inspire them to develop a better tomorrow. We needed, the thinking went, to remember. We needed to remember

---

[187] Fyodor Dostoyevsky, *Brothers Karamazov*, trans. David Magarshack (New York: Penguin, 1958), Book 5.

[188] Paula Hamilton, "A Long War: Public Memory and the Popular Media" and Catherine Merridale, "Soviet Memories" in *Memory: Histories*.

for our own welfare and good. Memory was more than real: it was life. It was essential to existence.

The past was restored.

World War II magnified this shift. In the aftermath of the enormous devastation and loss of life the War unleashed upon the planet, a wave of physical and spiritual disintegration perhaps embodied most acutely in the horrors of the Holocaust, memory became even more vital. More than ever, people felt as if they needed to remember what had happened, that they needed to train themselves to never let the memory of these events, these singularly shocking events, leave them. Even if the world no longer made any sense, and even if meaninglessness and a complete absence of permanent value had triumphed, humanity needed to remember its past. In the wake of this deluge of trauma, the people of the West realized that memory is essential, individually as well as collectively, something thoroughly essential to human existence. They must not forget what happened.[189]

People must, as the Cibecue Apache Indians observe, use "memorial traces," memorials, commemoratives, and monuments, to find a past which, through successive generations of recollection and recall, has been lost, "largely invisible" to the living.[190]

Out of this came countless monuments to the War's memory, multiple attempts to enshrine and make known, for all time, the fact of its mark on the past. We think here

---

189 *Memory,* Whitehead, *ibid.*; *Time Maps, op cit.*

190 See Keith Basso, *Wisdom Sits in Places: Landscape and Language among the Western Apache* (Albuquerque: University of New Mexico, 1996).

of the many memorials erected in countries throughout the world to honor and remember those who lost their lives fighting in the war. We also think of our earlier mention of the Holocaust, as well as the nation of Germany's ongoing efforts to preserve the Nazi concentration camp at Auschwitz for public viewing and meditation.

Unfortunately, humanity's subsequent journey through the twentieth century left it with too many more occasions to remember, too many more reasons to remind itself of what it had done. Over and over, people were forced to elevate memory as an agent of healing and completion. From Cambodia's Killing Fields Museum, that nation's attempt to remember the horror of the Pol Pot regime; Srebrenica's Srebrenica Genocide Memorial, the Bosnian effort to remember the 8,000 victims of the 1995 Serbian massacre; the Irish peoples' commemoration, held every Easter, of the day in 1916 on which their ancestors began to fight for their independence from Great Britain; the Armenia Genocide memorial complex, dedicated to the memory of the 1.5 million Armenians who perished in the 1915 Turkish massacre; and, sadly, many, many more memorials, people remember. In every way, humanity's continued corporate fracturing has caused people, more than ever, to view memory as integral to the life of the world.[191]

---

[191] See, again, our previous citations on the Holocaust; *Genocide in Cambodia: Documents from the Trial of Pol Pot and Leng Sary,* ed. Howard J. De Nike *et al* (Philadelphia: University of Pennsylvania, 2000); and *Srebrenica Massacre,* Jesse Russell and Ronald Cohen (Book on Demand, 2012). On a more obscure but nonetheless significant event in the United States, consider the purposeful reconstruction of the New York townhouse that was leveled by an explosion in March of 1970, victim of

Furthermore, more than ever, it is this "collective memory," this "socially framed" network of "memories of individual experiences," that, in increasingly incisive and powerful ways, that has come to bind humanity together. It has become the primary cohering force in our world.[192]

We also note that, even if these memories, collective or not, tend to do for those who hold them, torture, they must remain. As Tom Wingfield notes at the end of Tennessee Williams's (1911-1983) *The Glass Menagerie*,

> "I reach for a cigarette, I cross the street,
> I run into the movies or the bar and buy
> a drink, I speak to the nearest stranger—
> anything that can blow your candles out!—
> for nowadays, the world is lit by lightning!

---

a botched bomb making attempt by members of the Sixties radical group the Weathermen (*The New York Times,* June 9, 2014.) On the other hand, consider Primo Levi's comment in his *If This is a Man,* trans. Stuart Wolf (New York: Orion, 1960), 139, that, "Memory is a funny instrument . . . one day there will be no more sense in saying: tomorrow." Even if we should remember, perhaps we should not. Where does it really leave us? It's exceedingly difficult to say. "History," he writes earlier (p. 123), "has stopped." Consider as well Eli Weisel's *Night,* trans. Marion Wiesel (New York: Hill and Wang, 2006), his highly incisive and unbearably memorable account of his time in the concentration camp at Auschwitz.

192 Maurice Halbwachs, *On Collective Memory,* ed. and trans. Lewis A. Coser, the Heritage of Sociology (Chicago: University of Chicago, 1992). For another cultural perspective, see David Grua, *Surviving Wounded Knee* (Oxford: Oxford University, 2016).

> Blow out your candles, Laura—and so good-bye."

Although Tom wants Laura to erase her memory of him, Laura does not wish to. Though his memory will torment her, she believes it must remain, remain with her for the rest of her life. Oddly, it makes her feel alive.[193]

Similarly, although it was written some decades before the *Glass Menagerie,* Ernest Hemmingway's (1899-1961) *Farewell to Arms,* his novel invoking the human angst of World War I, captures this dichotomous character of memory aptly. In describing its main character's final actions, Hemmingway's narrative notes,

> "[After injuring himself fighting, and losing his wife and son at the latter's birth, the character says], 'I put on my hat, and walked into the rain.'"

In other words, "I want to remember, but I do not. Nonetheless, I must."[194]

On the other hand, even as monuments were being built, some urged that we should forget memory. We should strive, some argued, to forget the past. We should move on. We should rise above the bad memories of yesteryear and focus on what lies ahead, to embrace the present and future

193 Tennessee Williams, *The Glass Menagerie* (New York: Random House, 1945).

194 Ernest Hemmingway, *Farewell to Arms* (New York:

before us. After all, *contra* Freud, the argument went, can we really change the past?[195]

Ironically, however, all of these efforts required that people forget in order to remember. It put people in the position of remembering what they would rather forget in order to remember what they knew they never should forget. Consider the Jewish feast of Purim. Although most Jews would gladly forget Haman, the man who tried to exterminate every Jew in Persia during the reign of King Ahasuerus (known to us today as Xerxes), they do not. They wish to remember the glorious way that God delivered them from Haman's evil machinations.

Similarly, though they may not have wished to, on the first anniversary of the 2012 shootings at Sandy Hook Elementary School in Connecticut, many people gathered to remember. They gathered to remember the horror, they gathered to remember the pain. They gathered to remember the dead. They came together to hope and pray that an incident like this will never happen again. Despite the immense suffering involved with remembering the events of that terrible day, they wanted to remember. They knew

---

[195] Theodor W. Adorno, *Negative Dialectics*, (New York: Bloomsbury Academic, 1981); Brian O'Connor, "Adorno on the Destruction of Memory" in *Memory: Histories*: Gilles Deleuze, *Proust and Signs* (Minneapolis: University of Minnesota, 2004); Keith Ansell-Pearson, "Deleuze and the Overcoming of Memory" in *Memory: Histories.* See also David Rieff, *In Praise of Forgetting* (New Haven, Connecticut: Yale University, 2016), which argues that we must remember "carefully" so as not to let our memory overwhelm what he terms our "moral responsibility" to forgive and move on.

that in order to heal and move on, they must first stand still in memory.[196]

For the last few years a journalist named Serguei Parkhomenko has led a grassroots campaign to remember and commemorate the victims of Stalin's purges. Called "Last Address," it seeks to tell "in full" the horrific effects of the late dictator's paranoia about political and cultural dissent to his regime. When a victim's family, despite the agony of doing so, comes forward to identify a lost loved one, the campaign hangs a memorial plague at this person's last known address. It recognizes this person in memory. Although Parkhomenko abhors Stalin, he nonetheless believes it important to remember those on whom the so-called "Man of Steel" inflicted untold grief and sorrow. It is worth recalling the heartbreak, it is worth recalling the pain. It is good to remember.[197]

So it has been that as the twentieth century has moved into the twentieth-first, humanity continues to recognize that even if it is traumatic and best left alone, memory must persevere. Every effort should be made to connect the past with the present and future, every effort must be made to blend commemoration with forgetting, remembering with overcoming, and recollection with letting go.[198]

Yet as postmodernity has continued to permeate the West, encouraging an intense commitment to the

---

[196] See the analysis on http://www.cnn.com/interactive/2012/12/us/sandy-hook-timeline/

[197] Noah Sneider, "Remembering the Disappeared," *The Atlantic*, December 2015. See also the works of Svetlana Alexievich, whom we mentioned earlier.

[198] For the full story of Purim, see the book of Esther in the Hebrew Bible.

shapelessness of values, the loss of permanence, and the absence of God, humanity has striven in vain to make this connection viable. Memory still remains elusive, no more than a reflection, and a highly subjective and aimless one at that, of a lonely and unattached self. Absent a solid foundation of meaning and given to a social construction of the self, Western humanity has come to increasingly see that what people might have remembered they really do not need to. It has no point. Though it is subjectively important and real, it is, in a manner of speaking, not really worthwhile or there. It's not a perception, and it's not a thought. It is memory, vastly important yet as empty as many people now perceive the world itself to be.[199]

What can we now say? Curiously, in some ways, we have come full circle. The peoples of the ancient near east viewed memory as an experience, an experience by which they thought about the past. They remembered to recall what had been, they remembered to create what could be. Whether it was funerary rituals, prayers for relief from plagues, acknowledgment of a covenant, or aid in battle, the people of the ancient near east realized that memory was important, a vital part of a meaningful existence, a natural and inevitable part of their lives, something in which they engaged innately. It explained why the world, and their lives in it, were the way they are. But that's all it was. Aside from perhaps the Hebrews, most people didn't take time to think about what memory was in itself or what

---

[199] So Jacques Derrida, *Writing and Difference,* trans. Alan Bass (Chicago: University of Chicago, 1978); and Richard Rorty, *Philosophy and the Mirror of Nature* (Princeton, New Jersey: Princeton University, 1979).

its broader implications for their lives might be. Memory simply happened.

With the Greeks and Romans, people made memory an art, a talent at which they worked to master. Memory was an essential part of every person's education, a necessary part of all study. No one should lose it; no one should forget what she had inscribed on her "wax tablet."

The Middle Ages maintained memory as an art, a special ability which every good student was called to master, a task on which she (though we are striving for pronominal consistency, we should note that almost all students during this time were male) was meant to specifically focus. Memory took on spiritual overtones, too. Led by Augustine, people began to think about memory as a spiritual experience. They came to frame memory in the idea of God, meditating on how God's memory and theirs might fit together. Grounded in notions of *memoria* and the soul, they concluded that it was God's presence that vitalized memory and made it meaningful.

As Europe entered the Renaissance, however, and began to move away from traditional notions of God, ideas of memory took new focus. Although people retained memory as an art, they did so by constructing what they called "theaters of memory," elaborate mental scaffolds in which they "hung" their remembered thoughts and recollections. Memory became the art of being able to walk through the scaffolding to find that for which one was looking and bring it to the forefront of her mind. Memory fused oral tradition and written record together. And it was always present.

Yet memory remained a mystery: why must we remember to remember? And why must we remember in order to forget?

With the Enlightenment, humanity's view of memory shifted once more. No longer was it an art. Now it was an experience, an experience framed and enabled by the centrality of human consciousness and the self. The product of perception and perception only, memory was that which people used to affirm and grasp their place and experience in the world. In elevating reason above all else, people made memory an experience of the mind that formulated and explained the experience of humanness. Later, shifting the focus yet retaining the primacy of subjective experience, the Romantics rendered memory an experience of the heart, never sure, never there, but there nonetheless.

Consequently, memory became, more than ever, a perception of the present that recalled a past that actually never was, precisely because what had been is always changing. Although memory was reality, it was a reality that is not really real, for it could not define what real could be. Along with everything else, it is in constant flux. The past is gone, the future a myth, and the present was all that remained, yet amorphous and elusive as ever. Memory was nothing more than modernity's affirmation of the emptiness and fleetingness of existence.

As humanity carried this view of memory into the twentieth century, however, it realized, on the heels of two incredibly destructive wars, that the past was important after all. People grasped that they needed to remember the worst of what they had been so as to avoid becoming the same in the future. Humanity gave new acclaim to memorials and commemorations, fresh impetus to recollection and recall. We must, people resolved, never forget the past.

Nonetheless, people continued to wonder. They continued to wonder about themselves and the memory they found themselves possessing, they continued to struggle with memory's meaning. Though humanity has made memory the epitome of consciousness, it has also made it the ultimate mystery. Why do we remember? Why do we bother?

Indeed, why? In her *The Constitution of Selves,* Marya Schectman describes a person as a being who is in possession of an "explicit narrative" of journey. She is a being who has developed and experienced, in the course of her life's many paths, "beliefs, values, and desires." In other words, a human being is a person who constructs and, she hopes (although H.M.'s case leads us to question this), remembers. Nonetheless, as Schectman, and others, are quick to point out, in a world absent of historical or metaphysical meaning, whether or not a person's memory defines her does not matter. Life, and its memories, simply happen. And why should we suppose it could be otherwise?[200]

Hence, while we have in some ways come full circle and come to view, as did our ancient ancestors, memory as experience and nothing else, in other ways we have done far more. We have reduced memory to an experience that really doesn't have anything to remember. We have pushed memory into a remembrance that remembers nothing, a recollection

---

[200] Marya Schectman, *The Constitution of Selves* (Ithaca: Cornell University, 2007). See also Schectman's *Staying Alive: Personal Identity, Practical Concerns and the Unity of a Life* (Oxford: Oxford University, 2014), and Galen Strawson's review in *London Review of Books,* June 18, 2015.

of a past that was never there, a strand of a present that never had form or definition, anyway. Everything, yet nothing, matters.

Where do we go from here?

We turn to God.

THE SPIRITUALITY OF MEMORY

So what *does* God have to do, as we asked at the beginning of this meditation, with memory? What does remembering have to do with God? Can we leave memory as an existential foundling of a shattered world and ourselves content with the passing and evanescent moment? Or should we point memory, and ourselves, toward the metaphysical, the omnipresent metaphysical in which our physicality finds purpose and meaning?

In short, how can we understand most fully what memory has to do with who we really are?

Let's look at what we have decided thus far. One, we established that memory is integral to our sense of self. With memory, we see and focus ourselves in the world. Memory is the clearinghouse for what we perceive and experience, the fulcrum of what makes us who we are. In our present world, the fractured and disparate world of postmodernity and socially constructed—and bottomless—"self," we use memory to bind and keep our "selves" together. Memory anchors our life, at least for a moment, even as it breaks it apart. We are our memory, and memory is us.

Two, we saw that memory is not material. Although memory "remembers" material events and things, it is not tangible in the sense that, say, an apple is tangible. We cannot pick up a memory as an object and look at it. We sense and "see" it in our brains, but we do not "see" it as external perception, do not see it as we do a bumblebee or flower. Memory is not visibly real. As William James observed, memory is "unseen," even though within our brains it is "seen." On the other hand, memory *is* what we perceive and create, albeit with the neurons of our brains, in the consciousness of our minds. We know we have a memory, and we know that we experience it. Our memory is more than real to us.[201]

Three, we noted that not only does memory remember a material event, it remembers immaterial ones as well. Memory remembers what we dream and imagine, and memory remembers what we suppose or think. It even remembers what does not or may not ever exist. It remembers things that perhaps will never be. And it remembers things we do not consciously try to remember. We cannot fully control or decide what we remember. Nor can we fully control how or what we recall about a memory. Like a bobcat in a forest, ever present yet rarely seen, memory lurks about our brains, manifesting, looking, sensing, categorizing, but never "showing" its full self. As Freud observed, in many ways, we are captives of our memory. We have it, but we don't; and it has us, but it doesn't. Memory is always

---

[201] William James, *Varieties of Religious Experience* (New York: Modern Library, 1902), 53-77.

becoming something other than what it is now; it is ever cresting beyond the present moment. It's always becoming new, even while, we noted, it remains old.

Four, we saw that forgetting is crucial to memory. If we remember everything, we're not really remembering anything. Conversely, if we cannot forget, we cannot really remember: what is there to remember if there is nothing to forget? Memory is as much about remembering as it is about forgetting. If we do not forget, we become like Bill Murray in the movie *Groundhog Day,* doomed to repeat and remember the same day over and over and over again. Nothing is ever new. We cannot revise, we cannot reshape, we can only recollect the same thing over and over and over again. And what does life really become?[202]

Oddly enough, however, we remember forgetting. We remember that we have forgotten something. And we often remember what we have forgotten. We just don't "know" it at the moment. We remember that we knew something, and we also realize and remember that now we don't.[203]

---

[202] *Groundhog Day,* Columbia Pictures, 1993. In addition to Jill Price, whom we mentioned earlier, consider David Baldacci's *Memory Man* (New York: Grand Central, 2015). It's the story of a man who remembered everything—absolutely everything—but could not always grasp how to deal with this in what turned out to be a rather tumultuous life.

[203] We see an amusing picture of this in a popular television show from the Sixties, *Get Smart. Get Smart* featured a rather zany spy named Maxwell Smart (played by Don Adams). Smart, who worked for CONTROL, made it his mission to vanquish the forces of the other side, aptly named CHAOS. Unfortunately, Smart could never remember his Chief's directives. Too often,

This, then, is memory. Simultaneously binding and loosening the self; resting in yet not part of materiality; remembering the possible as much as the impossible; and absent without disappearing, memory is unlike any other cognitive function. Although it creates, it creates nothing tangible, nothing we can physically hear, touch, or see. We cannot physically take hold of memory, nor can we consistently direct it. We do not always know that we are remembering, and we do not always know how we are remembering. Memory is a puzzle, a conundrum whose particulars elude ready definition, an enduring condition, yet an enduring condition that is entirely transient and formless. Memory is a singularly peculiar mystery.[204]

In truth, memory is almost otherworldly. It's here, but it's not; everywhere, but nowhere. We know and believe it's here (or there), somewhere, but we also know that this somewhere is a somewhere that is not "there" for long. As Bergson observes in the opening pages of his *Matter and Memory,* memory is that which lies at the "intersection of mind and matter," the phenomenon that connects, in the human being, material and ethereal, and spirit and matter. Linking together inner rumination and

---

the Chief gave Max a lengthy list of instructions for his next assignment, then ask, "Did you get all of that, Max?"

"Er, not all of it," Max always replied.

"What part did you not get, Max?"

"Well, Chief, the part after you said, 'Listen, Max.'" In other words, Max had not remembered a thing. But he knew that he had forgotten it. He just didn't "remember" *what* he had forgotten. He knew, but he did not. See *Get Smart,* created by Mel Brooks, which ran from 1965 to 1970.

204 *Matter and Memory,* 85

outward experience, connecting and fusing mind, heart, and spirit, memory centers us even while it deepens us, grounding us as much as it extends us, stretching and guiding our vision between what we see and what we do not. It brings us to the liminal, the border, the boundary, the formless membrane between physical mystery and the invisible and unseen presence encompassing it all. Memory demonstrates that materiality does not fully explain us.

In illuminating the gone and vanished, and reconstructing the lost and disappeared, memory puts people on the edge, the edge of knowing and quotidian caprice, the precipice on which the finite mind is constantly dangling. It thus opens a door to the spiritual and transcendent. Taking us into the vexing limitlessness of consciousness and imagination, the rim of reality and truth, memory pushes us into the tumbled maw of angst and emptiness in which, to draw a page from the Danish philosopher Søren Kierkegaard, we find God.

Emergent, complex, ethereal, and mysterious, memory is a door, a door that opens into an even greater mystery in turn: the mystery of God. Apprehending, disclosing, touching, and clarifying, memory offers a way into Augustine's question, "Where indeed is the human being, if it is 'not contained' within something else, if it is not housed in and linked to the transcendent—God—the ultimate picture and framework of reality?" In memory, we enter into that "ultimate picture" of reality, for it is in memory's perplexing intricacy that we see more fully the logic and presence of the one whose sensibilities necessarily animate the cosmos. In stepping into memory, we step into the foundation of being. And in stepping into the foundation of being, we step into God. We come to see and understand what is most important and true, we come to grasp and experience what is most real. Furthermore, when we understand memory as it is, we come to understand ourselves as we are and, one day, will be. In memory, we unfold and reflect humanity's richest essence and most profound point.[205] Fusing immanent experience with transcendent meaning, we see the past, we see the present, we create the future. With memory, we touch the puzzling exchange of evanescence and eternality that comprises the weight and purpose of existence. In memory, we see it all.[206]

In memory, we open a window into God.

Hence, as it opens us to the complexities of our beingness and the presence of transcendence and God, memory affirms our inherently spiritual essence. It shows us that we are more than matter, yet more than spirit, too. Memory underscores to us that we are at once physically present and ethereally absent. It reminds us that we are creatures of spirit, body, *and* soul, a constantly merging union of this world and that which created it. With memory, we are neither robots nor electrical impulses, deterministic whims who never think or imagine beyond their present form or physical presence. We are rather creatures who experience, imbibe, and reflect the fact of transcendence, beings who are bent and inclined to

---

205 See Warren S. Brown, "The Brain, Religion, and Baseball: Revisited" in *Fuller Magazine,* #5; and Christof Koch, *Consciousness* (Cambridge, Massachusetts: MIT, 2012.

206 *Confessions,* X, XII. See also Thomas Nagel, *View from Nowhere* (Oxford: Oxford University, 1989).

ponder what is beyond their immediacy, to wonder what is outside of their present experience of time and space, people who are inherently disposed to think about and invest in the metaphysical and beyond.[207]

---

[207] See John Searle, *Making the Social World* (Oxford: Oxford University, 2009); Searle, *Mind, op cit.;* and James Kugel, *In the Valley of the Shadow* (New York: Free Press, 2011) We should also remind ourselves that unless we possess extraordinary powers of insight or, like Moses, Mohammad, or any number of other prophets, are the fortunate recipients of direct communications from God, we cannot see the spiritual realm. Can we prove it's there? Not empirically, but then again, outside of identifying a specific place in the cortex where a particular memory is lodged or occurred (and even this does not allow us to "see" the memory), we cannot prove memory empirically, either. Yet on the basis of our experience, we believe it is there. Moreover, although we are definitely physical and material beings, we experience some things that are decidedly immaterial, things like consciousness (even if, as some claim, we do not know we are; see Michael S. A. Graziano, *Consciousness and the Social Brain* (New York: Oxford University, 2013)), passion, justice, love, hate, and the like. There is much more to us than meets the material and naked eye, things that we know are there, but things which we cannot present as tangible phenomena or entities. Granted, these are questions outside the scope of this book, but they are cited here to make the point that it seems that deep within the human being resides an intangible something, a deeper longing, an immaterial impulse. Some of course will say this means nothing. They insist that human beings possess an ability to reason, transcend, and emote simply by virtue of the neurological capacities with which they have been born. Although we engage in transcending activities, we do not do so in the umbra of a transcendental presence. On the other hand, this doesn't explain how something that is thoroughly material (the brain) can produce things that are inherently immaterial (love or passion). Yes, we can understand

More than ever, we realize we are, as one writer put it, heteronomous, beings of worldly physicality even as we are creatures of supernatural spirituality.[208]

The Hebrew Bible tells us that God created the human being in his image and likeness, as a spiritual being, a "living soul" (Genesis 1:26). As spiritual beings, humans have a unique relationship with God, a special inroad into and affinity with the transcendent. Out of all the creatures on the planet, humans can consciously and intentionally communicate with God. To be made in the image of God is to enjoy a unique dialogical window into God. It is to know existence as more than a crinkled collection of moments, more than a mélange of points of time, more than raw instinct. It is to know and experience existence as infused with transcendent activity, larger meaning, and soulful purpose. To be made in God's image is to consciously understand oneself and life as they really are: meaningful creations of a meaningful, loving, and intentional God.[209]

---

the processes, and yes, we can understand the evolutionary motives for them, but we cannot explain *how* such a thing can be. How can a material world be filled with immaterial things? It's not logical. Neither, in a way, is the spiritual: why the spiritual in a material world? But that's the point. Both conclusions should tell us that we are dealing with something that though we cannot readily grasp it, we know intuitively that it is there.

[208] Merolyd Westfall, "Kierkegaard: In Praise of Heteronomy" Baylor University Center for Faith and Learning, Conference on Soren Kierkegaard, October 31 – November 3, 2013.

[209] See Michael Horton, *The Christian Faith* (Grand Rapids, Michigan: Zondervan, 2011), Part 3, and Hans Schwarz, *The Human Being: A Theological Anthropology* (Grand Rapids: Wm B. Eerdmans, 2013).

It is our creation as living souls who are spiritual beings that enables us to see and experience memory as spiritual phenomenon, to enjoy remembering as a work of matter as well as a walk of spirit. It is the fact of us being living souls that centers us, in memory, in God. If God is, as theologian Paul Tillich loosely described him, the "ground of being," then it is our experience as living and spiritual souls that embeds us in this ground. Our spirituality marks and clarifies the mnemonic processes that run through us. It is therefore as living souls and spiritual beings that we experience memory in its fullness. We touch our own memory of life and its endings, and we embrace God's memory of us, our life, and its endings, as well. Mediating amidst us and our memories, suffused as they are with God and his remembrances of us, our spiritual nature and our creation as living souls enable us to experience the heart of memory, the source and presence of seminal truth. It allows us to know life's most profound mystery, and to see, feel, and engage the fundamental structures and intimacies of the cosmos, the deepest framework of thought and recall. So positioned, we hear God speak, and we listen; so ensconced, we sense God's movement, we feel our spirit impel our soul. Our spirituality, the manifestation of our fashioning (and this is what the Hebrew word used to describe the creation of Eve literally means), in the divine image, upholds and engenders a life lived in the memory of a living God.[210]

We can therefore say that if God is indeed there, and if we are indeed spiritual beings created by him, made to remember and be remembered, we cannot separate our

---

[210] Paul Tillich, *Systematic Theology* (Chicago: University of Chicago, 1951), Vol I, Part II.

longing for meaning from our capacity to remember. They are inseparable. God is as much the grounding of what it means to remember as he is the grounding of existential understanding. It is in our experience as spiritual beings who remember that we see God's presence in life most clearly, and it is in our spiritual capacities that, upon death, we will grasp most fully the fact of divine remembering and meaning that auger and superintend the richest and most unshakeable truths of existence.

So: God exists as God, and we exist as spiritual beings whom he has created. As such, we can communicate with God, and he with us. We remember God, and he remembers us. We walk with God in a special relationship of thought, matter, and memory.

Now let's define God. Although we will rely largely on Christianity for this definition, we acknowledge that most of the world's religions share its basic picture of the divine. Generally speaking, people who look at the world through a spiritual lens share very similar conclusions about the beingness and character of God. They broadly agree that certain things must always be true about God if he is to be a meaningful element in the experience of life and memory.

What are these things? One, we say that God is, in some way, creator and sustainer of the universe. Although we may say that natural processes contributed to bringing the world into its present form, we affirm that it is ultimately God who provided the initial spark) from which the universe emerged. Before there were quantum fluctuations or "nothing" nothingness, there was God. Apart from God, even these would not exist. God is the ultimate beginning of the cosmos. All origins rest in his power and intentions.

Nothing would be here unless God had purposed it to be so.[211]

This means that God is the source of the order by which the universe functions. In creating the universe, God created and enabled its physical laws and set them in motion. Apart from him, they would not be. The world is not an autonomous entity. It is dependent on God for its working. Yes, its cosmological laws stand separate from God, but if God had not devised them, they would not exist. (And if he ever stopped thinking about them, they would cease to function.)

Moreover, because God created it, the cosmos has meaning. It is not an accident. Because God thought about the cosmos, it exists; because God continues to think about the cosmos, it continues to exist. God's memory, his active remembering of the cosmos, upholds and sustains all that is. The universe is thought about, the universe has point. There is a reason, an externally constructed reason, why it—and we—are here.[212]

From this, we make our second point. God is omniscient. God knows everything. God knows everything that is, and God knows everything that is not. He knows everything that might have been, everything that could have been, everything that has been, and everything that will be. God knows everything about everything. God knows us, and God knows the world, its past, present, and future,

---

211 For a comprehensive discussion of the varying ways that the peoples of the world have viewed God as creator, see David Leeming and Margaret Leeming, *A Dictionary of Creation Myths* (Oxford: Oxford University, 1994).

212 *It's All in a Word: God, Life, and Meaning, op cit.*

thoroughly and intimately. God knows and remembers it all. We therefore remember in a world that is remembered in turn, absolutely and completely, by God.[213]

Three, God is omnipotent. God can do anything. There are no limits on his power. God is absolutely capable of doing and effectuating anything he chooses to. He answers to no one. All the universe is subject to God's judgment and authority. Nothing and no one can defeat him, and nothing and no one can overcome him. His power is total.[214]

For this reason, we say that God is sovereign. God controls everything, absolutely everything, by the sheer

---

[213] As beings with a pitifully limited knowledge of reality, however, we have difficulty fathoming a being who knows absolutely everything, things that are happening, things that will happen, even things that might have happened. Unless God possess this level of omniscience, however, he is of no point in memory. How else could he remember everything about anything, and how else could he be the ultimate repository and arbiter of what is remembered? God's omniscience, his often frightening and thoroughly incomprehensible knowledge of all things, is essential to memory, our memory as well as the world's memory of itself.

[214] We must insert a caveat here. Although God is omnipotent, God is holy (see Leviticus 11:44), at once and simultaneously. God is as holy as he is omnipotent. Given this, God will not do anything that would undermine this commingling of his attributes. He is always consistent, he is always together. God is simple, that is, he is wholly and fully complete, always and forever set apart (the essential meaning of the Hebrew (*qodesh)* and Greek (*hagia)* words for holiness) from everything else in the creation. God is uniquely and absolutely moral, totally and unilaterally holy. He stands fully alone in his moral probity. None can touch him. As he told Moses when he spoke to the prophet from the burning bush, "Remove your sandals, for the ground on which you stand is holy" (Exodus 3).

force of his will. Nothing happens without God allowing it, and nothing happens without God knowing about it.[215]

As an old hymn goes,

> "Holy, holy, holy! Though the darkness hide thee, though the eye of sinful man thy glory may not see, only thou art holy; there is none beside thee, perfect in power, in love and purity."[216]

Four, God is eternal.[217] This means that he has no beginning or end. God does not have a starting point, and he did not have a cause. God is causeless. In a universe full of

---

215 This of course raises a host of issues, principally the age old question of God and evil. If God is omnipotent, why does he not stop evil in the world? Fully and properly answering this question is a task outside the scope of this book, but we will nonetheless keep it in mind as we proceed, as it affects how we see God and how and why he remembers. As Psalm 33 puts it, "For He [God] spoke, and it was done; He commanded and it stood fast. The Lord nullifies the counsel of the nations; He frustrates the plan of the peoples. The counsel of the Lord stands forever" (Psalm 33:9-11a). While this may be easy to say, understanding its full import and implications is an entirely different proposition.

216 "Holy, Holy, Holy!" Reginald Heber (1783-1726).

217 A slippery concept, eternal refers to a condition or state (finding a word to describe it is difficult) which has no beginning or end. Eternity has no starting point, for it has always been "existing," and it has no ending point, for it will "exist" indefinitely. It will never end, for it never really began. What's the difference between eternity and infinity? Although eternity describes something in relation to time, infinity describes a concept of space *and* time. In addition, as John D. Barrow points out in his *The Infinite Book* (New York: Pantheon, 2005), given the idea of infinity, we finite

causes and effects, God is the only cause without a cause in turn. He has always been. God will never end, for he never really began. Before time and space began, God was, and when time and space end, God will still be.[218]

---

beings cannot conceive of an infinite space and infinite time for we would need an infinite amount of time to do so!

218 Although we finite beings find this idea exceedingly difficult, if not impossible to grasp, we should recognize that unless God is eternal, always and forever existing, we will have a great deal of trouble explaining how the world came to be, much less why memory exists. Consider the prevailing theories about cosmic origins. In sum, there are only two ways that we can think about how the world came to be. Either it, in some form, has always been, and always will be, or it had a beginning. Many of the ancient Greeks opted for the former. Struggling to understand how a material world could have risen out of nothing, they concluded that the essential and foundational matter (the *Urstoff*) of the world has always been. The "stuff" out of which the world has come is eternal. Then, at some point, some indecipherable point of eternal space and time, it birthed the world we know today.

Modern science, however, has demonstrated conclusively that the cosmos had a beginning. It is not eternal. Yet questions remain. If the cosmos is not eternal, out of what did it come? Was *that* substance eternal? Either way, unless we posit the existence of a causeless and eternal creator God, we are left wondering: how did it all begin?

Moreover, unless God is eternal, any idea that he could have anything to do with memory collapses under the weight of its own contradictions. If God cannot remember indefinitely, endlessly, and forever, and if God was not around, remembering, before the world began, he is of little use to us and memory. If God could not think eternally, the world could not exist. If God cannot remember eternally, the world will not, in its present or, one day, potentially renewed form, last. In other words, if God can't

Five, God is personal. God is not a blob of plasma, nor is he a formless something floating around in space and caprice. God is a personal, communicative, and interactive being. God has personality, God has feelings; God has values, and God has intention. This is in part why those who believe in God do so, and this is in part why they pray to him. They believe he hears them, and they believe that he responds to them. They believe he's a personal being just as they are personal beings.

Moreover, only if God is personal would we even wish to consider his role in memory. A blob is of little use to us. Even if it could remember us (and if it did, it would not be a blob, anyway), how would this help us in the broad span of eternity, space, and time? How would we benefit from the memory of a dollop of dust?[219]

Most importantly, as a personal God, God loves to remember the spiritual beings—you, me, and everyone else who has lived and ever will live—he made.

So: God is the eternal, omniscient, and sovereign creator. He had no beginning, nor will he have an end. God knows all things, and God remembers all things. Moreover, God is absolutely sovereign. In all the universe, God is the ultimate lord, arbiter, and judge.

Now that we have, broadly speaking, defined God, we are ready to take the next step and answer the question we posed at the beginning of this chapter: how does God remember?

---

remember, who can? And if no one can remember, how could the world ever be? And what will happen to it? Furthermore, what will happen to us? Where will we be?

[219] See Genesis 1:26. See also the *Qur'an,* 11:90.

We'll address this question in multiple ways. We will first explore further how our affirmations about ourselves as spiritual beings and our understandings of the nature of God determine the shape of memory and remembering in our experience. Next, we will explore and ponder various expressions of life and its possibilities as to how these reflect and express God's role in memory and how we experience it as such. Finally, as we come to a definitive understanding of how grounding memory in the fact of God gives it a form and meaning and import it could not have otherwise, we will observe how in the end memory becomes for us, we spiritual yet fallen beings, the immutable basis for ultimate purpose and human destiny.

MEMORY AS PRESENCE, PRESENCE AS GOD

"Oh, still remember me!" said the Irish poet Thomas Moore (1779-1852), who is perhaps most famous for helping to burn Lord Byron's memoirs after his death. "When I am dead, my dearest," penned British poet Christian Georgina Rossetti (1830-1894), who wrote under the name of Ellen Alleyne, "If thou wilt, remember, and if thou wilt, forget; remember me when I am gone away, gone far away into the silent land."[220]

Please, please, at all costs, these poets pleaded: remember me!

So said musician Warren Zevon, whose poignant words about remembrance and memory we looked at earlier. For

---

[220] Thomas Moore, "Irish Melodies" in *Barlett's Familiar Quotations,* John Bartlett and Justin Kaplan, eds.
(Boston: Little, Brown and Company, 1882); Christina Georgina Rossetti, "Song" and "Remember" in *ibid.* See also Christina Georgina Rossetti, "The Covenant Threshold" in *Poets, op cit.*

all his manic behavior, Zevon was as human as Moore, Rossetti, and the rest of us: he wished to be remembered.[221]

Moore, Rossetti, and Zevon capture, for all of us, the heart of the otherworldliness of memory. They underscore that unless we are like Meursault, the emotionally vapid Frenchman inhabiting the heart of Albert Camus's chilling novel, *The Stranger,* a person who does not love, pretend, believe, or regret, we do not want to die unremembered. They remind us that we wish to be remembered, to be recalled and thought about after we leave this world. We do not want to be forgotten. We do not want to die and have ourselves and our lives fade away as if they had never been or never been known. We wish for our memory to last, to last for perhaps as long as eternity. We long for memory to extend beyond us, to rise above the temporal and contingent, to penetrate the hiddenness, the mystery that surrounds us all; in short, to linger beyond the grave.

Regardless of how we see such things, we yearn for memory to be transcendent. The darkness of death is frightening enough; the darkness of being forgotten—when we can do nothing about it—is even greater.[222]

Significantly, sometimes it is not so much that we wish to be remembered as it is that the events and experiences we endure in our lives be recalled. As a letter written by one Salmen Gradowski which the Allied liberators of Auschwitz discovered as they examined the grounds of the camp's

---

221 *Wind, op cit.* See also Crystal Zevon, *I'll Sleep When I'm Dead: The Dirty Life and Times of Warren Zevon* (New York: Ecco, 2008).

222 Albert Camus, *The Stranger*, trans. Stuart Gilbert (New York, Vintage, 1942).

crematorium states, "May the world at least behold a drop, a fraction of this tragic world in which we lived."[223]

Though she knew she would never live to talk about her experience of the Holocaust, Gradowski wished for the world to know, even if it is only a little bit, about what had happened to her and her fellow sufferers. She wanted the planet to know about the millions of otherwise forgotten.

So have we earlier noted how Jews the world over gather on May 4, International Holocaust Memorial Day; so have we observed how on the eleventh day of September, year after year, thousands of Americans meet at memorials built to honor those killed in the 2001 attacks on the World Trade Center; and so have we mentioned how every July 11, the day in 1995 that invading Serbian forces mercilessly slaughtered almost 8,000 defenseless Bosnian Muslims, the relatives and descendants of the dead men and boys join hands and remember them. American, Bosnian, Jew: we never want the world to forget what happened to our brethren.

As we begin to consider God's role in memory, we therefore make two observations. One, it is one thing to remember. Indeed, as we have already established, it is good and necessary to remember. Moreover, like it or not, it is inevitable: we cannot help but remember. Two, on the other hand, it is quite another to *be* remembered. To wish to be remembered, as we noticed in reading the words of Moore, Rossetti, and Zevon earlier, is fundamental to human wellbeing in a way that simply remembering is not. In our longing to be remembered, we say that although remembering can be meaningful as well as useful in the

---

[223] Nikolaus Wachsmann, *KL: A History of the Nazi Concentration Camps* (New York: Farrar, Straus and Giroux, 2015), frontispiece.

course of living our life, it is in *being* remembered that we taste the essence of human existence most profoundly. In being remembered, we touch our deepest longing, our most aching desire: our wish, our almost ethereal wish, regardless of how we view the afterlife, to be remembered beyond the grave. As we pass out of this life, we wish for those with whom we have walked through its tangled mix of joy and sorrow to remember us. We do not wish to be forgotten.

And it is in this longing to be remembered that we experience most fully the memory of God.

How? Let us note first that, God or not, memory is fleeting, frighteningly fleeting. In his novel *Cloud Atlas,* David Mitchell paints a world spread over six different episodes of time, some past and some future, working out multiple story lines too complex to detail here. At the end of the book, when every plot has been satisfied and every story line completed, one of the characters reflects, with his father-in-law, on his life goals. He shares that he would like to work to end the slave trade (this portion of the novel is set in the eighteenth century). Bristling with contempt, for he sees no good in pursuing such, as he sees it, unprofitable activity, his father-in-law remarks, "Only as you gasp your dying breath shall you understand your life amounted to no more than one drop in a limitless ocean!"

To this, the younger man replies, "Yet what is any ocean but a multitude of drops?" For the older man, life begins, ends, and is then forgotten. Time moves on, passage continues. Accomplishment means nothing, and memory is a myth. We live and die as nameless and unnumbered drops in an interminable and endless sea. The younger man, though he knows he will die one day, too, still believes that he ought to try to do something that he deems meaningful. He still believes in the transcending worth of his life and its impact on the world. Even if everything, as his obdurate father-in-law asserts, will one day slip into a bottomless ocean, this man believes that some things are worth doing, that some things will endure. The world will remember the footprints he makes in the field of human history. His work will last. His efforts will be remembered.[224]

Or will it? Again, either way, God or not, this young man's memory, the memory of him and what he did, remains fleeting.

In the opening scenes of *Dead Poets Society,* first year teacher John Keating (played by Robin Williams) takes his students out of their classroom into the adjoining hallway and tells them to look at the photographs of alumni past. Then he says,

> "Because we're food for worms, lads! Because we're only going to experience a limited number of springs, summers, and falls. One day, hard as it is to believe, each and every one of us is going to stop breathing, turn cold, and die! I would like you to step forward over here and peruse the faces of the boys who attended this school sixty or seventy years ago. You've walked past them many times, but I don't think you really looked at them. They're not that different from you, are they? Same

---

[224] See *Cloud Atlas* by David Mitchell (New York: Random House, 2004).

> haircuts. Full of hormones, just like you. Invincible, just like you feel. The world is their oyster. They believe they're destined from great things, just like many of you."

As wonderful as life is, John Keating insists, its time and the memories it engenders, are achingly transient and thoroughly fleeting.[225]

Unless we are famous (and fame, as anyone who has studied history knows, is a relative term), we will not be remembered. Our immediate survivors will remember us, yes, but once they are gone, no one will be left to remember us. Although our survivors may tell others about us, those whom they tell will not remember us as we were but only as we have been described to them. They will not be remembering *us*. Indeed, even if tell-all biographies are written about us, they will not present *us*. The best they can do is present an *image* of what their authors conclude, on the basis of research and study, we once were. *We*, each one of us, each one of us as individual selves, will not be genuinely remembered. Like the faceless and vanished people behind the intriguing yet sociologically opaque remnants of the Anasazi civilization of the American Southwest, we are gone forever.

It is as if no one ever knew us at all.[226]

Once more: God or not, memory is fleeting.

---

[225] *Dead Poets Society,* Touchstone Picture, 1989. See also http://genius.com/Tom-schulman-dead-poets- society-carpe-diem-scene-annotated/

[226] Craig Childs, *House of Rain* (New York: Little, Brown and Company, 2006).

Former Soviet dictator Josef Stalin's daughter, named Svetlana Stalina at birth, but who later immigrated to the United States and died as Lana Peters in 2011, wrote about her father extensively. Her books became international best sellers. Yet only she physically knew her father as he was. Only she knew Stalin as one with whom she had lived in this world. Only she knew Stalin as one who played games with her, who put her to bed, who fixed her breakfast; only she knew him as a human being who raised a daughter (however poorly, she made clear in her memoirs, he did so). The rest of us can only read her recollections of him. We can come to know a great deal about Stalin, yes, yet we will never know him precisely as *he* was. We have not grown up with him, we have not walked through a park with him, we have not celebrated our birthday in his presence. We have not been his child. Only his daughter did, and now she's gone, too. Though Stalin's name lives on, in the eyes of most people, we might add, for the worst possible reasons, the immediate memory of him will forever evade us.[227]

For all of his might and power, Stalin and his memories are now irretrievably gone, no more than a wisp in a nearly infinite flood of broken remembrance.

As my siblings and I sorted through family mementos and paraphernalia after our mother died in 2010, we came across numerous photographs of people of whose identity we had no inkling whatsoever. Some may have been great grandparents, others great-great grandparents. We had no

---

[227] Of course, Stalin's closest associates knew him, but not as a parent. See, most recently, Rosemary Sullivan, *Stalin's Daughter: The Extraordinary and Tumultuous Life of Svetlana Alliluyeva* (New York: HarperCollins, 2015).

idea. None were labeled. We had only known one of our great grandparents. For the most part, we were looking at people whose lives and memories we had never—and never would—know. Before us these photos sat, mute testimony to many, many lives that had been lived, lives that were surely important to those who lived them, lives to which we had distant linkage, yet now lives whose significance, sadly, eluded us. We saved some photographs: we wanted to preserve a few remembrances of our origins. We reasoned that even though we would never know the people behind the photographs, and even though we would never know anything about their lives, we ought to remind ourselves that they had, at one time, existed. We believed we ought to remind ourselves of our past. We agreed that we wanted to retain some permanence amidst the impermanence standing before us.

For most of the photographs, however, we decided that however much those depicted in them may had shaped or molded who we are as a family today, given that we had no idea whom they depicted, we should, regrettably, discard them. To us, the people at whom we were looking were as distant as peasants living in seventh century China. Other than an undefined and cloudy relationship to our family tree, we knew nothing about them. For those who had known them, for those who once took pleasure in looking at photos of them, these people were important, perhaps greatly so. But we had not known them. We did not even know who they were. Their memory had vanished completely.

Furthermore, when my siblings and I one day leave this planet, and our children go through the photographs we chose to save, these photographs we saved of people we never knew, they will be looking at people and lives even more distant than they were from us. They will be looking at people who, in some cases, lived over a hundred years before they were born. They will likely struggle with relevance, too. Why, they may think, should we keep these photographs? Why should we preserve memories we never had? We never knew these people. For us, they never really existed.

So it will be for all of us. When we die, our memories, our memories of our lives, our parents, our grandparents and other relatives—aunts, uncles, cousins, and the like—will die with us. Though our children may read our journals, though they may remember our stories, at that point that's all these will be: words from the grave. Whoever had spoken them is gone forever.

As Kate Winslet, playing Rose DeWitt Bukater in the movie *Titanic*, when asked, after she is rescued and the movie is drawing to a close, about her lover, Jack Dawson (played by Leonardo DiCaprio), remarks, "I only know him as a memory." Jack's face is now no more than a visage, an elusive glimpse of a lost life, a life that, even though it opened Rose's eyes to the possibilities of a much larger world, is now hopelessly gone. Did Jack even exist?[228]

As the writer of Ecclesiastes observes,

> "There is no remembrance of earlier things;
> and also of the later things which will occur,
> there will be for them no remembrance

[228] *Titanic,* Twentieth Century Fox, 1997. Echoing Rose's thoughts with words that delight every history teacher, Ecclesiastes 7:24 further notes, "What has been is remote and exceedingly mysterious. Who can discover it?"

> among those who will come later still" (Ecclesiastes 1:11).

Precisely. Pondering the aftermath of a funeral, the day on which a deceased's survivors, still grieving over their loss, put him to final rest, Ecclesiastes further notes, "For man goes to his eternal home while mourners go about in the streets" (Ecclesiastes 12:5). While the deceased's loved ones continue to mourn him, he himself has gone definitively on, his life and person now far, far away, permanently consigned to eternity. He lived, he died, and now he's gone. No one will ever see him again. Only his survivors remain, left to carry on with their lives.

And one day, they will be gone, too.

As the narrator of Kurt Vonnegut's *Cats Cradle* often says, "So it goes." God or not, does memory, any memory at all, *really* matter?[229]

So: is the father-in-law in *Cloud Atlas* right? Did Thomas Moore, Christian Georgina Rossetti, and Warren Zevon speak correctly? Do Ecclesiastes' words ring true? Do we really come into this world to live, die, then vanish, with no reason, no memory, no remembrance at all? Are we in fact brought into this world only to be discarded and forgotten? Does memory mean anything at all? Will it not continue to happen?

Of course it will. God or not, memory happens. In the *Epic of Gilgamesh,* widely considered to be history's first written meditation on mortality, its protagonist, Gilgamesh, the (partly) legendary king of Uruk, speculates often on

[229] Kurt Vonnegut, *Cat's Cradle* (New York: Barnes and Noble, 1998).

death. As he mourns the passing of his companion Enkidu, Gilgamesh says,

> "When I die, shall I not be like Enkidu [gone forever]? Woe has entered my belly. Fearing death, I roam over the steppe."[230]

Gilgamesh is overcome with the fleetingness of existence. What does it all matter? So does the "ale-wife" later say to him,

> "Gilgamesh, where do you roam? The life you pursue you shall not find. When the gods created mankind, death for mankind they set aside, life in their own hands retaining."[231]

You, too, Gilgamesh, will die. You, too, will die without ever knowing what life really means. And, the ale-wife later adds, in words that echo John Keating's words in *Dead Poets*

---

230 "The Epic of Gilgamesh," trans. by E. A. Speiser, *Ancient Near Eastern Texts,* 88-90. Briefly, the *Epic* recounts the story of Gilgamesh and Enkidu, the one a king, the other a "wild" man who, after a liaison with a woman, realizes the fact of his humanness and, subsequently, meets Gilgamesh. Quickly becoming friends, the two men find adventures all over the world until Enkidu dies. See also the pleas in the 59th chapter of the Egyptian *Book of the Dead,* that the supplicant "not die a second time in the netherworld." (*Book of the Death, op cit.).*

231 *Epic, ibid.*

Society, "Eventually you will be as forgettable as a grain of ocean sand! But be happy!"[232]

Of course! Even if life means nothing, and even if we do not matter, everyone, even if it is only for a brief instant, is remembered. Across the planet, regardless of place, circumstance, or condition, everyone, even if for only one brief "shining moment," is remembered. Somehow, some way, memory captures all of us. No one can elude its arms, no one can escape its grasp. We're human beings. We live, we die. We remember, we are remembered. God or not, we all live and die in the compass of memory. God or not, memory happens.[233]

Furthermore, as we noted, God or not, memory, in this life, ends. Be it the memory of the people of *Cloud Atlas;* that of the eager young men of *Dead Poets Society;* or the memory of the shattered Rose DeWitt Bukater of *Titanic;* one day, regardless of whether and how eternity lies in wait, memory ends.

Many years ago, we had some friends who, after a great deal of trying, brought a baby into the world. Sadly, this baby was born severely deformed. It would only live three days. Our friends had been made aware, prior to the child's birth, that this would happen, but chose to bring the baby, a little boy, to term, just the same. They named him right away and, after he died, held a memorial service for him and buried him in the family plot in the local cemetery. They

---

232 *Ibid.*

233 I have borrowed this phrase from William Manchester's book on John Fitzgerald Kennedy, *One Brief Shining Moment* (New York: Little Brown, 1983).

will not forget this baby. Though they had only known him for three days, they will always remember him.[234]

Although my friends, committed evangelical Christians, firmly believe that they will one day see their little boy again in heaven, this will not erase the certainty that when they are dead and gone, all earthly memory of this boy will be dead and gone, too, terminally consumed in the black hole of their mortality. One day, this baby will be completely forgotten, a child, as the Red Queen once described Alice in Lewis Carroll's *Through the Looking-Glass,* "without any meaning?" Who will know?[235]

Ten days after giving birth to her daughter Mary, the Mary who, as Mary Shelley, would go on to write the nineteenth century novel *Frankenstein,* Mary Wollstonecraft died. Although her husband William Godwin told Mary often about her mother, Mary really had no memory of her. It was almost as if her mother had never existed. Like my friends' baby, like the wandering Alice, all time and memory of her had vanished.[236]

A number of weeks after we moved into the home where we now live, as we always do when we enter a new

---

[234] My friends' one time hopes and aspirations for their baby echo those of the anonymous elegist who wrote, in the wake of actor Richard Burbage 1619's death, "and, with him, what a world are dead [all] . . . that lived in him have now for ever died." See Stephen Greenblatt, "How Shakespeare Lives Now," in the April 21, 2016, issue of *The New York Review of Books.*

[235] Lewis Carroll, *Through the Looking-Glass* (New York: Dover, 1999), chapter 9.

[236] Stephen Hebron and Elizabeth C. Denlinger, *Shelley's Ghost: Reshaping the Image of a Literary Family* (Oxford: Bodleian Library, 2010).

community, we joined a local church. One of the first things we learned about the pastor was that he and his wife had had a son who, tragically, passed away from leukemia at the age of thirteen. Al often referred to Nicholas in his sermons, and when asked how many children she had, his wife Vicki always replied, "Three" (they had two others). Every year on the anniversary of Nicholas's death, the entire family visits his grave. They remember. Even though Al is no longer the church's pastor, even though many of those who knew him during his tenure have moved on, and even though progressively fewer and fewer people who attend this church know about Nicholas, he is remembered. He will not be forgotten.

Nicholas's family will of course continue to remember him to the day they die. But what does it matter? Is not Ecclesiastes correct to say, as he often does, that "all is futility?"

Maybe. A number of years ago, my now grown son spent eight weeks volunteering at the Mother Teresa Home for the Destitute and Dying in Kolkata, India. Every day, he told me, he and staff from the Home went into the streets of the city, looking for people in the final stages of life, people about to slip out of this life without notice, companion, or friend. People whom the world had forgotten. When my son and the staff workers brought these people into the Home, they ministered to them. They bathed them, tended to their wounds, kept them warm, and stayed at their bedside. Usually, these people were dead by the next morning, their life gone without a sound.

Their memory was gone, too.

So did they really matter?

Marilynne Robinson's *Lila* opens with the account of how a much abused child's on again, off again caretaker, Doll, one night snatches her up and spirits them both away from the child's parents' home. Did Lila's parents make an effort to remember Lila? Not really: they barely remembered Lila while they had her in their house. Too many times, they made clear they had little use for her.

Doll, however, remembered Lila. She wanted Lila to be remembered by other people, too. Doll wanted Lila to know the warmth of memory. And she succeeds. As the story continues, Lila comes to meet the Reverend Ames, who eventually becomes her husband. Lila then experiences being remembered in a singularly intimate way. In addition, she came to be remembered by many other people in Gilead, the imaginary town in which she lived. She did not live, and will not die, without notice.

Nonetheless, as Lila herself notes in her later years, even in Gilead, "There were the people no one would miss." All the wonder, all the glory, all the joy: when these people left the planet, they were, in every way, gone forever.[237]

As all of us will be. God or not, one day, we all will be forgotten.

Tom Vincent was a hermit who lived on the side of California's San Gabriel Mountains' 9,000 foot Mt. Baden-Powell for over 50 years. A recluse, he made every effort to keep people away from him, freely firing his rifle at anyone who dared approach his habitation. One day, however, Tom became very sick, so much so that he could no longer live on his own. As it turned out, he was dying.

[237] Marilynne Robinson, *Lila* (New York: Farrar, Straus and Giroux, 2014), 258.

Fortunately for Tom, the local postmaster, the only person with whom he ever talked, learned of his illness and took him down the mountain to a hospital. After a few weeks, Tom died, the postmaster still at his side. He didn't die alone, he didn't die unremembered. Briefly, perhaps very briefly, Tom saw a window into the world that he had not opened before. He saw that the world was not a completely cold place. He saw that life had not been a travesty; he saw that memory mattered. There was love, there was heart, there was recall. Tom left this planet knowing that his memory, the memory of him, would last beyond his present existence.

But did it? Only as a footnote to the history of a little known mountain range in Southern California. Otherwise, regardless of what he thought when he passed, now Tom and his memory are forever gone. He's vanished.[238]

Does Tom still matter? One of my aunts, my father's only sister, succumbed to liver disease in her fifties. Although she never married, she had a dear friend, Jeanne. She and Jeanne traveled and explored together for decades, jointly experiencing people and cultures the world over. The day before Velma died, Jeanne visited her. Neither knew it would be their last time together. When Velma died the next day, she was alone, alone as she had been most of her life. Yet we have to think that in her final moments, she remembered the friendship she and Jeanne shared, that she remembered that someone who loved her deeply was thinking of her. We have to think that she knew she was not dying forgotten.

---

238 See the article in the 2009 *Desert Gazette*, http://desertgazette.blogspot.com/2009/09/tom-vincent-was-hermit-that-lived-on.html.

Jeanne died in 2015, nearly thirty years after Velma's passing. Her will stipulated that her ashes be scattered at the same coordinates of the Pacific Ocean as Velma had hers so done. Jeanne wanted her and Velma to be together, metaphorically speaking, forevermore. In her remembering Velma this way, Jeanne will affirm their individual—and corporate—worth. She will establish that their lives were important, their time worthwhile, and that their memories are good. Their remembrances will be forever.[239]

Or will they?

As he lay dying near the close of the movie *Saving Private Ryan,* Stephen Spielberg's award winning movie about D-Day in World War II, Captain John Miller (played by Tom Hanks) says to Private Ryan (played by Matt Damon), "Earn it." In other words, Private Ryan, I died—I gave up my life—in order to find you and get you home to be with your mother (Ryan's three other male siblings had all been lost in the War). Remember me, Private Ryan, remember me. Remember what I did for you—and live it.[240]

After Private Ryan dies, however, will anyone remember John Miller, the man who rescued him? We would hope so, but we will not fully know. So does the slogan of the organization Wounded Warrior Project, a group dedicated to serving the physical and emotional needs of those wounded

---

[239] For more, read Jeanne's memoir, published shortly before her death, *A Meaningful Life: Memoir of a Lady Therapist* (Seattle: CreateSpace, 2015).

[240] *Saving Private Ryan,* Amblin Entertainment, 1998.

in combat since 2001, contend, "The greatest casualty is being forgotten."[241]

While we cannot disagree with this sentiment, how do we, in this life, stop this from happening?

Memory is the paradox of being human. Even if it will not change anything, even if it will not bring anyone back, we remember. Whether it is small or large, trivial or profound, memory enables us to attach meaning and purpose to the joys and losses of existence. Even if life means nothing other than it will one day end, we will always wish to remember. We do not like to think that we live and die in vain and without point. We do not like to set our lives in the burnishes of the rock band Ten Years After's song, "As the Sun Burns Away," their achingly depressing, almost Schopenaueran paean to the utter mediocrity and vanity of life and living. We do not like to think of ourselves as trapped in a circle of meaningless turns and random events.[242]

---

241 Regrettably, however, in 2015, two of Wounded Warrior's top executives were forced to resign over questions regarding how they spend the money donated to the organization, and its founder began talking about returning to restore the reputation of the organization. See http://www.nytimes.com/2016/03/11/us/wounded-warrior-board-ousts-top-two-executives.html?_r=0

242 "As the Sun Still Burns Away," written by Alvin Lee, from the band's *Cricklewood Green*, Deram Records, 1970. On Schopenhauer, see Arthur Schopenhauer, *World as Will and Representation*, Vols. I and II, trans. E. F. J. Payne (New York: Dover, 1966). See also Stephen Cave, "Imagining the Downside of Immortality," in the August 28, 2011, edition of *The New York Times*, in which he observes that, "Knowing we will die defines our lives." We remember now because we know that we will one day no longer be able to do it. In the face of impending loss, we

And we do not like to think that our memories are nothing more than a vast and unexplainable waste. Like the son-in-law in *Cloud Atlas;* like my friends and their three day old baby; or like Velma and Jeanne, we want to think that life is meaningful, and that our memories of it are similarly so. We want to think that our memories are, and always will be, wonderful and inherently meaningful parts of our lives. Fleeting or not, we see our memories, even if they seem hopelessly pointless, as the essential "stuff" of existence. We believe our memories frame our days and years on this planet.[243]

Yet we also know that if there is no God and no afterlife, our memory will not last. And what will we then do?

In *Living on the Edge: The Winter Ascent of Kanchenjunga,* author Cherie Bremer-Kamp writes eloquently about her 1985 attempt to climb Kanchenjunga, which at 28,169 feet is the third highest mountain in the world. Tragically, the person with whom she partnered to do the peak, Chris Chandler, perished along the way. He succumbed, unexpectedly, as he had much experience climbing at these altitudes, to cerebral edema. Although Cherie did everything she could to keep Chris going and connected to the work of scaling the mountain, in the end, she could not stop the inevitable. After Chris died, Cherie left him, propped on a slope, ice axe in hand, gazing over the valley out of which they had come some days earlier. His body is likely still there today, frozen for an earthly eternity.

---

strive to fill our lives with memories today. We use our memories to confirm the fact of our existence.

243

As Cherie recounts the episode, when Chris knew he would die, he did everything he could to bond with her, to stir her, to fill her with the memory and thought of him. Although we will never know what went through Chris's mind as he finally drifted into the grip of mortality, we certainly can conclude that he did not wish to go unforgotten. He wanted to be remembered.[244]

And if, and only if God is there, he will be. Before Rob Hall, a mountain guide from New Zealand who, along with six other people, perished on the slopes of Mt. Everest in 1986 (a story documented in Jon Krakauer's best-selling *Into Thin Air*), left for Nepal, he told his wife that rescue on these slopes is impossible, that, "You may as well be on the moon." Yet Hall's awareness that people were remembering him surely sustained him as later in the expedition, trapped by cold and darkness on the upper slopes of the mountain, he drifted into the grip of death. Although Hall was acutely aware that he was fading into a place where no one else could follow him, he likely felt significant. He knew he was thought about; he knew he was remembered.[245]

For a while, he will be. As will Chris Chandler. Without God, however, one day, one perhaps distant but nonetheless inevitable day, they will not. Unless there is God, and unless there is eternity, Chris Chandler and Rob Hall are gone, irretrievably gone.

---

[244] *Living on the Edge: The Winter Ascent of Kanchenjunga,* Cherie Bremer-Kamp (Layton, Utah: Gibbs M. Smith, 1987).

[245] *Into Thin Air,* Jon Krakauer (New York: Doubleday, 1997). See also the movie *Everest,* Crosscreek Pictures, Walden Media, and Working Title Films, 2015.

And no one will care. Thousands of miles from the Himalayas, signs posted at several places in the upper reaches of the backcountry of Colorado's Rocky National Park tell every hiker who passes by them that, "Mountains don't care." If you, the hiker, die in these mountains, the mountains will not care one whit that you're gone. It will not matter how important you had been to people. Like Chris Chandler, Rob Hall, or Steve Fischer, another guide who perished on Everest the same night as Hall, like all other backpackers and mountaineers who die alone, you're gone.

And although you will want to be remembered, only God, and the mountain, will really know where you are.

Again: that's the point. Over and above it all, God, if he is indeed there, knows. Over and above it all, God will remember. In God, memory will endure. Without God, however, no one, absolutely no one, will, in the excruciatingly lengthy and unknowable fullness of space and time, ever do likewise.

When mountaineer Walter J. Starr went missing while climbing in the Minarets of California's Sierra Nevada in 1940, scores of his fellow climbers went looking for him. They never found him. To this day, Starr's body, probably a skeleton by now, lies alone, eternally apart from all knowing, grasp, and time. Though his name remains, an authorial line in a guide book to the John Muir Trail, the most famous hiking trail in the Sierra, the man Walter Starr is forever gone. He's barely a fleck in an unfathomably turbulent sea of memory.

If there is God, however, Starr, and Hall, Fischer, and Chandler as well, will continue to be known. Memory will continue.[246]

After Christopher Hitchens, a highly outspoken atheist, died in 2011, his wife and publisher released *Mortality,* a series of reflections on the death that he knew awaited him imminently (he succumbed to cancer at age 62). In the book, Hitchens repeatedly stated his conviction that life ends definitively at death, and that once he was gone, he was irretrievably gone. He insisted that he would never have another shot at existence. It's over. But in making these assertions, Hitchens also underscored the worth of existence. He emphasized that his life had had a point. He was asserting that he, and his memory, meant something, that he and his memory had value. He believed that his existence had been known, had been known beyond himself.

Perhaps Hitchens sensed that, as John Rember put it in his memoir of living in the Sawtooth Mountains of Idaho, he had lived to glow "brightly in the moment of decay, to remember the brightness of others, and to feel the faint beat that remains in the things they touched." His life had had worth.[247]

Yet Hitchens also knew, knew very well, that because, as he saw it, there is no God, one day, nothing, he and everything else, will matter. It's futile.[248]

---

[246] Even today, Walter A. Starr, Jr., *Starr's Guide to the John Muir Trail and the High Sierra Region* (San Francisco: Sierra Club, 1964), remains the best guide to this spectacular 220 mile trail.

[247] John Rember, *Traplines: Coming Home to Sawtooth Valley* (New York: Vintage, 2003), 237.

[248] Christopher Hitchens, *Mortality* (New York: Twelve, 2014). But see the recently published *The Faith of Christopher Hitchens* by

An atheist friend of mine, Alan by name, once told me, "I know that even though I'll be gone after I die, I will live on. I'll become part of the planet. I'll be remembered." Though Alan will not know how he will be remembered, he believes that, metaphorically speaking, he will be. He will be part of what he sees as the unbelievably vast mnemonic energy of the universe. He believes he will be, to quote "Mrs. Ramsey," one of Virginia Woolf's most memorable characters, continue to be "woven" into the memory of those who knew him.[249]

Mike, another atheist friend of mine, says similarly. "My energy," he insists, "will carry on after I'm gone. There's no afterlife, but I will live on."[250]

Maybe so. Yet if the cosmos is impersonal, a massive and unplanned conglomeration of dust, flesh, and plasma, how

---

Larry Alex Taunton (New York: Nelson, 2016) which, based on a lengthy and illuminating relationship that Hitchens had with an evangelical Christian, offers a far more nuanced perspective on what Hitchens precisely believed.

249 Virginia Woolf, *To the Lighthouse,* as cited in Victor Brombert, *Musings on Mortality: From Tolstoy to Primo Levi* (Chicago: University of Chicago, 2013), 79.

250 As Philip Pullman so poetically states in *The Amber Spyglass,* "Even it means oblivion, friends, I'll welcome it, because it won't be nothing. We'll be alive again in a thousand blades of grass, and a million leaves; we'll be falling in the raindrops and blowing in the fresh breeze; we'll be glittering in the dew under the stars and the moon out there in the physical world, which is our true home and always was." Buzzy Jackson, ed. *The Inspirational Atheist* (New York: Plume, 2014), 45.

can it really remember? Though memory may cover all, will it really cover meaning?[251]

Moreover, are we really creatures who are, as Virginia Woolf once described us,

> "Advancing with lights across the waste of years to the rescue of some stranded ghost . . . waiting, appealing, forgotten, in the growing gloom"?[252]

Maybe someone will remember us, then again maybe not, but either way it does not matter, for we will be lost in a mnemonic "gloom," never, as Psalm 49:19 describes it, to "see the light"?

And then whose memory will it be? When Larry, a friend of mine who died of cancer in 1993, his widow, Edna, wrote to me to say, "He died surrounded by love." What greater thing than this? Though Larry, never one to be sentimental about death, realized that his passing was, in biological terms, simply the end of a human gene pool, he nonetheless appreciated being remembered. He appreciated the company of his wife and two children, he was grateful for their presence. Larry died happy: he was loved, he was remembered.

---

251 So does Ecclesiastes 6:12 say, "Who can tell a person what will be after him/her under the sun?" Unless a conscious and omnipotent moral purpose is working in the universe, we really do not know, the nature of our essential constituents notwithstanding, what will happen to us.

252 Virginia Woolf, "Lives of the Obscure," excerpted in Thomas Mallon, *Essays on Writers and Writing* (New York: Random House, 2001).

Once everyone who knew Larry is gone, however, what will happen? Moreover, what will happen when, after *everyone* has lived, died, and moved on, and all that remains is what the writer Oliver Sacks described as "the heavens' beauty" that is "inseparably mixed with . . . death?"[253]

If there is no God, absolutely nothing. And we may well wonder whether one astronaut's observation in the movie *Europa Report* that, "compared to the knowledge yet to know, what does your life matter?" is really in fact true.[254]

Yet paradox remains. If we feel we are remembered, we feel we are loved. We feel we are cared about. We feel fulfilled, whole and complete. We're tethered, we're connected. We have lived for a reason. As the Corrs sing in their "Breathless," even if tomorrow never comes and all we have is right before us, we can be—indeed, we *ought* to be—happy to just have each other, for in the big picture we, we little human beings, are all the love we need.[255]

We will cling to our memory to our last breath.

If on the other hand we engage our memory convinced that, in the biggest possible picture, it means nothing, do we not deny where we have been? Do we not prevaricate all of our earthly assumptions? If we genuinely believe that once we're gone, everything, life, goodness, and remembrance, is over, why do we do bother?

Well, we might say, we have family, and we have friends. Evanescent or not, our memories are us. They define our lives. We love them, we treasure them.

---

253 Oliver Sacks, "My Periodic Table," *New York Times,* July 26, 2015. Sadly, Sacks died in September, 2015.

254 *Europa Report,* Start Motion Picture, 2013.

255 See "Breathless," written by the Corrs, AllMusic, 2000.

And oh, how we do. After my father died in the autumn of 1983 and my three siblings and I had only our mother to love and care for, we all of course tried to carry on. We returned to our own lives and obligations and did what we could to refocus and keep going. However, we were profoundly aware that our mother was very alone, living on her own in the house in Southern California she and Dad had shared for twenty-five years. And we also knew, knew in the very depths of our hearts, that although like us Mom had many challenges with which she had to deal, she continued to think about us. We knew that even if no one else was thinking about us, Mom was. We knew that even if everyone else on the planet forgot about us, our mother would not.

This knowledge made all of us feel immensely better. Though we continued to struggle with our loss, we did so knowing that someone else was struggling with us. We were not alone. Someone loved us deeply, someone cared for us greatly. Someone remembered us. Someone else, someone very dear to us was remembering us, someone on whom we could call, anywhere, anytime, someone who was, simply, there. In this memory, this affirmation of our worth, we felt richly blessed.[256]

Even though we knew that this sense of memory would not last, and even though we knew that the hope it brought us was ephemeral, we kept it. We cultivated its hope, we nurtured its possibilities.

---

[256] In contrast, consider the dedicatory words on the frontispiece of Samantha Baskind & Larry Silver, *Jewish Art: A Modern History* (London: Reaktion, 2011): "And to all those who have no one to mourn for them."

Even if we knew that the earth would one day crumble and disintegrate and we along with it, we enjoyed, deeply, being remembered.

Many years before Dad died, I went on a snowshoeing expedition in the winter snows of the Sierra Nevada (a range I mentioned earlier in regard to mountaineer Walter J. Starr, Jr.). As I always did in my mountain forays in those days, I went alone. And I told no one, not even the rangers, about my route. I wanted to be totally detached from the world.

One afternoon midway through my trip, I looked up through the steadily falling snow to realize that I was lost. I had somehow misread my topographical maps and had taken a path well off my planned route. I had no idea where I was. The forest looked as empty as a beach at dawn.

I soon grasped the hopelessness of my situation. No one, absolutely no one knew where I was. The rangers and my parents knew I was in the backcountry, but that's all. They had no clue as to my precise location. I was frightfully alone.

Trying not to panic, I stopped where I was and set up camp. The next morning, I looked at my maps again. Joy: I figured out where I was! Perhaps I would make it after all. As I set off, now able to find my way, I thought constantly of Mom and Dad. I knew they were thinking about me, I knew they cared about me, I knew they were remembering me. Though to the rangers I was just another mixed up kid, to Mom and Dad I was one of their greatest treasures. I knew they'd do anything for me. I knew they would not forget me.

As snow continued to fall and as temperatures held cold and steady, this knowledge sustained me. It inspired me, it heartened me. I fought my way back to my starting point knowing that hundreds and hundreds of miles away in a house in Los Angeles, two people were thinking daily about me. I was remembered. I was not forgotten. I knew that when I emerged from the mountains, I could return to these people, these two people who loved me so dearly, and enjoy their active and continuous memory of me. I had value, I had worth.

And I did not care whether this sense of being remembered would last a month or a year. I didn't care that when I one day died, it would be gone. I wanted it for today.

At this juncture in my life, that's all that mattered.

For most of us, memory's temporality notwithstanding, we are remembered out of love. Our parents and friends remember us because they love us, our colleagues and associates remember us because they respect and admire us. Those who remember us do so because they genuinely care about us. They are sorry we are gone.

Sometimes, however, we remember people not because we love them, but because we fear them. We remember them in darkness, a darkness engendered by the shadows and pain they brought into the world. Consider the many tyrants and dictators who have trod the pages of history. From the Assyrian king Sennacherib to Mongolia's Genghis Khan to the Gupta monarch Asoka before he converted to Buddhism; from Maximillian Robespierre of the French Revolution to the barbaric Pol Pot of Cambodia to Uganda's Idi Amin, who would want to remember them? Most people are happy they're gone. Indeed, most people would prefer that they had never existed.[257]

[257] For instance, the infamously perverted Marquis de Sade (writer of *Justine* and *One Hundred Days of Sodom*) wished to

Nonetheless, these people lived, and they died. And their memories remain. We cannot escape them. If nothing ultimately matters, if nothing ultimately lasts, however, do we care?

Ironically, we know we do. As we observed earlier, even if we believe our memory of these people vanishes at death, we cannot help but remember, today, and likely for the rest of our days the unrelentingly bitter agony that these people brought into the world.

After all, we are only human.[258]

---

be remembered not for his love or affection but for his sexual and sadistic predilections. And Jack the Ripper, the furtive and merciless slasher who terrorized Victorian London, loved that he achieved public notoriety. He loved that his twisted deeds would be what people remembered about him. Also, consider how much Joseph Goebbels, Hitler's propaganda chief, mourned the passing of his leader. He wished that the Fuhrer would live forever. He wanted what he saw as Hitler's "greatness" to be remembered forever. See Peter Longerich, *Goebbels* (New York: Random House, 2015).

[258] See Stéphane Courtois *et al, The Black Book of Communism*, trans. Jonathan Murphy and Mark Kramer (Cambridge, Massachusetts: Harvard University, 1999). So, too, consider that despite the various terrors (Great Leap Forward and Cultural Revolution) which Mao Zedong visited upon the Chinese people in the years he ruled the country, even today, many Chinese continue to unapologetically revere his name. On this, see Philip Short, *Mao: A Life* (New York: Henry Holt, 2000). Yet compare these scenarios with Ecclesiastes 8:13, which tells us that, one day, the memory of the "wicked will be forgotten." Although from our earthly vantage point, "one day" could well be centuries away, we can nonetheless believe that it will eventually come, and thoughts of the "wicked" will be no more (we will enlarge on this thesis later).

Unbroken tells the story of Louis Zamperini, a standout high school and college runner who served in the U.S. Navy in World War II. Shot down over a lonely stretch of the Pacific Ocean, Zamperini and a fellow survivor drifted over 2,000 miles of open sea to finally, and inadvertently, land on an island controlled by the Japanese. Zamperini subsequently spent eighteen torturous months in a Japanese prison of war camp. One of the guards at the camp, who was nicknamed the "Bird," had a special hatred for Zamperini, and did everything he could to make his life singularly miserable.

After the War had ended and Zamperini had returned to the U.S. and gone on with his life, did he continue to remember the "Bird"? He certainly did. Although at one point he even returned to Japan in an effort to find the "Bird," Zamperini did not do this because he had wonderful memories of him. He did so because of the pain he remembered the "Bird" had inflicted on him. He remembered the "Bird" for all the wrong reasons.

But he remembered him still. How could he not?[259]

Similarly, when Boston Marathon bomber Tamerlan Tsarnaev's survivors tried to identify a cemetery in which to bury him, they met with opposition almost everywhere they looked. No one wanted him. No one wanted his horror, no one wanted his tenebrosity. No one wanted to remember him.[260]

---

259 Laura Hillenbrand, *Unbroken* (New York: Random House, 2014).

260 See http://www.cnn.com/2013/05/10/us/virginia-boston-suspect-burial/ for additional details.

Conversely, once Tsarnaev's brother is executed, and all of the two brothers' relatives are gone, will *anyone* remember Tsarnaev? Sure. They will not be able to help it. But they will not remember him for good reasons.

Does this, however, really matter? Does it really matter that no one will remember Tsarnaev or the "Bird" with love? If there is no God, if there is no transcendent purpose, it will not, absolutely not. If the world is accidental, if the world is nothing more than a blip of gravity and quantum field, morality and memory mean nothing, nothing at all.

If presence implodes at death, it will not matter how anyone is remembered.[261]

Consider the epitaph of Aleister Crowley, the self-proclaimed British pagan and Satanist, which reads,

> "He had the gift of laughing at himself, most affably he talked and walked with God, and now the silly bastard's on the shelf, we've buried him beneath another sod."[262]

---

261 On this, see Paul Kalanithi's best selling memoir of his imminent passing, *When Breath Becomes Air* (New York: Random House, 2016), in which he observes, "To make science the arbiter of metaphysics is to banish not only God from the world but also love, hate, meaning—to consider a world that is self-evidently *not* [emphasis his] the world we live in. That's not to say that if you believe in meaning, you must also believe in God. It is to say, though, that if you believe that science provides no basis for God, then you are almost obligated to conclude that science provides no basis for meaning and, therefore, life itself doesn't have any."

262 Laura Ward, *Famous Last Words* (London: Robson, 2004), 130. See also Lawrence Sutin, *Do what thou wilt: a life of Aleister*

Crowley had it absolutely right. Absent a larger moral compass or framework, we remember in a vacuum. Bereft of a God, we are indeed just another layer of sod. Whether it is the most evil of people or the finest person we know, once they are gone, regardless of how, love or not, we remember them—and they remember us—we do so in nothingness, utter and categorical nothingness. Good or bad, right or wrong, it will not matter. Everything has vanished, decisively obliterated in the aphonic sea of human futility. We lived, they lived; we died, they died. And whether we and they did good or ill does not ultimately matter.

In a senseless world, a world devoid of and apart from circumspection and judgment, a world without larger moral point, memory is pointless.

As we observed earlier, however, we make this assertion in paradox. All of us, every last one of us, even if we believe life has no larger compass or meaning, cannot help but live, and die, with memory. It's who we are. Even if we believe we will one day lose it all, even if we are certain that nothing will ever "be" again, we remember.

And we wonder why. Why do we remember if one day we will not? Why do we remember even if we would rather not? Why do we remember if we will one day be remembered no longer? What's the point?

Wait! Larger moral point or not, doesn't memory affirm human worth? It certainly does. Memory means that people have a point. It says that people have purpose and value. When we remember someone, we are thinking that somehow, some way, this person is worthwhile. She has importance, she has significance. Regardless of how we

---

Crowley (New York: St. Martin's Press, 2000).

see any other person, and irrespective of how we view the meaning of existence, we believe that this person is special. We have noticed this person, we have set her apart. We have given her a place, a unique moment of station in our life.

In the same way, when we hope that a person remembers us, we are saying that *we* have value, that we have a measure of significance. We are affirming that we are worth knowing, that we are deserving of love, and that we have meaning. We affirm our human dignity. We are regarded, we are thought about. Our experience of being remembered makes us feel pictured, imagined, and pondered. In what appears to be a cold and insouciant universe, a cosmos with no apparent rhyme or reason, the thought of being remembered helps us to feel meaningful. Even if the universe is without a heart or soul, even if existence is capricious, and even if there is no God, our knowledge, at the point of passing, that we are being remembered helps us to see that we have significance, that we are more than errant glacial rocks. It enables us to be pleased that we have lived.[263]

Our memory, our own as well as the memory others have of us, is one way that we affirm life is good. It is our acknowledgement that life is important, that it is worthwhile. We use memory to say that when all is said and done, we are happy we have lived. Memory lets us remind ourselves that we are not sorry that we were born. With memory, we are pleased with our days on this planet, we are grateful for the opportunity to live. Sure, some of our memories are filled with hardship and tragedy, but most

[263] A glacial rock is one that has been dragged and scraped by a glacier over many thousands of years rather than being dumped summarily in a random place on the landscape.

of them have populated our life with moments of pleasure, even some times of profound bliss. Our memories tell us that life is sweet. They tell us that there is a reason why we are here. There are explanations, important explanations, for why we lived as we have, for why our lives have gone as they have. Our memory tells us that life has real point, that our years have purpose and meaning.

Memory and being remembered also tell us that the *universe* is a place of purpose. There is a reason why it is here, there is a reason why it is the way it is. The world is not an accident, the cosmos is not happenstance. Memory reminds us that larger meaning exists. Weaving moments, days, and weeks together, it underscores the value of everything that is. Indeed: we would not remember if we did not believe that some things are worth remembering, if we did not believe that life is more than something that, in philosopher and mathematician Bertrand Russell's (1872-1970) view, "just is."[264]

Yet as my atheist friends Alan and Mike might say, there is no meaning. But there is, they add, purpose. Fair enough. But how can we posit purpose without meaning? Why would we remember if we believe that what we remember has no meaning? Why would we think that memory is purposeful if what it remembers is pointless? Unless existence has meaning, while we might still find memory to be important, even purposeful, as we might life itself, in the end, we would be ignoring the obvious. Who are we kidding?

We cannot have it both ways. Either we remember in a meaningful universe that is filled with meaningful beings

---

[264] Bertrand Russell, *Why I Am Not A Christian* (New York: Touchstone, 1967).

or we may as well not remember at all. What would be the point? Lives would be lived, lives would be enjoyed, and lives would be remembered, but lives would be fruitless as well. Grand and lovely though memory might be, in truth it would be no more than an evanescent spurt of sentience, a quirk without a home, a pop of *something* unaccountably irrupting from an irredeemable void. It cancels itself even as it happens. And everyone and everything, every last grain of sand and every last human being, will be flotsam in the emptiness of an immense and futile burst of a life of unexplainable and thoroughly vapid presence.

No, memory does not matter unless we live in a meaningful universe. And the only meaningful universe is one that is an intentional universe. Otherwise, although memory will still happen, in fact it does not. It can't remember, it won't remember, and it will not be remembered. In a cosmos devoid of intention, memory, good or bad, right or wrong, will remain forever inchoate, interminably doomed to reflect the unbearable angst of a totally vain existence: we are, then we are not.

What's an intentional universe? An intentional universe is a universe that someone intended to be here. It is a created universe. Like a sculpture or musical composition, present only as the intentional work of a conscious being, an intentional universe is here because someone, a deeply conscious someone, purposefully and directly enabled it to be so.

An intentional universe can only be one that has been created by God. Only an intentional universe is one driven by and infused with purpose; only an intentional universe is one of lasting transcendent and moral sensibility. An intentional universe has a plane of enduring purpose in which all things come about and all things happen, a plane outside of which nothing occurs or happens. It is a universe in which purpose encloses and discloses all things in it.

Absent the intentionality of God, memory, existence, and universe have no real moral point. Indeed, they have no point at all.

Why? Because God, and God alone, created and sustains the universe, only God validates and enables memory, uniquely granting purpose and point to the plethora of recollections that erupt and flood endlessly through our existence. God gives epistemic weight to our weeks and months and years. He stops memory from underscoring life's absurdity, instead shaping and using it to affirm life's marvel and worth. With God, memory upholds the meaningfulness of the universe. No longer is memory simply one more experience in the seas of subjectivity and particularity. Now it is an explanation, a transcending explanation that demonstrates and authenticates the necessity of existential *and* metaphysical meaning for human thought and endeavor.

Not so fast, some might say. Echoing Plato's long ago words in *Phaedrus*, many of us insist that, God or not, we are all souls who will, in some form, exist forever. We matter. Transcendent purpose or not, though we will one day die, we will still live. We will carry on. Universe moral framework notwithstanding, as souls, we will last forever. The cosmos's rhythms will continue, and the balance of the universe, the omnipresent patterns of karma, being, and non-being, will endure. Things will not disappear altogether. Nor will we.[265]

---

[265] Plato, *Phaedrus,* trans. R. Hackforth (Cambridge: Cambridge University, 1952). See also the writings of Buddhism and

Perhaps. Perhaps we, or our souls, will live forever. Perhaps our souls will remember us. Perhaps our souls will remember each other. Perhaps existence will never end. Everything we know about the nature of the universe, however, militates against this happening. Every scientific theory of origins and ends points to a day when the cosmos will no longer be.

And unless this realm of souls can sustain itself, it will end, too. Unless this human "presence" of spirit and soul has independent energy and momentum, it will not outlast a dead universe. It is not a creator, and it is not a redeemer. Nor is it moral. It has no basis for ensuring that itself, much less conscious existence, will be, in some form, meaningful or permanent. How can it? It's no more than rhythm and balance. And where do these come from?

Charles Dickens's *Christmas Carol* tells the story of how, seeking to "cure" the financier Ebenezer Scrooge of his chronic selfishness and greed, three ghosts visit him on Christmas Eve. One by one, they take him through various stages of his life. The first, the Ghost of Christmas Past, gives him a tour of the Christmases of his childhood, letting Scrooge see that he has not always found the holiday so odious or difficult. The next one, the Ghost of Christmas Present, offers him a window into the Christmas at hand, unfolding for him a picture of how those he knows, particularly his hard working assistant, Bob Crachit, are celebrating Christmas this year. He hears his name mentioned, he hears

---

Hinduism on the eternality of the human soul in, respectively, Nirvana or Brahman. In these, time and space never really end: death is only another stop on an endless continuum of birth and rebirth.

people talking about him. He hears some mention him with pity, others with despicability and scorn. Scrooge is shocked. Finally, the Ghost of Christmas Future shows Scrooge how he will be remembered after he dies. He sees that no one, absolutely no one will remember him. No one will care that he is gone, no one will mind that he is no longer on the planet. Indeed, he sees that people seem to feel that the world is better off without him.

Then, the story goes, Scrooge changes. He wakes up Christmas morning full of mirth and good cheer. Gathering himself together, he goes out into the streets, shouting good wishes to everyone he sees. He gives away money, he gives away food. He is a new man.[266]

In an unintended universe, however, why would Scrooge care? And why would anyone bother to not care about him? There would be no reason to do either one.

Really? At first glance, it seems as if people like Christopher Hitchens and my friends Alan and Mike, people who view death, though they may find it unfair, maddening, or frustrating, with relative equanimity and calm, to be people whose lives challenge this thesis. At first glance, they seem to be people who have embraced life's fleetingness and are ready to accept death when it comes. They seem to be people who believe that even if life and its memories are fleeting, sentient existence remains unbearably sweet. They have no quarrels with the finitude of existence. In the end, they do what author Elisabth Kubler-Ross observed many

[266] Charles Dickens, *A Christmas Carol* (Santa Fe: Small Town, 2009).

decades ago about people and death: they accept it.[267] Life has been good, yes, but it has to end sometime, and that time appears to be now.[268]

No, transcendent morality and purpose do not really matter.[269]

Maybe so. Maybe it doesn't matter that there is no eternity, afterlife, or God, and that our memory is the present, and only the present. Maybe it doesn't matter that although we may die knowing we are remembered, as soon as we expire we will know nothing at all, and that it will not in fact then matter to us how many people remember us. Maybe it doesn't matter that we who remember do so more for us than those we remember, as we believe that it will not matter to them, anyway. After all, one day, everything will be nothing. There will be no one left to know.

Furthermore, maybe it doesn't matter that our lives do not continue indefinitely. Maybe reality is in fact sufficiently true as we physically perceive it, its memories complete unto

---

267 Elisabeth Kubler-Ross, *On Death and Dying* (New York: Macmillan, 1969).

268 As clothing manufacturer Patagonia founder Yvon Chouinard remarked in the Patagonia 40th Anniversary Catalog, "I've accepted the fact that I'm going to die someday. I'm not too bothered by it. There is a beginning and end to all life—and to all human endeavors."

269 Either way, people like Alan and Mike will die knowing that they will be remembered. Whether it be the memory of their loved ones, colleagues, admirers, or relatives and friends, doesn't matter. They are being remembered. They will not be forgotten. They depart acutely cognizant of the weight, achievements, relationships, and memories of the lives they lived. And they die believing in their heart of hearts that they need nothing more.

themselves. Maybe life is no more than life, and memories no more than memories. Maybe life begins, filling itself with memories, thrilling and dazzling memories, then ends, the significance and power of its memories gone, collapsed into a tangle of faceless chemicals and fading material moments, slowly putrefying remnants of the vexing joy and incongruity of existence.

Maybe so. If no one remembered us beyond our immediate survivors, or if no one remembered the worlds of our lives—and the world as a whole—it would not change the quality of our lives. It would not alter the fact of our presence, would not eliminate the fact of anything we did. We still would have lived, we still would have been human beings in the world. We still would have been here, and nowhere else. No, remembering and being remembered in a faceless and empty universe would not change the fact of existence. It would simply serve to reinforce its fleetingness, and the general pointlessness, as physicist Steven Weinberg once said, of the universe.[270]

Maybe memory does not need a larger moral framework.

Maybe. We may well be able to live and die and never mind or miss that life has no overarching purpose, or that there is no genuine reason or point for us to be here. That we will die without being remembered, that one day the universe itself will no longer be thought of or remembered, that in the big picture we were no more than an infinitesimal point on an enormously large canvas, is really of no consequence. We enjoyed our life, we had our fun, and that's all we need. Sure, we're "useless passions," to repeat French philosopher

[270] Steven Weinberg, *Dreams of a Final Theory: The Search for the Fundamental Laws of Nature* (New York: Vintage, 1993).

Jean Paul Sartre's words once more, but we were here, and we lived responsible, purposeful, and upright lives.[271]

Yet life is only wonderful and death tragic if there is moral point. And in an impersonal cosmos, there is none. As biologist and atheist Richard Dawkins, once asked about life's meaning, responded, "That's not a valid question." He's right. Absent a God or moral framework, there is no reason to ask about meaning. Why would we?[272]

We are therefore like the denizens of Sir Walter Scott's (1771-1832) *The lay of the last minstrel,* people who, though they have lived, will one day die, and do so, he says, "Unwept, unhonored, and unsung." It's over.[273]

Can we really live this way? In *The Fault in Our Stars,* two high school students, Augustus Waters and Hazel Grace, meet at a support group for young people who are dealing with cancer. Hazel is still struggling with hers; Augustus's is in remission. As things progress, however, Augustus's

---

271 *Being and Nothingness, op cit.*

272 See Jesse Bering's *Belief Instinct: the Psychology of Souls, Destiny, and the Meaning of Life* (New York: W. W. Norton, 2011). On the other hand, as Thomas Nagel argues in his review of Samuel Scheffler, *Death and the Afterlife* (Oxford: Oxford University, 2014), perhaps the imminent end of life and memory will serve to "heighten rather than diminish" the value of a life's experiences. If there is no tomorrow, people will find fresh impetus to maximize their today, indulging in what Nagel terms, "a desperate wish to give them [their lives] an intense final realization in experience before the lights went out for good." (Or put another way, *carpe diem.*) See Thomas Nagel, "After You've Gone," *The New York Review of Books,* January 9, 2014. Nonetheless, this still doesn't answer the question of why life came to *be* in the first place.

273 Walter Scott, *The lay of the last minstrel* (Charleston, South Carolina: Nabu, 2011).

cancer returns. He becomes terminal, and eventually dies. Although he's realistic about the facts of his demise, he still weeps inwardly at his fate. He does not want, he often makes clear, to fade into oblivion. He wants to stay. He wants to be remembered.[274]

As do all of us. In a meaningless universe, however, why do we bother?[275]

We would not. Indeed, we *cannot.* As George Borrow (1853-1932) puts in his memoir *Lavengro,*

> "There's night and day, brother, both sweet things; sun, moon, and stars, brother, all sweet things; there's likewise a wind on the heath. Life is very sweet, brother; who would wish to die?"[276]

Augustus's angst is only meaningful if it happens in a meaningful universe. And as we observed, a universe can only be meaningful if it is created, intentionally planned, purposed, and made by a living and personal God.

---

274 John Green, *The Fault in Our Stars* (New York: Penguin, 2014).

275 In his short story "Oblivion," David Foster Wallace presents an amusing picture of this fact of existential emptiness. After checking themselves into a "somnology" clinic to deal with issues of snoring and inability to sleep, a married couple endures several rounds of testing and counseling only to find that, in fact, they've been dreaming the whole thing. They have been living their life as one big dream: in the end, it didn't really matter. See David Foster Wallace, "Oblivion," in *Oblivion* (New York: Little, Brown and Company, 2004).

276 As quoted in Robert MacFarlane, *The Old Ways: A Journey on Foot* (New York: Penguin, 2012), 19.

When we reject the idea of God in memory, we therefore reject more than God. We reject the fundamental nature of reality. We reject the fact of the universe's innately and necessarily transcendent structure and origin. We miss that reality can only be its fullness if it is, as Immanuel Kant put it long ago, noumenal as well as phenomenal, physical as well as metaphysical and that we are, as we observed earlier, heteronomous. We ignore that we and our reality are more than the sum of our parts. We overlook that our very mnemonic complexity begs the fact of the metaphysical, that who we are demands the existence of God, an omnipotent creator God in whom all things cohere and find meaning. We forget that personal beings cannot have come from, much less live in, an impersonal universe.[277]

God in memory reminds us that reality is more than what seems materially real, that what is materially real is only so because something bigger than it is real, too. It means that the universe does not exist in a vacuum, that it is more than individuated asseverations and conclusions of form, experience, and perception. God in memory, and God remembering the cosmos make it true, true in the deepest sense of the word, true not because it is here but because whatever has enabled it to be here *is* truth, absolute and morphological truth. We know that we live in a purposeful and loved cosmos.

Furthermore, we understand that apart from God's memory, that is, God remembering us and all other things, the universe has no real point. God's memory enables us to know why, to know why we are here, and why we and the universe remember and are remembered in turn. The

[277] *Critique of Pure Reason, op cit.*

memory of our creator allows us to see that the universe is more than the object of whimsical and insipid human desire, more than a little splash in an incoherence of nothingness, more than a twist of strings and inflections. We realize that because the universe is remembered, it is neither lonely nor alone, but is thought about and cared for. It is supposed to be here. As are we.

But for the memory of God, the universe would not happen, and but for the memory of God, the universe would not last.

Pushing God away from memory therefore defies reason itself. It ignores the meaning of space, it rejects the nature of time. It leaves us without any way to say that life, its experiences, and its memories have any real value. God and God's memory ensure that our memories are not accidents, happenstances of birth, remembrance, and death, silly and momentary spurts on an accidental and undesired canvas. They are not the inaccessible work of a purposeless cosmos, random and groundless assertions of worth in a universe which has none. With God, our memory has credible foundation, value, meaning, and point. With God, the past indeed needed to happen, and the future is far more than a mirage of volatility and caprice.

Moreover, to jettison God from memory is to sever ourselves from who we are. It is to divorce ourselves from our true selves, our uniquely personal human moment and presence. It to cause to us to overlook that we are consciously spiritual creatures, spiritual creatures endowed with rich sensibilities of the empyrean and divine.

Memory without God leads us to forget that we are beings who live in an open universe. It is to overlook that we live as creatures perched on the edge of eternity, creatures living before an endlessness that is constantly making itself known in our present experience. Without God in memory, we do not know that our present recollection and recall are but shadows standing before the veil of another, overwhelmingly richer day.

Centering memory in God enables us to say, as did the Sanhedrin leader Zerah in the film *Jesus of Nazareth* upon seeing the empty tomb on Easter morning, "Now it all begins." In God, the resurrected Christ, memory, everything present and bouncing about us, becomes the door to a truth exceeding our wildest and most creative dreams: life begins again.[278]

What does this mean for us? It demands that we delete, totally, the naturalistic equation of birth, life, and death. Not only will we remember and be remembered in this life, we will remember and be remembered in another life as well. And we will be conscious and aware that we are doing and being so. We will continue to be aware that people are remembering us, and we will continue to be cognizant that we are remembering them. This life is not it. Memory will not run away, memory will not leave us. No longer will it be transient, no longer will it vanish in a moment. Even in death, memory, and life, will go on.

Everything that we had enjoyed in this life, everything of which we have fond memories in this existence will therefore, in some way, continue. Whatever we had known in this earthly life we will know in the next, and whatever we had experienced in this present existence we will carry

[278] See Franco Zeffirelli's *Jesus of Nazareth,* ITC Entertainment, 1977.

into the one to follow. Who and what we had been in this life we will take, in some way, into its successor. We will continue as ourselves, we will continue as we are, we will remain "us," conscious, aware, and cognitive beings, for all eternity. We will "be"—and everything that this had comprised or will comprise—forever. Nothing will have an end. Although life as we had known it will be over, it will be "born again," and continue, eternally and without end.[279]

Moreover, God in memory demands that our memory, hitherto frighteningly empty, will now become unspeakably full. Remembrance will not be, as the prophet Isaiah puts it, "wiped out" forever. Quite the opposite. "The dead will live, their corpses will rise, and those who lie in the dust will awake and shout for joy" (Isaiah 26:14, 19). Imprinted into an afterlife, limed into a second dawn, memory is transformed, transformed in ways that are beyond our puny imagination's ability to grasp. Joyously writhing in the hands of a divinely ordered afterlife, memory becomes something entirely and completely new.

In this, our present therefore changes completely. We now live and remember knowing that we will do so even after death. We frame our present with the future, and this not an earthly future. It is a future that is eternal. Our ken expands exponentially, our universe broadens infinitely: our world discloses as it had not before. We set our lives in a tremendously greater span of meaning.

Those who loved us do, too. When we die, though they mourn us, they know that they will be mourning and

---

279 Or as N. T. Wright puts it in his *The Resurrection of the Son of God* (Minneapolis: Fortress, 2003), we will live a "life after life after death." Life will continue, yet will become totally new.

remembering a person who continues to exist. They will be remembering a person who is aware that she is being remembered. They know we will live on. They know they will see us again. They know that because God remembers us, they can, too, and that it will not be in vain.

Knowing that the eternal and omniscient creator, the one who set all things into motion, the one who oversees all things, the one from all life has sprung is remembering us, our loved ones will live assured that we are not forgotten. They will live out their days secure in their knowledge and conviction that the people they are remembering—us—will exist forever. The memory of us will never die.

Though nothing will get old, nothing will remain the same.[280]

And life will not be what Eleanor Marx, daughter of *Communist Manifesto* and *Das Kapital* author Karl Marx, once described as "a sadness" that "comes upon us almost too painfully for endurance." Quite the opposite: life will become profuse and inexhaustible. It is eternal.[281]

When I was in Los Angeles a few years ago, I breakfasted with two people whom I had known for almost forty years. At ninety years of age, they knew their time on this planet was drawing to a close. At point in our conversation Ruth said to me, "I know I could die anytime, but I'm ready.

---

[280] This assertion raises very difficult questions about memory and forgetting, which we will address later.

[281] Rachel Holmes, *Eleanor Marx* (London: Bloomsbury, 2014), 304. Also, we do well to note that although Marx has received the bulk of the credit for the *Manifesto,* he in fact shared authorship with his loyal patron Friedrich Engels.

I know that I have a glorious future." Ruth believes in eternal memory, the eternal memory of God. She knows that upon her death she will be in a place, a personal place inhabited by a personal God, a personal God who never forgets those who believe in him. She knows that when she dies, she will continue to consciously remember and, more importantly, continue to be consciously aware that she is being remembered. She knows that her awareness of remembrance and memory will continue forever, and that what she had experienced in this life will not die but carry on, gloriously and indefinitely. Her remembering will have neither boundaries nor border; it will be the ground and impetus of a life shorn of all earthly restriction and surcease. Ruth's memory will glimmer in the light of eternity.

Ruth knows that God will remember her, always and forever.[282]

Putting to rest all materialistic claims to the nature of reality, setting memory in the workings of an eternal God reminds and assures us that although as countless religious thinkers have suggested, we humans (and our remembering and being remembered) are evanescent and perishable, this will not be so forever. One day, earthly memory will no longer bind us; one day, our mortal connection to memory will cease. One day, our memory will be permanent and *im*perishable, a victim of dust and passage no more. One day, we, now supernaturally transformed and irrecoverably changed, will remember and live a new life in which we

---

282 In fact, as this book was going to press, Bob, his wife, children, and grandchildren at his side, all of them singing hymns together, passed away. He was 91.

will remember again and again and again: forever. No longer will this world's canvas of memory be "all we [could possibly] need."[283]

With God, we remember with transcendent measure, redeeming significance, and comprehensive explanation. We experience memory as inherently meaningful. We understand that what has happened means something, and that what we remember about it means something, too. We know that there is moral weight and meaning for all remembrance and memory, good and bad. Ensconced in the hourglass of eternity, we know that we live and die and remember in the umbra of a realm that unpacks and clarifies everything we do not now comprehend or see. All questions are dispelled, every contradiction is erased. Our memory becomes bigger than its individual parts, the harbinger of supernality, a metaphysicality of passion and recall undergirded with truth and lasting energy and power. Oblivion reigns no longer.

And the sundry and countless days, nights, months, and years of mnemonic grasp and embrace will all, profoundly and marvelously, remain.[284]

---

[283] So contends David Peterson, *On the Wild Edge: In Search of a Natural Life* (New York: H. Holt, 2005), about the current state of existence: when it's over, it's over

[284] While we will later try to paint a more precise picture of what this experience of memory in the next life will look like, we will say for now that regardless of how we attempt to envision the nature of the afterlife in this life, we cannot fully know, this side of death, what it will be like. And we do not know, precisely, what we will be like in it. For now, we can only say that with God, in death, memory becomes permanent, eternally permanent and, significantly, eternally personal, in a way it could not be before.

How could it be otherwise? As we noted previously, in addition to being eternal and omniscient, God is

---

This notwithstanding, we note that with the possible exception of Confucianism (although in the *Analects,* the collected saying of Confucius, the "Master" occasionally refers to a heaven, it is believed that he is not referring to heaven in a physical sense. (*The Analects of Confucius,* trans. Arthur Waley (New York: Vintage, 1989), Book XII.)), the major religions of the world all hold to some type of afterlife. For Islam and Christianity, it is resurrection in bodily form and eternal and conscious communion with God (or Allah, which is the Arabic word for "God"). For Buddhism and Hinduism, it is eternal oneness, conscious or not, with the source or balance of reality, be it Nirvana or Brahman. (See *Hindu Scriptures, op cit.*). Depending on the branch of Judaism, it is bodily resurrection and eternal exchange with God; an indefinable experience of goodness, righteousness, and meaning; or a void. (See Robert Coles, *The Spiritual Life of Children* (Boston: Houghton Mifflin, 1990); *Death and Dying, op cit.; Jewish Art, op cit.*) Even for those religions that assert bodily resurrection, however, it remains unclear exactly what this will look like. Bodily resurrection is a slippery term. Also, despite the continuing spate of near death experiences circulating through the world, particularly in the West, not one of these has yet proved amendable to physical study or duplication (see the two part article by Robert Gottlieb in the *New York Review of Books,* October 23 and November 6, 2014). The experience of eternity seems to come in all shapes and sizes. Although religious literature presents a range of perspectives on the content of the afterlife, in general, it does so on the basis of prophecies, words, and visions, and not from the standpoint of people who have actually experienced it. Granted, Matthew's gospel describes a time when Peter, James, and John witnessed the prophets Moses and Elijah in what appeared to be a transfigured heavenly state. However, those men did not experience this state for themselves. In the end, we are left with mystery.

personal. He will not remember as a faceless particle of energy or amorphous presence, a being devoid of perceptible content, an entity generating in eternal stasis, bound and tamed by ontological parameters which no one can experience or understand. Not at all. God will remember as a communicative and emotive being, one who is directly cohering with the eternity he inhabits and experiences. He will remember with palpable subjectivity and place, visibly presiding over eternity's world of remembering, orchestrating its ever open state of endless space and time and recollection and recall.

Of course. Only a personal God remembers us eternally; only a personal God will remember us as the personal and communicative beings we are. And only a personal God remembers—and, as we shall later see, come to know, in an overwhelmingly rich way—us as sentient and cognizant and conscious beings.

We will know and remember God in eternity as a personal and remembering being, too. We will experience memory after death as creatures who are attuned and responsive to the fact of our existence, however it will be comprised and defined, however it will inhabit and express eternity. We will remember as we are, and we will remember as *who* we are.[285]

And we will be remembered in precisely the same way.

---

[285] This is *contra* to Immanuel Kant's suggestion in his *Critique of Pure Reason* that, "a being, which we represent to ourselves as supreme among all possible beings, should, as it were, say to itself, 'I am from eternity to eternity, and outside me there is nothing save what is through my will, *but whence then am I* [italics in the original]?'" Although we at present cannot see neither eternity nor God, we know, on the basis of other evidence, that they both

Furthermore, this will be true even if we do not, in this life, know, sense, or see it. In his *Dementia: Living in the Memories of God* (a text which we mentioned in an earlier footnote), author John Swinton notes that even if a person with Alzheimer's disease stops "remembering" that God remembers her, God continues to "remember" her. Even as this person fades slowly and steadily into a consciousness of unimpeded darkness, she remains a member of God's family. She remains one of his beloved, a treasured person whom he is continually bringing "into being" in his eternal mnemonic vision for her. One day, when she is on the other side of this existence, she will cognitively experience God's memory of her once more. Once unaware, she will now be exceedingly so. Once God chooses to remember us, he remembers us regardless of how our physical or mental disabilities might now prevent us from consciously remembering him. His memory is certain, his thought forever.[286]

Yet to fully experience this level of memory, we must live this life first. We will not know and remember God as a personal being in eternity without first being a creature of time, an "experiencing and remembering self."[287] Unless we live in time, we will not experience memory, and without time our memory cannot be. Time without memory is time

---

exist. We know that we live in a world which an eternal God created. See *Critique of Pure Reason, op cit.,* A613, B641.

[286] *Dementia: Living in the Memories of God, op cit.* See also Margaret Lock, *The Alzheimer Conundrum: Entanglements of Dementia and Aging* (Princeton, New Jersey: Princeton University, 2014); and Sue Meck (with Daniel de Visé), *I Forgot to Remember: a Memoir of Amnesia* (New York: Simon and Schuster, 2014).

[287] Daniel Kahneman, *Thinking Fast and Slow* (New York: Farrar, Straus & Giroux, 2011), 236.

that never happened, and memory without time is memory that never was. We remember in this life in layers, layers and sheaves of time, ruffles and folds of moments, days, and years in which we live and breathe and cogitate, again and again and again.

If we do not know memory in time, we will not know memory in eternity.

As we must experience time, so must we experience space. Without space, earthly memory cannot exist, and without memory, present space is a blank. We need time to create memories, and we need space to know them. We must experience memory in space and time before we can know their otherworldly counterparts; otherwise, we need not bother being human beings. We cannot remember, and be remembered forever if we do not remember, and are remembered, today.

Our remembering in the frame of present space and time is the foundation and prelude to our remembering in the frameless eternity beyond it.

Speaking of the coming resurrection of Christian believers, Paul writes,

> "You fool! That which you sow does not come to life unless it dies; and that which you sow, you do not sow the body which is to be, but a bare grain, perhaps of wheat or of something else . . . . and so is the resurrection of the dead. It is sown a perishable body, it is raised an imperishable body." (1 Corinthians 15:36-37; 42)

Because we are now flesh, one day we will be spirit. A creature of present space, a creation of earth bound time, memory is constantly foretelling its larger eternal self. Our current material journey of memory in space and time will one day enable us to experience existence and memory without either one.

This is why, those many billions of years ago, when the eternal and eternally remembering creator God created the cosmos, when God purposed the humanity he had made, he did so in space and time.[288]

"And God spoke and said, 'Let there be light.'" So begins the third verse of Genesis 1. With light, the appearance of illumination and perspicacity, comes passage. Whereas the darkness of the preceding verse ("And the earth was formless and void, and darkness reigned over the deep" (Genesis 1:2a) brings abysses of opacity, the light is transparent, moveable, malleable. We see it, we feel it, we move through it. We grow, we change. We step into the beginning of time.

With the dawn of day two (metaphorically speaking), mortal space, heretofore present only in the mind of God, begins, too. God separates the waters above from the waters below, creating the heavens (not *the* heaven but the sky) and

---

[288] For those readers who are interested in such things, I state that, generally speaking, I am taking the position that the earth is considerably older than the 7,000 to 10,000 years that certain biblical theories of origins have argued that it is. Though we could debate the differences between these views at length, we will not do so here, as it is beyond the scope of this book. For a quick comparison of the two viewpoints, see the Institution for Creation Research (www.icr.org) (for the "young" earth perspective) and Reasons to Believe (www.reasons.org) (for the "old" earth viewpoint).

earth. Space is born, born to us, born for us. Illumined by light yet subject to darkness, bordered and propelled by the shifts of time, space is birthed (Genesis 1:6-8).

So memory is born, so memory comes to be. As the cosmos finds time and place, movement and passage, structure and form, living, breathing, moving, and transforming, so it finds memory. People remember, animals remember, and the universe becomes itself. Memory comes, and memory goes; remembrances are made, and remembrances fade away again. Because God remembers and creates, memory, space-time memory, comes to be. God remembers what he makes, and what he makes comes to remember in what has been made. In God's memory, working, generating, and compelling space and time, we remember.[289]

More importantly, in the space and time God creates, we are remembered, too. Through it all, God remembers us. He remembers us today, he remembers us tomorrow, and he remembers us in every tomorrow to come.[290]

Nothing happens without God.

As we draw this chapter to a close, we note several things. One, without God, memory is fleeting. While mountains, oceans, and everything else on the planet are born, exist, and populate and impel memory, one day they will all collapse and go permanently missing, never to return. And we will not know it. Nor will the cosmos know about us.

---

[289] See *Universe from Nothing* and *Grand Design, op cit.*

[290] It's worth nothing that although God is infinite and beyond and apart from our earthly parameters of quantity and spatiality, he remembers, for our sake, in space and time. God communicates himself in space and time; he expresses himself in finite passage and history. He adapts to our world.

Although we and the cosmos will live and die together, making memories in ever expanding planes of space and time, in the end, when we and it are gone, everything will be over, irrevocably over. There will be no remembrance, recollection, and past to ponder; no present and future to formulate and consider. Once the web of time and space that memory occupied dissipates, memory dissipates, too, drowned and dissembled in the mists of a ghostly and futile cosmic longing. We will ache for it, we will pine for it, but we will not catch it. It will be gone.

Two, we observed that to ignore God in memory is to ignore the fundamental nature of reality. Ignoring God in memory overlooks the fact of presence, personality, and metaphysicality. It fails to account for the spiritual compulsions of the cosmos.

It also fails to account for the spiritual nature of human beings. Divesting God and memory fails to address how despite insisting there is no meaning, human beings persist in assigning purpose to their lives just the same. It is to reject what cannot be rejected if we are to uphold and validate what is necessary to describing the human being and the cosmos in which it lives. It is to dismiss that the origins of the universe must necessarily be considered, intentional, and personal. Jettisoning God in memory is to set aside what and who we and the universe most are and can only be.[291]

Three, we noted that in the hands of God, memory's richest power is that it will not end. In God, memory is eternal. Death therefore does not end memory; it lets it begin. The world may fracture and fall, but memory will never stop. It is the work of an eternal God, the forever

291 *Moral, Believing Animals, op. cit.*

movement of a forever God, the eternal personal narrative of an eternally personal being. Life's end is a gate to its beginning, a window to its greater presence, a mnemonic pathway into a world in which the present is past and past present, today, tomorrow, and evermore. In God, today's memory is tomorrow's reality, the coming future's felt goal and dream.

In sum, because God is there, although memory may well "flee" from this existence, it will not vanish altogether. It will not disappear, it will not find futility, and it will never disappoint. It will remain, a divinely endowed and dynamic expression of personal beings, personal beings who have been uniquely created by a personal God. In the person of God, memory will not run madly without purpose, spinning like a rat on a wheel without point, but move through existence with definitive aim and vision.[292]

"God is the God of the living," observes author Carol Zaleski, "and our memories are safe with him."[293]

Indeed. In God, memory will endure, and in God it will last, forever a mirror and picture of an actively personal and eternal universe. In God, memory speaks, and in God, it acts. In God, memory manifests the power and truth of all that is, and all that can possibly be.

---

292 For the phrase "a rat spinning its wheels in a cage" I am indebted to the song "Bullet with Butterfly Wings," written by Billy Corgan and sung by the Smashing Pumpkins, Virgin Records, 1995.

293 Carol Zaleski, "The Memory of God," *Christian Century,* February 22, 2012.

GOD IN MEMORY, GOD OF MEMORY

What do we now have? In essence, we see that to reject God in memory is to forget about the nature of the universe, and to overlook God in memory is to overlook the real meaning of who we are. It is also to fail to note that life will continue beyond the present. In God, memory has import and value, and in God, memory endures. In God, memory is present, meaningful, and forever. In God, God's eternity and eternal vision, memory sustains, and memory preserves. Upholding and preserving what we lose upon death, retaining and renewing what we would otherwise see fade away, memory links body, mind, spirit, and soul together, draws them from the temporality of the present into the timelessness of eternity, sealing the worth of every moment of our lives. In God, memory supersedes and overcomes all intimations of evanescence, inadequacy, and an ineluctably mortal destiny.[294]

---

[294] So an analysis of the Southern Arapaho ghost dance observes that this dance "expresses the impossible dream of a people who

We can now make several additional points. One, in that God remembers eternally and forever, God, unlike you and I, does not forget.[295] Nor does God want to forget. God's memory is thoroughly intentional and inescapably permanent. Whereas we often remember things without expecting to do so (and frequently remember things we would rather forget[296]), God remembers eternally; he remembers eternally because he is the eternal and omniscient God. Remembering is an integral and essential part of who God is. Indeed, it *is* who he is (just as his other attributes are also *who* he is[297]). In addition, while every living being, as part of its beingness, in some way, remembers, God is the only being who remembers with totality. God's memory

---

have lost everything but memory." Absent any earthly surcease, the dance is all they have. See Thomas Powers, "A Tale of Woe and Glory" in the May 7, 2015, issue of *The New York Review of Books*.

295 Although we will return to this later, we will pause here to note that Judeo-Christian theology holds that in regard to confessed sin, God indeed forgets. When a person confesses her sin, God forgives and, in a way that we likely will never comprehend, forgets it. Never again will this sin present a barrier between her and God. It's over. See Psalm 103:12 and Jeremiah 31:34 for more. In regard to other things in terms of God's forgetting, however, we have more territory to cover and, in due time, we will.

296 Recall our earlier mention of Jill Price, who could remember, literally, everything that she had ever experienced, pleasant as well as unpleasant, continually and all the time. *Borges and Memory*, 119-122.

297 See *Christian Faith, op cit.* Additionally, consult Anthony Thiselton, *Systematic Theology* (Grand Rapids: William B. Eerdmans, 2016).

eclipses, encompasses, and surpasses all other memory, all other thought. It is absolutely complete. God's memory is the memory of a creator and maker, the memory of someone who remembers because he eternally loves and appreciates and treasures what he has made. It is the memory of a mother, it is the memory of a father, it is the memory of love for one's offspring.

But it is far more. God's memory is the memory that is only possible in someone who is the sole author of life in the cosmos. As the world's creator, God remembers the world he has made. And he remembers it with absolute love, mercy, righteousness, and care. His remembering is entirely selfless, pure, and full. God's memory holds and effects every happenstance and possibility.[298]

Two, not only does God remember, he wishes to *be* remembered. Like you, like me, as a personal being, God, even though he is God, the sovereign and holy creator, nevertheless wishes to be remembered. He wishes to be remembered by those whom he has made. Furthermore, like you, like me, God wants to be known. He wants to be known and remembered in mutual relationship with his human creation. God wants for our memories of him to be simultaneous with his memories of us, to know us as we have come to know him. Personal, interactive, and mnemonic, God longs for genuine emotional and collective connection with his cosmos.

---

[298] Technical talk of existence and predicate aside, we are to understand that God's existence is one with his essence. Who God is, is what God does, and vice versa. See *Christian Faith, op cit.* and *Systematic Theology, ibid.*

We earlier noted God's commitment to remembering the Hebrew people. What we did not note, however, were God's constant reminders to the Hebrews that memory is a two way street. I will remember you ("O Israel, you will not be forgotten by Me," he says in Isaiah (Isaiah 44:22)), yes, but you must remember me, too. God longed to enjoy the love and loyalty of his chosen people. He wanted earnestly to be remembered by them. Yet God also believed that because he remembered his people, they should remember him, too. They should remember their God. They should remember the promises he made, they should remember from whom their blessings have come. They were not to forget their creator. As God remembers, eternally, he wishes to be remembered, eternally, as well. In the eyes of God, remembering and being remembered link intimately and forever together.[299]

---

[299] This conclusion is fraught with controversy as well. Much of it centers on the effects of Jesus' birth, death, and resurrection on determining who God's people really are. Though this discussion is outside the scope of this book, we will say that most interpretations of the New Testament state that in light of Jesus' time on earth, the definition of who is one of God's people has changed, profoundly. It moved from one based primarily on family lineage to one based solely on a decision of faith (although as the New Testament also points out, faith had in fact been the operative covenantal word all along (see Romans 2-4)). As a result, how God continues to remember his covenant and what the covenant is today continues to stir much controversy. What is not disputed, however, is that God remembers his promises. Again, full discussion of the religious and political implications of many of these points is outside the purview of this book. The central point is that, above all, God is a God of promise. He *always* remembers.

God did not wish for his people to be like those who "did not know the Lord, nor yet the work which He had done for Israel" (Judges 2:10).

So did Moses tell the gathered nation, "Beware that you do not forget the Lord" (Deuteronomy 8:11. "Remember His [God] wonders," encouraged the psalmist, "which He has done" (Psalm 105:5). "Remember your creator in the days of your youth," urges Ecclesiastes (12:1). Indeed, the central burden of most of the Hebrew Bible is to describe how God sought, patiently and repeatedly, to convince his people to remember him and, alternately, how he responded when they did not. As the Chronicler noted,

> "The Lord, the God of their fathers, sent word to them [the Hebrews, his people] again and again by His messengers [the prophets], because He had compassion on His people and on His dwelling place, but they continually mocked the messengers of God, despised His words and scoffed at His prophets, until the wrath of the Lord arose against His people, until there was no remedy." (2 Chronicles 36:15-17)

Yet as we also observed, even when the Hebrews appeared to forget about God altogether, even when "there was no remedy" to their willful ignoring of their creator, there actually was. Despite everything that they had done, God still remembered his people. "I will leave a remnant," he told Ezekiel (Ezekiel 6:8), a "remnant of the house of Israel," he advised Isaiah (Isaiah 46:3), a remnant through whom he would continue to remember and bless his people.[300]

So would God continue to do in the Christian community which formed in the wake of Jesus' resurrection in the early part of the first century CE. God indicated repeatedly that he wanted to call out a people, a people—man, woman, and child—a people who came to trust in the redemptive work of Jesus, to enter his eternal family. His remembrance and communion, his intention to preserver

---

[300] Consequently, the Hebrews lived and died believing that whatever else God may have decreed or worked in their lives or the life of their nation, he would continue to remember them. Even death would not eradicate God's memory for them. God's memory would last, they were convinced, would last infinitely beyond the dark shoals and judgment of a fallen people and broken universe. The Hebrews would not be forgotten in Sheol (the Hebrew notion of afterlife); they would not be consigned to the "dung heap" upon death (Psalm 16; 73). Until the end of time, and beyond, the Hebrews believed, God would remember them—and they were to remember him. God's memory, theirs of him and his of them, was the Hebrews' ultimate comfort and solace. This brings up discussion of the Jewish conception of the afterlife. Although much could be said about ancient and modern Jewish conceptions of the afterlife, let us say here that, broadly speaking, Sheol represented for the ancient Hebrews the realm of the dead, the netherworld, the place to which people would go, in some way, upon death. This of course does not include those whom God "transmuted" bodily to heaven, people like Enoch (Genesis 5) and Elijah (2 Kings 2). Again, precise delineation of these matters lies outside the plane of this book. We say now only that then, and for many Jews today, the afterlife is entirely attainable and unquestionably real.

a people to himself, God proclaimed constantly, remains eternal.[301]

Nonetheless, God's mnemonic expectations have not changed. As he expects the Jew to remember him, as he expects the Christian to remember him, so he expects everyone else to remember him, too. Memory will always be a two way street for God and the human being. Although despite this truth we can still chose to not remember God, we will never fully evade God's desire—and insistence—that all people must, eventually, remember him. Because in the end only God's memory will remain standing, inviolate and firm, our feeble attempts to forget him will come inevitably to naught. The two way street of God, memory, and human being will always hold true.[302]

Three, because God remembers and wishes to be remembered as well, we can conclude that, in some inscrutable way God wants, maybe even needs us. God enjoys us, God delights in us, God appreciates our company. This is not to say that God depends on us to exist or express himself. God doesn't need us to be God, and God doesn't need us to do what he does. It is to say, however, that because

---

[301] Yet as the eleventh chapter of Paul's letter to the church at Rome indicates, despite the divine favor that has been given to the Christian community in this age, God will continue to remember the Jewish people until the end of time—and beyond. Precisely how this will happen, however, remains unclear.

[302] Although we will explore this idea more later on, we should nonetheless note that for those within God's family who fail to remember God in their lifetime, they will nonetheless remain in his active and mnemonic love, now and forever. For those who in their earthly time choose not to remember God's remembering of them, the outcome will be much darker.

God is a personal God, he is as desirous as we to be in relationship with companionable living beings. As most of us do nearly every day, God enjoys connecting with other sentient beings. Moreover, although God can very well communicate with himself and himself only (this is particularly clear in the notion of the Trinity), this does not obviate that God wishes to communicate with his creation, too. He enjoys its fellowship. We might even say that God enjoys the creation's companionship in order to fully be who he is. Like you, like me, like almost every creature on this planet, God, being a personal being, a naturally inclined and personal and communicative being, finds fulfillment in the company of beings beyond outside of himself.[303]

Sacred texts the world over concur. "Allah remembers [those he loves]," states the *Qur'an*, and ensures that they will participate in the "resurrection of the dead." (Sura 75). The *Mahabharata,* the great epic of the founding of India, mentions frequently that Krishna and Arjuna, the deities who are the saga's central protagonists, enjoy interacting with and remembering human beings. They have a special fondness for the human creation. Similarly, the *Rig Veda* states that Indra (one of Hinduism's chief gods) cares for and "remembers" people (7, 16). The *Bhagavad-Gita* (the "love of God"), actually a part of the *Mahabharata,* talks of how God indicates that "one must love in order to be

---

[303] Consider, however, the belief of many Reconstructionist, Conservative, and Reformed Jews that God needs his people to alleviate the pain of the world. God depends on his people to help him improve human lives. He counts on humanity's partnership to do his healing work, his *tikkun olam.* My thanks to Rabbi Jonathan Kohn of Chicago for this helpful insight.

loved." So does, the writer goes on to suggest, God want to love, communicate, and remember. And he wants to be remembered in turn.

Still other religious perspectives frame God in exactly the same way. From the shaman religions of Siberia to the dream visions of the Mojave Indians to the gods of tribal South America, we see repeatedly that however a religion defines God, its adherents insist that he loves, communicates, and remembers—and wants to be remembered in turn. They state forthrightly that God wants to be with humankind, that he enjoys the company of the people he made. Without fail, they believe that God wants to communicate, love and, significantly, be needed and remembered in turn.[304]

To review what we have so far, we state that one, God does not forget; two, God wishes to be remembered as much as he wishes to remember; and three, God, in some way, needs us.

What's next? We face a challenge. If God is the infinite and ultimate "rememberer," the one in whom all memory finds its point and end, and if God is the one who, by creating space and time, enabled memory to exist and be, then for God to participate in *our* memory, our limited and earthbound memory, is for him to step into something of which he is not necessarily a part. It is for him to become something he is not. God remembers and communicates eternally, yes, but we remember and communicate in

---

[304] See *The Bhagavad-Gita,* trans. R. C. Zaehner (Oxford: Oxford University, 1966); *Mahabharata,* retold by William Buck (New York: Meridian, 1987); Anna Reid, *The Shaman's Goat* (New York: Walker & Company, 2002); and Lawrence E. Sullivan, *Icanchu's Drum* (New York: Macmillan, 1988).

temporality. We do not remember indefinitely, and in this life we are not remembered indefinitely. This side of eternity, we and our memories have an end. God's memories, however, do not. They exist forever.[305]

As the French mystic Simone Weil observed, "God is not present to the soul and never has been." In other words, although God is, in this life, spiritually and metaphysically speaking, with us, he is not necessarily physically present to us.[306]

Moreover, given who God is, that is, omnipotent, eternal, morally absolute, and supernaturally invisible to the earthly eye, it seems that, absent other evidence, people would tend to remember him for his might and authority only. Yes, as Paul pointed out, humans are bent to see even God's invisible attributes in the created order, but a person may not necessarily be able to translate her experience of visible creation into a working image of an invisible God (Romans 1:20). She may only see a creator's majesty and power. Unless she connects a number of dots, she may not directly see God's benevolence or care.[307]

For this reason, let's unpack God's memory. Let's unravel, carefully, some of the many layers of God's infinite memory. And let's do it in six ways: memory as love; memory as hope; memory as faith; memory as trust; memory as wisdom; and

---

[305] A point Lesslie Newbigin makes in his *The Gospel in a Pluralist Society* (Grand Rapids: Wm. B. Eerdmans, 1989), 184-197.

[306] Simone Weil, *Waiting on God,* trans. Emma Craufurd (New York: G. P. Putnam's Sons, 1951), 137.

[307] Romans 1:20 reads, "For since the creation of the world His [God] invisible attributes, His eternal power and divine nature, have been clearly seen, being understood through what has been made, so they [unbelievers] are without excuse."

memory as knowing. By examining God's memory in the light of these six characteristics, we can gain a richer picture of how an infinite memory, God's memory, can become real and meaningful to us in this earthly reality. We will then see more precisely how we can make God's memory of us, his eternal watchfulness and care for us, integral to our being, make it a living and active part of who we are. As a result, we can come to understand more deeply how we can make the fact of God's remembering, and our remembering him, our own, our own sacred trust and possession, as we seek to walk in active relationship with our creator.

First, love. As the prophet Malachi asked of God, "How do you love us?" (Malachi 1:2).

How, indeed? We have already looked at God's covenantal love for the Jewish people. We have also considered God's love for the early Christians. We now use these to underscore a fundamental point: ultimately, God is love (1 John 4:9, 16). Although as we have observed in a previous footnote, God is righteous, just, and holy simultaneously and at once, foremost he is love. Over and above all, God is about love.

God loves every human being, totally, absolutely, and completely, now and for all eternity.[308]

Nowhere do we see this expressed more clearly than in the person of Jesus Christ. In Jesus, whom we earlier identified as the Jewish (and universal) Messiah, the one who came to free all human beings from the chains of moral bondage, God makes his love known, unmistakably known, to all humanity. As the apostle John writes,

---

308 As we shall see, however, this statement is far more complicated than it at first glance seems.

> "And the Word [Jesus] became flesh, and dwelt among us, and we saw His glory, glory as of the only begotten from the Father, full of grace and truth . . . For the Law [the Torah] was given through Moses; but grace and truth came to be through Jesus Christ. No one has seen God at any time; the only begotten God [Jesus] who is in the bosom of the Father, He has explained Him." (John 1:14, 17-18).[309]

In Jesus, God presents his love and grace, clearly and visibly. In Jesus, God expresses, expresses with the utmost perspicacity and clarity, the love that is what he most is. Jesus is the most profound material picture of God's love for his human creation. Born, as we noted earlier, as a human being ("the Word became flesh"), Jesus lived as a human being, freely and gratefully moving for thirty-three years among those whom he created. When Jesus died, died as a human being at the age of 33, tortured and killed on a Roman cross, he effected atonement for all human transgression and sin (1 John 2). And when after the "third day, according to the Scriptures" (1 Corinthians 15), Jesus rose, he rose as the same physical and material being he had been on earth before. He remained like those whom he, as God, had made. Neither ghost nor phantom, Jesus thus confirmed the power of God's love to overcome death and sin.

---

[309] For a detailed exposition and explanation of the full significance of these verses, see my *It's all in a Word, op cit.*

For this reason, today, tomorrow, and forever in eternity, Jesus presents, indeed, *is,* the fullest picture of God's love for us.

As the letter to the Hebrews puts it, "Jesus Christ is the same yesterday and today and forever (Hebrews 13:8).[310]

By displaying (and thereby explaining) himself in the person of Jesus Christ, God made clear, made abundantly clear that when all is said and done, he wishes to be remembered most for his love. In Jesus, God made plain that his deepest desire is to love human beings, to enter into their space and time experience to commune with them and set them free: to know, fully and intimately, those whom he created. The life, death, and resurrection of Jesus tell us that for all that remains of human history, God will continue to work, continue to work steadfastly to shape and direct the most powerful and fundamental forces of the cosmos to make known to all people, the people who are his most treasured creation, that he loves them. To love is the deepest desire of God's heart.

As it is for most of us. In a park near my home is a plaque erected in honor of a woman who had devoted her too short working life (she died of a heart attack at age 46) to working with the children who attended the day care facility that she ran at the local park district. It contains a quote from her, a quote others have also used, in various emendations, that reads,

> "One hundred years from now, it will not
> matter how big my house was or what kind

310 As most students of the New Testament know, despite many centuries of scholarship and study, we to this day still do not know who wrote this letter.

> of bank account I had. What will matter is that I made a difference in the life of a child."

When all is said and done, what matters most to Linda is that the children for whom she cared know that she loves them. At the end of time, when all accounts are settled and all debts are fulfilled, Linda, like God, and like almost all of us as well, wishes to be remembered most for her love.

Indeed. God does not want to be remembered for his power or authority. This is the remembering of fear. It is the memory of domination and arrogance. No: God wants to be remembered for his love. He wishes for us to see that because he loves us, he remembers us, and that if he did not love us, he would have no reason to remember us. God wants us to see that his love is inherent in his memory and remembering, for us to realize that he enters into our space time experience of memory and remembering because he loves us. God's love and memory are inseparable. God's love in memory lies at the heart of his vision for us and the world.

It is this memory of God's love that sustained the Hebrews; gave the early Christians hope; and impels the longings of those who believe in the *Vedas,* the *Avesta* (the sacred text of Zoroastrianism), or the *Qur'an.* It is this memory of God's love that penetrates every corner of the cosmos and every nook and cranny of the human heart. The memory in God's love infuses all existence with joy, purpose, and meaning. It is the memory of a love that birthed the world and sustains all human adventure and endeavor, a memory of a love without boundary or end.[311]

God's memory of love brings all memories together and gives them meaning and point. In God's love, the love that empowers and pervades the cosmos, we see our reason to remember the memory of God. In God's love, the love that purposes everything that is, we make our memory of him, and his of us, irrefutably living and personal, simultaneously present and eternal. In God's love, we see memory affirm all that is real and true. And we acknowledge that without God's love, without his love running through memory, neither memory nor love mean anything, anything at all.

As Paul tells the church at Rome,

[311] To reiterate and enlarge on our earlier words to this effect, we note, again, that for the Hindu, God's love is that Brahman continually sends Krishna to enlighten and aid them in their life journey. For many Native Americans, it is that the Great Spirit will bring them to a happy hunting ground. For the Zoroastrian, it is that Ahura Mazda, the bearer of light, will always overcome Ahriman and, one day, will send his followers Saoshyant, a savior. In every case, people remember God because they believe, be it in word or action, that he has demonstrated that he loves those who love and believe in him. Around the world, those who follow God, however they understand him to be, remember God out of affectionate loyalty to the one whom they believe has been and will continue to be loyal and affectionate towards them. See the *Mahabharata, op cit.;* the *Avesta: The Religious Books of the Parsees,* trans. Arthur Henry Bleeck (Boston: Adamant Media, 2001); Arlene Mirschfelder and Paulette Molin, *The Encyclopedia of Native American Religions* (New York: MJF, 1992).

> "For those whom He predestined, He also called; and these whom He called, He also justified; and these whom He justified, He also glorified. What then shall we say to these things? If God is for us, who is against us?" (Romans 8:30-31)

If God loves us, and if God remembers us, we need nothing more. As Jesus said to his disciples,

> "My sheep [believers] hear My voice, and I know them, and they follow Me; and I give eternal life to them, and they will never perish; and no one will snatch them out of My hand." (John 10:27-28)

Because in the person of Jesus God entered into space and time, and because in Jesus God presented his memory of love in ways that humans could palpably grasp, we, all the people of the planet, know that we can experience God's love in memory as present moment as well as future journey. We see memory from both sides of life and death. And we wonder, with profound amazement and gratitude, how, as Mary, upon being informed she was to give birth to Messiah, asked the angel Gabriel, "can it be?" (Luke 1).[312]

---

[312] See the chorus from Charles Wesley's hymn "And Can It Be That I Should Gain": "Amazing grace, how can it be? That Thou, My God, shouldst die for me." Words by Charles Wesley, 1738; music by Thomas Campbell, 1825.

For we know that in this life we are only beginning to experience the fullness of this love. So does Paul tell the church at Ephesus,

> "[I pray] that you may be able to comprehend with all the saints what is the breadth and length and height and depth, and to know the love of Christ which surpasses knowledge, that you may be filled up to all the fullness of God." (Ephesians 3:18-19).

That God's love in memory, his love in memory which, though it is eternal, enters into space and time, exceeds all that we can, in this life, know and understand. Nothing is its equal, and nothing can surmount or withstand it. So Paul asserts in another part of his letter to the church at Rome,

> "For I am convinced that neither death, nor life, nor angels, nor principalities, nor things present, nor things to come, nor powers, nor height, nor depth, nor any other created thing, will be able to separate us from the love of God, which is in Christ Jesus our Lord." (Romans 8:38-39)

When we believe and remember God's love, God's love and the memory of love it bequeaths as our ultimate source of nourishment, salvation, remembrance, and meaning, we know and remember that God will love and know us, always and forever. In God's love, God's memory of love, the memory of love with which he loves us, and the memory of love with which we love him, loving and knowing never end.

With God's love in memory, no other memory matters. Moreover, with God's love in memory, with God loving us fully and unreservedly, we have no reason not to love God in turn.

And to love God, to paraphrase an old song, is to know and, naturally, remember him. In God's love in memory, our knowing and God's remembering, earthly as well as eternal, come decisively together.[313]

---

[313] See "To Know Him is to Love Him," words and music by Phil Spector. Doré Records, 1958. In addition, consider the words, "Love the Lord your God with all your heart, and with all your soul, and with all your mind" (Deuteronomy 6:5; Matthew 22:37; Mark 12:30; Luke 10:27).

We have learned what it means for God to love us. Yet what does it means for us to love God? For the Hebrew and Jew (the bulk of Jesus' first century A.D. audiences), the heart was more than a physical organ. To think about the heart (*leb*) was to think not just about the physical organ we today call the heart, but to think about the lungs, stomach, kidneys, liver, and everything else that fills the central portion of the human body, as well. It is to think, to a significant degree, with one's entire person. To love God with one's whole heart is to love God with the entirety of one's being. It is to love, and be loved, with all of that which drives our memory forward.

As to the soul, the Jews considered the soul (*nepesh*) to be the mark of humanness, that which distinguishes the human being from the other animals, that which enabled people, and only people, to enjoy an active and meaningful interaction with God. The soul makes people whom they are. As we observed in our reading of Genesis 2, only Adam was created by God as a living soul. Though God breathed life into all the animals, he did not endow them as living "soul[s]" (Genesis 2:7). To love God with all of one's soul is to therefore walk in a memory of God's love that centers what makes one a human being. It is to remember

God's love grounds all other dimensions of his memory for us. With God's love, his memory begins, and in God's love, his memory for us will never end.

We have seen how integral God's love is to his memory, how seminal it is to the way he remembers us. Now let's consider the role of the second dimension of God and memory in the six we mentioned earlier, the dimension out of which the experience of being loved inevitably flows: hope.

God is a God of hope. For God to remember us is for him to hope for us, to hope for our welfare, to hope for our wellbeing. It is for God to hope *in* us, to hope in our life, our life on earth, and our life in eternity. When God remembers us, when God remembers us with love, his love in memory,

---

as a creature who is fully aware of the real meaning of life, space, memory, and time.

On the other hand, as they did the heart, the Jews viewed the mind (*leb*) as the center of understanding and physical and mental function. Indeed, some translations render the Hebrew *leb* interchangeably, sometimes using "mind," and sometimes using "heart." To love God with one's whole mind is to love God with all the mental energy and capacity that one can summon, and to therefore remember God with all that enables a person to live and function.

In every way, then, to love God, to love God in memory, is to give oneself—all of oneself, the heart and soul and mind of who one is—to him. If we are to know God, we must love him. And if we are to love him, we must give ourselves unreservedly to him. As on their wedding day a husband and wife pledge themselves to one another "until death does them part," so does the one who is known by God totally dedicate herself to God. It is a relationship of absolute and unyielding commitment.

he grounds our lives in hope, his eternal hope, his hope for us, his hope in us.

And we can hope in God. We can hope in God in this life, and we can hope in God in the next. Always and evermore, we can hope in God. We can hope in what our memory tells us, we can hope in what our memory remembers. We hope in memory's love, ours and God's. God's hope is memory's energy and driver; it gives memory life and impels it forward. God's hope is our memory's *raison d'etre,* its reason to be. The certitude of God's hope, a hope brimming with his memory in love, makes our memory real, connected, and worthwhile. We remember with hope, and we hope with memory. God's hope as memory sets memory at the very heart of what it means to be human. It makes memory the linchpin of how we see ourselves and the fact of our existence. It places memory as the foundation of our enjoyment of our life. As we cannot live without hope, God's hope, so we cannot live without our memory, our memory of God's hope in memory, that creates and sustains it. Our knowledge of God's hope for us is central to our belief in God's memory of us.

Furthermore, we can hope in God because we know that God is omnipotent, entirely able to do whatever he purposes to do. His hope for us is certain, his hope for us is sure. The hopes God has for us are destined to be fulfilled. Nothing can stop God from consummating his hopes for us. For God to remember us with hope means that we can rely unreservedly in his wishes for us. For God to remember us is to love us; and for God to love us is to hope for us, to hope for our days on this earth, and to hope for our coming and everlasting union with him, in memory, in love.

God's hope, God's hope for us, is integral to how his memory, his memory of love, remembers us.

What is God's hope? God's hope is a memory of times past that becomes a confidence in times to come. It is the future in the present, a future predicted and foretold in what is past, a future whose roots have been planted, its foundations secure. An expectation of future that creates joy in the present, God's hope projects past remembrance onto present experience, weaving living memory into what can be expected in the life years to yet come. God's hope is a promise that what we have known and experienced and remembered have value and worth. It is a promise that we have a reason to remember what has been, and just cause to believe in what will be. God's hope promises that the shape of our memory past prognosticates and scaffolds the shape of our memory future. God's hope validates the promise of his memory, just as God's memory validates the promise of his hope. Absent God's hope, his memory of love means little. Vested in God's hope, God's memory, his memory of heart and his memory of love, means everything.[314]

As John Calvin (1509-1564) put it,

---

[314] And the past, the past that, as Romanian novelist Zaharia Stancu's *Barefoot* describes it, is often no more than a feeling that, "Your whole body is drenched in sweat, salt water springing from yourself, and your mouth burns, and your lips crack, and your blood—what remains of it—rushes into your eyes," is forever gone. Zaharia Stancu, *Barefoot,* ed. Frank Kirk (New York: Twayne, 1971), 454-455. Whatever happens, meaning remains.

> "Hope is nothing else than the expectation of those things which faith has believed to be truly promised by God."[315]

God's existence ensures the reality and expectation of our mnemonic hope.

God's hope permeates the entirety of our life of memory. Working in every last tendril of the cosmos, God's hope encompasses and enables all other hopes, hopes significant and hopes mundane, on which we rely in our lives. Whether this is the hope grounded in the memory of a mathematical formula or the mechanics of replacing an appliance; the hope rooted in the memory of an exceptionally meaningful day, or the hope attached to an expected retirement pension, it is God's hope, God's hope in memory that, over and above all, enables, embodies, and sustains it. God's hope centers the universe and grants purpose to everything that happens in it. It makes memory's hope possible and true.[316]

God's hope also gives memory its point. It tells us that without God's hope and the meaningfulness it engenders, memory means little. If we cannot attach meaning to our recollections of what has been, we cannot attach meaning

---

[315] John Calvin, *Institutes of the Christian Religion,* ed. John T. McNeill, trans. Ford Lewis Battle (Philadelph ia: Westminster, 1960), Book Three, Volume XX and XXI.

[316] So does Jürgen Moltmann observe, "Hope's statements of promise, however, must stand in contradiction to the reality which at present is experienced." God's hope is always an affront to a fully disenchanted reality. Jürgen Moltmann, *Theology of Hope,* trans. James W. Leitch (New York: Harper & Row, 1970), 18. See also Harvey Cox, *The Secular City* (New York: Macmillan, 1965).

to what is to come. As only meaning begets meaning, so only meaningful memory enables real meaning, a meaning grounded in genuine form and possibility, to be.

Moreover, although we all find often tremendous meaningfulness in the cornucopia of earthly hopes, unless our universe is filled with the presence of a personal God, we should understand that, ultimately, such hopes have no real basis. If we do not believe the cosmos to be vested with meaning, if we believe the universe to be a random and unpredictable occurrence and that we are no more than erstwhile creatures who just happened to be born into it, we cannot argue that we have reason, any reason at all, to hope.

An eternal memory must be present. Absent this, absent a memory of everlasting love, we will live like Vann Nath, one of the few who survived twentieth century Cambodian dictator Pol Pot's Tuol Sleng prison and torture center. Nath later published a memoir about his experiences. In it, he writes, "After I was arrested, I lay down [in my cell], resting my arm across my forehead, feeling no hope at all. I thought about the day that they would take me away to kill me." In a world in which, as he later put it, no one "cared about human beings," there was no reason, absolutely no reason to hope. It was all gone.[317]

Consider what we said about God's ability to remember. As we noted, God never forgets. His memory is forever. When we hope in God, we therefore hope in truth. We hope in a memory which has always been and always

[317] Vann Nath, *A Cambodian Prison Portrait*, trans. Moeun Chhean Nariddh (Bangkok: White Lotus, 1998), 29, 35. When Nath's captors realized he had exceptional painting skills, they set him aside to paint portraits of prison life as well as Pol Pot himself.

will be, a memory which therefore will never, ever stop remembering. We hope in a person who has promised to remember us forever, a person whose mnemonic capacities are indefatigable and without end. Regardless of what befalls us, we know that this hope will always be there, will always exist. It will always exercise material effect. It's grounded in an eternal, omnipotent, and omniscient God.

And it is the hope of this memory, the memory of a God whose presence inhabits the whole of the cosmos, inculcating it with purpose, vision, and meaning, a memory that is always present, in life as well as in death, that is most real and true. To hope in this memory is to hope in that which makes life as it most is: a journey in and through the love of an all-knowing and supernatural creator.[318]

Unlike the hope of physical prowess, mental acuity, medical or quotidian practicality, or hope for hope's sake, this is a hope that speaks out of the seminal truths that govern the fullness of what enables existence. It is a hope of memory that is centered in and flowing out of the eternal presence and power that made the universe. Metaphysical in nature, infinite in scope, it transcends all other hopes. It's unshakeable. It's God.

God's hope in memory stretches our hope beyond what is earthly possible, extending, enfolding, and communicating the true intention of time, space, and eternity. God's hope speaks of transcendence and supernal destiny, arcing over what we do not presently see, lifting up our lives, our lives of the fleeting moment and day, and weaving them into a greater tapestry, a tapestry bringing together present

---

[318] On wonder, see William P. Brown, *Wisdom's Wonder* (Grand Rapids, Michigan: William B. Eerdmans, 2014).

materiality and coming eternity. It is a hope that embodies the heart of reality, physical as well as metaphysical, the primacy of presence from which all things, natural and supernatural are birthed, comprised, and defined. God's memory as hope expresses and reflects the fundamental structure of the universe. In it, all other hope is empowered and contained.

Consider Ecclesiastes 3:11:

> "He [God] has made everything appropriate in its time. He has also set eternity in their heart, yet so that man will not find out the work which God has done from the beginning even to the end."

Apart from God, God in memory, God in the hope of memory, we will hope, perhaps bravely, perhaps not, but, either way, ultimately in vain. We hope in the broken shards of a meaningless cosmos, never seeing and never grasping, "What secret force hides in the world and rules its course." Moreover, we may never know that we are failing to do so. We may never know we are hoping in vain. Though we will live with joy and die with hope, ambitions, and longings, we will never be able to prove why we should be pursuing either one.[319]

Because of the abiding fact of God's hope in the world, we come to see all other hope in a profoundly different light. We see that although God or not, there is hope, it is only

---

[319] *Goethe's Faust,* trans. by Walter Kaufmann (New York: Doubleday, 1963), Part I, 382-383.

in a divinely endowed universe that hope has any genuine form and basis.

This holds true whether our hope is hope we think about or hope we do not. For instance, consider our cardiovascular system. In the course of a normal day, we rarely think about our cardiovascular system. We assume that it will work, day after day, month after month, and year after year. Beneath our outward confidence, however, we know, know almost instinctively, that we "hope" that it does. We "hope" our heart continues to beat for many years to come.

In a pointless and unremembered universe, however, why would we, indeed, *how* could we hope for such a thing? What would be the point?

This notwithstanding, more often than not, we consciously think about our hope. Sometimes it is a hope in what we can do. If we are athletes, we hope that our bodies will "remember" to perform in the way that we believe we have trained them to do so. We hope that we will do well. We hope that the time we have spent getting our body to remember how to act under the challenge and duress of a particular event will bear fruit and we will find success.

In a profile many years after she had won the first women's Olympic marathon in the 1984 Olympics in Los Angeles, runner Joan Benoit described the training routine she followed to do the race. Living in the state of Maine, she said, meant that she had to run through very harsh winters, and endure much snow and cold to maintain her conditioning. Although she could likely have found more amendable training conditions elsewhere, she preferred to stay in her home state. "I do what I can do," she said, "and in the spring I see how prepared I am to race." In other words,

Benoit hoped that her body would "remember" what she had trained it to do.[320]

The March-April 2015 issue of *AARP* (American Association of Retired People) *Magazine* featured an article about bridge and its benefits for memory and mental clarity. It pointed out that people, people well into their nineties, who play bridge for many years have trained their minds to remember, be it cards that have been played or trump calls other players make. Moreover, as these people continue to age, they hope that they can continue to play, to continue to remember. They hope that their mnemonic systems remain intact. Consciously or not, they, like Joan Benoit, hope they continue to remember.[321]

Having spent over forty years backpacking and climbing mountains at altitudes above twelve thousand feet, I feel as if my body is well conditioned to perform optimally at higher altitudes. Every time I enter the mountains afresh, I implicitly hope that my body "remembers" this conditioning; I hope that it will continue to function at the levels I believe I have trained it to do. Although I usually don't think about it, I nonetheless put my hope in my body's ability to "remember" what it has always done.

Either way, whether we know it or not, Benoit, the elderly bridge players, and I can only hope in memory because God remembers us. Apart from God, our hope in memory misses the point. Why would we bother? Consciously or not, we set our mnemonic hope in the fact of divine memory pulsating

---

[320] See the profile in *Runner's World* *http://www.runnersworld.com/tag/joan-benoit-samuelson*

[321] See *AARP Magazine,* http://www.aarp.org/magazine/, March/April 2015.

through the cosmos. We implicitly acknowledge that, in contrast to Richard Dawkins's words that trying to divine life's meaning is "not a valid question," it is rather the only question worth asking.

What about hope in what we have? Many years ago, some friends of mine were backpacking in the Alaskan bush when one afternoon, with little warning, a fierce rainstorm descended on them. With very few trees under which to seek shelter (they were hiking across mostly treeless tundra), they had few options. Then, remembering an emergency space blanket in one of their backpacks, they pulled it out and huddled under it, shivering and shaking, teeth chattering, hands and feet rapidly turning blue, body core temperature quickly dropping. It was all they could do. They wondered whether they would make it. But they hoped they would. They hoped in their space blanket, and they hoped in themselves.[322]

In his moving *Crazy for the Storm,* author Norman Ollestad tells the story of how, as he climbed out of the wreckage of a small plane carrying him and his father to a ski race in Big Bear, California, he realized that he was the only one to survive. He would need to hike out on his own. And he did. Thanks to the many things his father had taught him about outdoors survival, Ollestad left the downed plane on the mountain into which the pilot had

322 They survived. Tragically, however, a number of years after this, Chris, Claudine's husband, was diagnosed with Hodgkin's Lymphoma. Despite bringing all available medical care to bear on his condition, he died six months later at the age of 46.

crashed it and made it out safely. He had hope in what he had remembered, he had hope in what he knew.[323]

Centered in the material universe yet embedded in the eternal hope of its creator, my friends and Ollestad's experiences of hope in memory turned out wonderfully.

Yet they also underscore that if we are to suppose that the world has meaning, we must view the worth of these hopes in the fact of God. We must admit that all these hopes, these capable yet contingent hopes, reflect and affirm that above and beyond all experience, God's hope in memory is there, swirling, surrounding, guiding, and sustaining meaningful remembering throughout the cosmos. Our hope in what we have physically or mentally remembered occurs inside God's greater hope in memory that is, necessarily and whether we wish to admit it or not, upholding all the temporal hopes of the material universe.

So it is that we turn to an entirely different type of hope. This is not a hope in what we can see, a hope we can touch in the acumen of our physical abilities, but a hope in that which we cannot see, a hope that we can in no way view physically. It is a hope that hopes directly in God. It is a hope in which we, convinced of God's active presence in our world, believe.

And unlike hope that we can see, this hope exenterates all earthly connection and possibility. Though it is grounded in a commitment to the fact of God, it is nonetheless insuperably more challenging to sustain. In the early nineties, a woman I knew was told that her brother, her only sibling, was stricken with cancer and that his chances were not good. Immediately, she and her parents began

---

[323] Norman Ollestad, *Crazy for the Storm* (New York: Ecco, 2009).

to pray. And they hoped. As the months went by, they took John around the country, consulting various doctors and trying numerous approaches to halting the disease's relentless spread through his body. Though the situation looked bleak, they continued to hope, they continued to pray. They continued to hope and pray that they would find a way out, even if everything appeared to dictate otherwise. They hoped for what they could not see.

In a universe they believed to be pervaded by an eternal God, they believed their hope to be likewise. For them, in God, hope is present and though they could not now see it, future as well.[324]

Nearly thirty-five years ago, the husband of one of my wife's best friends was doing his usual after work run around the track in his gym when, without any warning, he collapsed and died of a heart attack. It was shocking. That night, a steady stream of people visited Suzanne. She told all of them that, "I have hope that things will get better." Suzanne knew very well that nothing would bring Al back. She knew very well that she had no concrete reason to think that in the darkness of the moment, things could get better. She had to hope in what she could not see. And she did. Suzanne believed in the hope of God, a hope she could not see, but a hope she was convinced was there.

---

[324] Sadly, in the end, they were unsuccessful. When they eventually realized that John's only contact with the world were his tubes and IVs, and that all signs indicated that this would never change, they made the hardest decision anyone has to make. They asked his doctors to disconnect John from his life support. He was nineteen years old. At the close of John's memorial service, we heard the Beatles' "Here Comes the Sun" coming out of the speakers in the sanctuary. It was his favorite song.

A number of years ago, a photo essay appeared in the *New York Times Magazine.* It featured photos of the bedrooms that some of the young men and women who had been killed in America's war in Iraq had left behind and to which, tragically, they now would never return. These bedrooms looked like bedrooms of a teenager, even a child. Stuffed animals competed with video players, brightly patterned spreads with military paraphernalia. Notes from Mom and Dad appeared along with high school textbooks. Some bedrooms had a Peter Pan feel, those of a person who never wanted to grow up, but who did, in the most poignant and final of ways. Memories flood every photograph.[325]

Do the survivors, the parents of these young and deceased, have hope? They of course will never forget their children. They hope that their sons and daughters did not die in vain; they hope that they died happy to be doing what they were doing; they hope that they have a better life than this earthly one; they hope that their lives had been worthwhile. Do they have reason to do so? They know their children are never coming back. But they believe it is better to hope than to not. Wrestling with a tangle of remembrances, convictions, and regrets, they try to hope. They try to find hope in their memories. They try to hope in what they cannot—indeed, what they may never—see.

Why? Because they believe there is a God. They believe that apart from the active presence of God, suffusing the cosmos with potential and meaning, hope, even hope that

---

[325] Ashley Gilbertson, "Shrine Down the Hall," *New York Times Magazine,* March 21, 2010. More recently, Ms. Gilbertson turned these photographs into a book, *Bedrooms of the Fallen* (Chicago: University of Chicago, 2014).

is solely earthbound, has no basis. If God is there, even the most distant and invisible and hopeless of earthbound hopes has reality, thoroughgoing tangible form and working presence.

When in the face of tragedy we hope in the memory of the God we cannot see, though we are acutely aware that nothing we do will return our lives to exactly what they were before, and though we know that however much we might wish our days to continue as they had in the past, they will not, we can still hope. We believe we have reason to trust in the proverbial light at the end of the tunnel; we have cause to imagine that things will get better. We know we can continue to believe in the virtue of existence.

Why? Because God is there. With God's hope, we can always look ahead. We can believe that the joy we find in our past memories of God means that we can hope in the memories we have of him going forward. As it flames like a bonfire on a winter night, we see the hope of God's memory burn brightly before us, an ever present blaze of time and memory, lifting us above our privation and despair.[326]

As theologian Lewis Smedes put it,

---

[326] A particularly poignant illustration of hope's metaphorical flame is found in American author Jack London's short story, "To Build a Fire." It's the account of a mountain man who in crossing a river, falls through the ice, getting dangerously wet in temperatures fifty degrees below zero. He soon builds a roaring fire and begins to thaw. Suddenly, and without any warning, a pile of snow slides from the overhanging tree and smothers the fire. Unable to start the fire again, the man eventually freezes to death. His dog then wanders off on its own. Hope vanishes forever.

> "Hope is the Creator's implant into us, His traveling children, on the move into a future we can imagine but cannot control. Hope is our fuel for the journey. As long as we keep hope alive, we keep moving. To stop moving is to die of hope deficiency."[327]

On the other hand, although without the fact of God, hope's flame burns meaninglessly, a futile flicker in a haunting and frigid night, we can certainly still hope. We can hope in what we see, we can hope in what we do not. Yet it is not the same. As philosopher William James said to his father in the latter's final hours,

> "As for the other side, and Mother, and our all possibly meeting, I *can't* say anything. More than ever at this moment do I feel that if that *were* true, all would be solved and justified. And it comes strangely over me in bidding you goodbye how a life is but a day and expresses mainly but a single note. It is so much like the act of bidding an ordinary good night. Good night, my sacred old Father! If I don't see you again—Farewell! A blessed farewell!"[328]

---

[327] Lewis Smedes, *Keeping Hope Alive for a Tomorrow We Cannot Control,* cited in *Fuller Magazine,* Issue #6, Fuller Theological Seminary, 2016.

[328] D. J. Enright, ed., *Oxford Book of Death* (Oxford: Oxford University, 2008), 185.

Did James feel convinced of the reality of an afterlife? No, he did not. Did James feel convinced of the meaningfulness of existence? No, he did not. But he expressed his hope that both were real and true. Without any reason to do so, he indicated his desire that life has a point, and that it would not end at death. Like John's parents, like Suzanne and her children, like the parents of the dead soldiers, James stood in his hope, his hope in his memory of goodness, the goodness not of God, but of his world. He hoped in what he had seen, yes, but he also hoped in what he could not see.

Ironically, tacitly or not, James affirmed the necessity of God, a God in whom, despite all visible evidence that may point otherwise, we have observed that genuine hope, tangible and lasting hope, is found. Otherwise, as James well knew, he might as well not bother hoping at all.

Or as Mary Shelley, whose name we mentioned earlier as author of *Frankenstein,* wrote to a friend after her husband Percy's death,

> "Thus beyond our soul's ken there is an empty space; and our hopes and fears, in gentle gales or terrific whirlwinds, occupy the vacuum; and if it does no more, it bestows on the feeling heart a belief that influences exist to watch and guard us, though they be impalpable to the coarser faculties."[329]

[329] *Shelley's Ghost,* 96. The circumstances of Percy's death contributed greatly to Mary's pain. On a day and in a moment she did not expect, Mary, along with Lord Byron, watched Percy drown

Even if she didn't see it, and even if she could not know it, Mary wanted to hope. And she wanted this hope to have a basis in fact. She wanted that for which she hoped to have ground, potential, and possibility. At that point, it was all she had.

Whether she knew it or not, Mary wanted to think there was a God. For unless there is a God, however understandable, poignant, and heartbreaking Mary's wishes may be, she should perhaps never utter them. In the absence of an active divine, her longings are as empty as a desert wind.

On the other hand, philosopher Simon Critchley, referring to a hope in God, once suggested that such hope is pitifully ignorant and entirely unrealistic. It is, he says, a "hopeless" idealism. It means nothing.[330]

Better, Critchley holds, to believe, as did French novelist Albert Camus, that "human truth lies in accepting death without hope."[331]

Perhaps. Let's turn Critchley's argument on its head and say that unless hope *is* in God, it is totally unwarranted. It is, to use his words, a "hopeless idealism." It solves nothing. In the absence of God, hope in the unseen is baseless, superstitious as well as ignorant. It is indeed hopelessly idealistic. While groundless hope may bolster spirits, it

---

after his boat capsized in the Bay of Spezia in Italy. He had never learned how to swim.

330 Simon Critchley, "Abandon Nearly All Hope" *New York Times,* April 20, 2014. See also Critchley's book, *Memory Theatre* (New York: Fitzcarraldo, 2014).

331 As noted in *Musings on Mortality,* 91.

cannot materially change the situation. It soothes, it heals, but it will not alter or change.

Groundless hope is no more than, to quote a citizen of the massive Dadaab refugee camp in southern Kenya, a "hope in the rain watchers even if one knew they can do nothing [for him]."[332]

Even if hope helps a person revise her attitude about her circumstance, it cannot undo what has happened. Nor can it guarantee the future. Ultimately, it is meaningless. If we are to hope genuinely in the unseen, we do well to ensure that we have a real basis for doing so. Without a material basis, though unseen hope can be very real to us, it ultimately has no power to directly affect our present condition—or anything beyond it as well. It does not exist. Unseen hope must have a real basis in a real reality.

And the only real basis for unseen hope is God. In his *Manual for Creating Atheists,* Peter Bogdossian admits that although he saw no reason for his mother to cling to what he considered to be a misguided and unfounded faith in God as she passed through the final hours of her life, he could not help but thinking that maybe, just maybe she had viable reason to do so. Maybe, just maybe, his mother's trust in God was not without reason or foundation. His mother's conviction and belief in the hope of God, he noticed, sustained and comforted her. It allowed her to die in peace. Bogdossian observed that although his mother couldn't visibly see her hope, her belief that it was unquestionably real allowed her to experience a tenderness, a profound and encompassing tenderness which she felt was gently ushering her out of this existence. It was a tenderness, he added, that

[332] Ben Rawlence, *City of Thorns* (New York: Picador, 2016), 61.

he was not sure he, as an atheist, would, when he came to his death, be able to duplicate.[333]

Apart from God, God in memory, God in the hope of memory, we will hope, perhaps bravely, perhaps not, but ultimately, in vain. It's the hope of a random and meaningless cosmos. We will live with joy and die with hope, but have no way to prove why we should be engaging in either one.

Writing a letter to a friend, Norwegian playwright Henrik Ibsen (1828-1906) described the nature of his earliest work, saying that,

> "[It portrays] the conflict between one's aims and one's abilities, between what man proposes and what is actually possible, constituting at once both the tragedy and comedy of mankind"[334]

Ibsen put it well. Absent God's hope, not only will we never know what hope really is, but we, finite beings that we are, will never fully undo the perennial discrepancy between what we wish and hope for and what we can actually accomplish and achieve. However much we admire and love the hope of this world, and however much we may appreciate the idea of unseen hope, unless we ground them in God, we will never find full satisfaction in either one.

Worse, we may never know it.[335]

---

[333] Peter Bogodssian, *A Manual for Creating Atheists* (Charlottesville, Virginia: Pitchstone, 2013).

[334] As quoted in *Ibsen's Selected Plays,* ed. Brian Johnston (New York: W. W. Norton, 2004), xi.

[335] We need to mention one caveat, however. We do not want to revere hope of God's memory as a hope that ensures that we will

What do we do? We acknowledge that the hope we place in this life will never be as responsive or meaningful as we would like it to be, for we exercise it in a finite and broken planet whose capacities to meet our wants and needs will always and forever be, though temporarily adequate, in the end thoroughly otherwise. We admit that placing our hope in this world is no more than a hope in hope itself, an exercise in fideism. We stop making ourselves victims of ourselves, we cease reducing reality to us and us only. We elevate the plane of our life vision, giving it a totality and moral absoluteness in which it can be measured. We then come to realize that we will no longer wander in a daze, a

---

always get what we want or need. God's hope of memory is far more complicated than that. Although all things being equal, we all would like to get what we think God ought to give us, to really trust in the hope of the memory of God is for us to see hope as a work of love and memory that does not so much grant wishes as it grants future and meaning. We understand that we trust in hope's present expression because we see its future promise. We understand that as we hope, we are remembering a hope that sculpts the very fabric of reality. We see that things or outcomes are not nearly as important as achieving greater identity and oneness with what is, physically, metaphysically, and all. We come to live this life in this world even as we crave to know the source and end of its desires and longings. It is in these that we find ultimate fulfillment in the promise of the hope of God's memory. We trust in God, we hope in God. We hope *for* God. We trust that even if life appears very dark, in God's hope, God's hope of memory, we will not address it with wishes and dreams, but with trust in the work of an eternally remembering God. We realize that life is not a closed circle, nor is the universe an endless line. There is more. We are confirmed in who we are now as well as who we will one day to be, for in God's hope, they are, in a highly profound way, the same.

fog of epistemological uncertainty and confusion, always knowing in part but never knowing in full.

We will know.

With God present, with God's hope infusing memory, although we may still find life confusing and difficult, we can live it with confidence, understanding that we live and die in the grip of a certain future, a definite dawn. We live in the aegis of a singularly powerful memory, a vividly personal memory that has and holds all things together. We touch a hope that is as real as life and reality possibly can be.

Furthermore, when we remember with this hope, when we remember God and he remembers us, we have decisively valid reason to believe that we can always be optimistic about our life. Even if we do not see this hope, even if we do not feel this hope, we have every reason to believe it is there. We have every reason to believe that, undergirded and guided by an eternally loving and ever present God, a God who has always been there and who always will be so, this hope is forever real and true. We know that this hope has form and face. Hope in us remembering God and his remembering us is a thoroughly viable hope.

And we do not live as the people of Émile Zola's novel *Germinal*, people consigned to working in a dank and unsafe mine until they literally dropped dead, people who remarked,

> "You see, the worst of it is when you admit that it can't ever change. When you are young you think happiness will come later on, and you hope for things; and then the same old poverty gets hold of you and you

> are caught up in it . . . Now I don't wish anyone any harm, but there are times when the injustice of it makes me mad.
> "And then, if only there were some truth in what the priests say, if only the poor of this world were rich in the next . . . No, when you're dead, you're dead . . . So there it is, we're done for."[336]

We know there is more hope than what we can presently see.

Yet we should also understand that to hope in God, and God alone, is to invest in a hope that we will find highly challenging. For it is a hope of memory that is asking, indeed, commanding us to live the visible and present moment by faith, by faith in the light of an unseen personal presence. It's a hope that demands that we set our hope in things invisible, a hope that is centered in realities whose essence is beyond us, realities which we cannot always touch or prove directly. It is a hope of memory that asks us to assert and believe that this present life is merely a shadow and foretaste of true and genuine existence. It is a hope of memory that invites us to believe that even if, given the limits of the

---

[336] Emile Zola, *Germinal,* trans. Leonard Tancock (New York: Penguin, 1954). Consider as well a passage from Jacob Riis's *How the Other Half Lives: Studies Among the Tenements of New York* (New York: Penguin, 1997), 129, quoted in Matthew Desmond, *Evicted* (New York: Crown, 2016), 115, which reads, "There is nothing in the prospect of a sharp, unceasing battle for the bare necessities of life to encourage looking ahead, everything to discourage the effort." All hope, all thought of looking for better things tomorrow, is gone.

world, "Everything is a dream" and will not last, all good things nonetheless *will* last, will last forever.[337]

When former Beatle George Harrison died of lung cancer in November of 2001, news reports mentioned that he passed away in the company of a coterie of Buddhist monks. He was, these reports said, at peace with his end. He was hopeful for what it portended. He believed in the promise, the promise of another life that he, rooted in his perception of things divine, had embedded in memory. He believed in his remembered hope, the vision of post death bliss he believed awaited him. Nourished and refined through years of study and reflection on this promise's present evidences, Harrison had every reason to let go of his earthly life without remorse or fear. He had every assurance that he could pass out of this time, this material plane of space and time, in peace.

He had absolutely every reason to hope that there was more.[338]

With God's memory as hope, we can live and die unafraid and without regrets. We can honestly believe that our lives are worthwhile. We can realistically find solace in the value of our past, and that the essentials of this life have always been more than the mere fact of its presence. As a friend of mine who passed away from brain cancer nearly forty years ago told me shortly before she died, "My hope is

---

[337] James Salter, *All That Is: A Novel* (New York: Vintage, 2016), epigraph. The full quote is, "There comes a time when you realize that everything is a dream, and only those things preserved in writing have any possibility of being real."

[338] See also Harrison's album, *All Things Must Pass,* Apple, 1970.

in Jesus. I know that he's been with me all this time, and I know that he'll be with me when I die."

Brenda died in hope, God's hope, a hope sustained by her memory, God's memory in and for her, her remembrance of God's constant life companionship. She died believing that her earthly memories of this companionship pointed to a future hope of companionship greater than anything she could presently imagine. She died with hope in her memory, the memory that, cultivated over ten years of trusting in God, persuaded her that God's promises were indeed real and true. Unlike the object of Dylan Thomas's memorable words, she went "gentle into the night." Like George Harrison, she died in peace. She believed and remembered the promise of her hope in the memory of God.[339]

As we close out this discussion of God's memory as hope, we note that one, God's presence of memory ensures the possibility of hope in the universe. Because God is there, remembering, we can find meaningful hope in this universe. Two, God's memory as hope enables us to understand that when we hope, we hope not in this life only, but in the life to

---

[339] Dylan Thomas, "A Refusal to Mourn Death" in *The Poems of Dylan Thomas* (New York: New Directions, 2003). The relevant words are, "Do not go gentle into that good night, old age should burn and rave at close of day. Rage, rage against the dying of the light." See also Stephen Jay Gould, "The Median Isn't the Message" in *Discover,* June, 1985, in which he calls death "the ultimate enemy" and wants to "rage against the dying of the light." In addition, consider David Rieff's poignant memoir about the final years of his mother, Susan Sontag, *Swimming in a Sea of Death: A Son's Memoir* (New York: Simon & Schuster, 2008), in which he repeatedly underscores that his mother, at all costs, did not want to die.

which it points as well, for both will one day come together in the grand counsel of God. Three, God's memory as hope tells us that we can trust in the essential structure of the cosmos. We can trust in the goodness of this incredible array of planets, galaxies, and stars. And why not? It has been created by a mnemonic and, necessarily, good and personal God.

Fourth, we realize that God's memory as hope allows us to envision and participate in the third dimension of God and memory: our faith and God's faithfulness.[340]

In the fifth chapter of his second letter to the church at Corinth, Paul urges his readers to, "Walk by faith and not by sight" (2 Corinthians 5:7). Though we cannot always see our hope, our hope of memory, he says, we must believe, in faith, it is there. We must believe in the fact of its presence. We must believe in its inevitability, we must believe in its certainty, its certainty of coming and fulfillment.

And, he adds implicitly, why would we not? Our faith and hope are in the eternal memory of an eternally faithful God.

Throughout the Bible, faith, hope, and God's faithfulness come constantly together. According to the writer of the letter to the Hebrews,

> "Faith is the substance of things hoped for, the conviction of things unseen . . . And without faith, it is impossible to please him [God], for he who comes to God must believe that he is and that he is a rewarder of those who seek him" (Hebrews 11:1, 6).

---

[340] See *All That Is, op cit.*

To have faith is to possess and experience that for which we hope. It is to experience in part today what we will one day experience in full. Faith is our conviction that that in which we believe and hope, though we cannot now see it completely, is already true. It is true now, and it will be true later.

More significantly, we believe in this hope because we have faith in that to which our memory of it points: the faithful remembering of God. Our faith is the substance (or evidence) of that for which we hope. Faith is the way we walk, the way we travel our life's highways and byways of hope in memory. With faith, we believe in the active presence of our hope and we live in its continuing promise and expectation. With faith, we keep going, and with faith, we hold steadfast, always believing in the certainty of what we do not now see. We trust our hope, we trust our faith, our faith and hope of memory, now and in every new day into which we come. As the writer says, we believe that if we have faith in God, God as the faithful and ultimate rememberer, God as the one who always and evermore loves and remembers us, we know that he will grant favor to the many roads and trails, whether up or down, of our lives. Secure in our hope of his memory, ensconced in our conviction of faith, we are convinced that God will always act on our behalf. Our faith expresses our expectation in God's memory and love for us, now and in eternity. Our faith and God's faithfulness drive the hope of memory; they uphold memory's power. They tell us that we are in good hands. Our faith and God's faithfulness enable us to believe that our hope in the memory of God is unshakeable and will always accrue to our lasting benefit. In faith, we affirm the worth of this life just as we do the next.

The prophet Jeremiah captures this sentiment beautifully in the third chapter of Lamentations. As he broods over the state of his nation, a nation whose people's failure to remember God brought them untold suffering and pain, including the destruction of the temple and exile to Babylon, he nonetheless writes,

> "This I recall to mind, therefore I have hope. The Lord's lovingkindnesses indeed never cease, for His compassions never fail. They are new every morning; great is Your [God's] faithfulness." (Lamentations 3:21-23)

Even in the face of God's studied rejection of his people, Jeremiah continued to have hope. He continued to believe, in faith, that God still loved his chosen people.

So it is for us. Our faith and God's faithfulness in memory lead us to trust that because, all things considered, God has remembered us in the past, he will do so in the future, and that however much we have set our hope in God to this point, we can continue to do so, again and again and again. Our faith in God's faithfulness allows us to let go of what we know, distress, pain, and all, about our present life situation and the dark memories it is generating. It enables us to instead believe that God, who knows and remembers infinitely more than we do, will redeem our troubles, that he will remedy our heartaches and futility with insight, cogency, and wisdom. We know that we can trust unreservedly in the eternally faithful memory of God.[341]

---

[341] We should note here that even those who do not choose to believe in God trust, too. They, too, exercise a type of faith. It may be faith in themselves and their capabilities; it may be faith in what they may perceive to be the basic goodness of the universe; it may be faith in the material options that they perceive are available to them; and more. Whatever that on which they rely may be, they trust. They trust in the hope of their memory, they trust in their memory of what has worked in the past, they trust that that which they assumed to be true to this point will continue to be true in the future. They trust in what they remember and, by extension, what they believe and know that will, in each and every circumstance, prevail.

For instance, I have a friend who, as an atheist, insists that he never exercises faith. Rather, he says, he engages in "reasonable expectation." If he encounters setback or hardship, he reminds himself that he has a reasonable expectation, based on his past experience, that he will be able to deal with it. He doesn't use faith, he says; rather, he uses his reason, reason that is in turn rooted in what he believes he knows. He reasons and believes that he always has sufficient evidence to support his reasonable expectation. He reasons and believes that he has concrete proof, proof sustained by his memory, to persuade and encourage his conviction that he will pull through.

Perhaps. But clearly, faith is faith is faith, and belief is belief is belief: either way, one is believing in the hope embodied in her memory. After all, we are finite. We cannot see everything. And we cannot always expect that what has worked or been so in the past will always continue to work in the future.

This is not to say that faith does not need support. It does. Otherwise, it becomes an exercise in fideism. It is to say, however, that to believe in the hope of memory is to believe on the basis of the past evidences embedded in this memory. There are reasons to believe, there are reasons to think that hope in a particular

In faith, hope finds its full weight and expression, and the hope of memory its deepest fulfillment. Real faith, faith with viable and genuine basis, creates memory that is aware of the full import and meaning of reality. Born in a vision of existence both physical and metaphysical, the faith of memory understands the world as it most is. It brings love, hope, and memory decisively together, coalescing and ordering them in the eternal purview of the steadfast faithfulness and compassion of God.

Both testaments of the Bible present hope and faith alike as a "confident expectation." Whether we engage in hope (Hebrew *yachal, qavah, tiqvah*; Greek, *elipzo, elpis*); faith (Hebrew *emeth;* Greek, *pistis*), or both, we are saying that we have every confidence and expectation in the unwavering goodness of the memory of God. Set in faith, secure in hope, we have absolutely no reason to think that God and his memory will let us down. We know, know beyond all doubt that we are not trusting a groundless wishing or empty longing, chasing a memory with no basis in form or fact. We are confident that even though we will not see the final picture of God's memory until we enter eternity, we can believe, believe this very moment, in faith, in its certainty. We can believe in the surety of God's loving and forever memory of us.[342]

---

memory, be it of God or the assumed inevitable consequences of the natural laws that govern the planet, is justified. Faith, of some kind, is essential to memory.

342 "*emeth*" in *Theological Dictionary of the Old Testament,* ed. G. Johannes Botterweck, Helmer Ringgren, and Heinz-Josef Fabry; trans. David E. Green (Grand Rapids, Michigan: William E. Eerdmans, 2004), Vol VIII; and "*pistis*" in *Theological Dictionary of the New Testament,* ed. Gerhard Kittel, Gerhard Friedrich;

Today, tomorrow, and for all eternity we know that we can place our trust, our full, total, and absolute trust in the grace and faithfulness of the memory of God. We know that God is faithful to his memory.

This brings us to note that faith's original meaning is not, as many moderns insist, believing in the absence of evidence. Faith's original meaning is "to trust." To have faith is to trust, and to trust is to believe in the integrity of the reasons for one's faith. When we have faith, when we have faith in the hope of memory, God's memory of faithfulness, we trust. We trust in the goodness, worth and, most important, truth, fact, and reality, of God's memory of us. We say that we are willing to trust, to trust from the bottommost depths of our heart, God and his memory of us with everything we are, have, and do. We set our hope unwaveringly in the fact and effectuality of the memory of God. We acknowledge that we are trusting in something that will last, something that has always existed, something from which all things have come, something that will always be reliable and sure: the memory of God.[343]

As the psalmist put it,

> "How blessed is the person who has made
> the Lord his trust" (Psalm 40:4)

In this we see the essence of trust and memory. To trust God in memory is to believe in the fullness of his memory

---

trans. Geoffrey W. Bromiley (Grand Rapids, Michigan: William E. Eerdmans, 1967), Vol. VI.

[343] See "Faith" in the *Oxford English Dictionary* (Oxford: Oxford University, 1971).

of us, to hope to the fullest extent possible in his faithful remembrance of who we are. To trust God in memory is to live fearlessly, vigorous in times of plenty, and confident and sure in days of downturn, always convinced of the presence and redemption of divine recollection and recall. It is to know and believe that God's memory for us, the memory written in the power of his love and hope for us, is ever present and unceasing. It is always faithful. To trust God in memory is to believe that no matter what happens, we are remembered, in hope and love, now and forever.

Of course, given our knowledge of the mechanics of this world, we know that setting our hope, faith, or trust in the things of this world frequently works. We know that we have the ability to manipulate the structures of this world on our behalf. To hope and trust in this world is not entirely unjustified or unfounded. As creatures of a highly technological age, we can indeed make the world work in our favor.

But not always. Sometimes we encounter situations from which the combined weight of all the technology on the planet cannot deliver us. Sometimes we will not be able to effect our own salvation. One day, we will hit a wall like the one that Pink, the protagonist of Pink Floyd's movie *The Wall,* frequently met, a wall of pain and angst that we will find supremely unconquerable. In that moment, we will not be able to, as a former colleague of mine, asked about what he would do when he met God in the afterlife (he is an atheist), remarked, "I'd talk my way out of it." We will have met our match. And we will see, see as we have never before, that however wonderful it may be, the world is in truth hollow, temporary, evanescent, and finite. It will not last. As John puts it,

> "Do not love the world or the things in this world. If anyone loves the world, the love of the Father is not in him. For all that is in the world, the lust of the eyes and the lust of the flesh and the boastful pride of life, is not from the Father, but is from the world. The world is passing away, and also its lusts; but the one who does the will of God lives forever." (1 John 2:15-17).[344]

We cannot disagree that the world is remarkable and grand. We cannot dispute that life on this planet is riven with astonishing beauty. Yet we cannot deny that one day it, its hope, and all its memories will end, forever. If the world and its memories are all in which we trust, we will ultimately be disappointed. When we reach our earthly end, hope, life, memory, and all, we reach the end of our trust, too. We will have trusted in vain; we will have trusted that which cannot be trusted. We will have trusted a trust of our own making, a trust that, in the moment we need it most, will leave us bereft, utterly alone before the maw of mortality.

Our darkness will be total.[345]

---

[344] Pink Floyd, *The Wall.* Metro-Goldwyn-Mayer, 1982.

[345] As poet Ted Hughes, husband of the angst driven (and suicidal) poet Sylvia Plath, puts it in his "Examination at the Womb-door," "Who owns these scrawny little feet? *Death.* Who owns this bristly scorched-looking face? *Death.* Who owns these still working lungs? *Death.*" [Italics, Hughes]. Although nothing inhabits mortality's end, nothing escapes it, either. This section

Although we may never know what ran through her mind as Lisa Bonochek Adams, who had blogged straightforwardly about her cancer from her initial diagnosis to the day of her death, took her final breath, we do know that, from her standpoint, once she was gone, everything she had known would be gone, too. While she had enjoyed and reveled in the world's adventures and pleasures, now, she believed, she and the world would forever part. She'd be definitively gone, her memories vanished, her hope and faith forgotten, lonely debris in a dismembered sea.

Although we are perfectly free to live as did Bonochek Adams, trusting in this world and this world only, we must realize that it is a trust that, absent the faithful memory of a God of love and hope, will, upon death, slip away as quickly as it had come. We will then not be merely alone; we will not *be* at all.[346]

On the other hand, to trust in the metaphysical, to hope and trust in a personal and eternal and faithful God, is to hope and trust in a hope whose foundations are entirely secure. It is to trust in a hope of memory that will never stop being a hope of memory, a hope of memory that will never diminish or depart. It is to trust in a memory that will last beyond the grave, a memory whose powers are infinitely greater than our own, a memory that knows, understands, and guides all things. We trust and hope in the memory of a being whose ability to circumscribe and superintend the ways of present memory far exceed our meager perceptions

---

of the poem appears in *Interrupted Lives,* ed. Andrew Motion (London: National Portrait Galley, 2004), 69, 76.

346 See Lisa Bonochek Adams, www.lisabadams.com/blog.

and speculations of what is possible. We trust in a memory of a hope that is everlastingly tangible, present, and true.[347]

With this trust, we do not limit our hope to the boundaries of the present moment. We enlarge it infinitely. We hope in the eternal significance of what has been made. We hope in a hope that, though it is now working in the shadows of the present, will one day be made fully manifest and complete, forever fulfilled in the eternal vision of the memory, hope, and faithfulness of God.

In this hope, in this hope engendered by God's faithfulness (and our faith in it), memory becomes a door, a door out of this life of limits into a life with none, a life suffused with a divine inexhaustibility of experience beyond our imagination. We see our possibilities grown unspeakably beyond anything that we can presently perceive them to be. As Paul writes to the church at Corinth,

> "Things which eye has not seen and ear has not heard, and which have not entered the heart of humankind, all that God has prepared for those who love him." (1 Corinthians 2:9)

Looking towards this day, we therefore marvel. We marvel at God's faithfulness, we exult in his faithfulness of hope and love, his faithfulness of trust and memory. Let us remind ourselves once more about what Jeremiah wrote in Lamentations,

---

[347] For additional discussion of this passage, see my *Thinking about God: Living the Considered Life* (Indianapolis: Author House, 2007), 33-44.

> "The Lord's lovingkindnesses indeed never cease, for His compassions never fail. They are new every morning; great is Your faithfulness." (Lamentations 3:22-23)

God's faithfulness, his faithfulness of memory, is solid, sure, endless, and forever.

Many centuries after Jeremiah penned these words, Paul wrote to the church at Philippi to say,

> "For I am confident of this very thing, that He who began a good work in you will perfect it until the day of Jesus Christ." (Philippians 1:6)

Once we acknowledge God's embedding of us in his memory, and trust his faithfulness of remembrance, his hope and love and care never stop rippling through our lives.

When we looked at God's hope and memory, we realized that it is the fact of God which enables the hope of memory to have any legitimate meaning. As we close out our look at God's faithfulness and memory, we see that, similarly, apart from God's faithfulness—and our faith in it—we have no reason to set our hope in memory. It is the faithfulness of God that ensures hope's reality in memory.

Put another way, we can say that, in the end, the basis of our hope in God's memory is nothing more and nothing less than the unwavering fact of the person of God.

We have discussed love and memory; hope and memory; faith and memory; and trust in memory. All of these could not happen, however, without wisdom. Why? As we have noted, memory can only happen in an ordered and meaningful universe. A meaningless universe is not a universe in which memory can be. Memory needs structure, and memory needs order. It requires a cosmos which has been intentionally and carefully planned and designed. Memory needs a personal creator. It will not exist in a cosmological genesis without a point.

Wisdom is this order, the fundamentally personal and created order that God built into the cosmos he made. In wisdom, God revealed himself, and in wisdom he designed and structured the patterns of life and creation. In wisdom, God ensured that the world's parts fit together, and in wisdom God ensured that the world would function rightly. In wisdom, God enabled memory to formulate, allowed memory to find its rightful place. Wisdom is God's memory, the mnemonic wonder of God's universe, the astonishment of remembrance planted and woven into the most intimate parts of what he made.

As a line from the hymn (often sung around Christmas) "O Come Emmanuel" asks, "O come, Thou Wisdom from on high, and order all things, far and nigh . . . "[348] Infused with God's creative power, the world is a living picture of God's wisdom, ordering and enabling, guiding and orchestrating, a continuous and constantly changing portrait of all that is. To live in the world is to live in the wisdom of God.[349]

It cannot be otherwise. As the author of reality, so is God the progenitor of its wisdom. Rightly did Job once observe, "God understands wisdom's way" (Job 28:23). God

---

[348] "O Come Emmanuel" ("Veni, Veni, Emmanuel"), adapted from Plainsong, Mode I, Thomas Helmore, trans. H. S. Coffin, 1916.

[349] *Wisdom's Wonder, op cit.; It's All in a Word, op cit.*

understands wisdom because he is its source, because he knows and defines it, and because only he can set it into the full sweep of the cosmos. He birthed it, he sustains it, and he uses it in the totality of his universal vision for what he made. Wisdom is the face of God, the manifestation of who he is, a living picture of his person in the world. To find wisdom is to grasp, to quote Job once more, "the fear [respectful awareness] of God" (Job 28:28).

Without God's wisdom, his wisdom which enables hope and faithful memory, though the universe may well remember, it will do so in pieces, disconnected and fractured pieces of striving and desire. Its memory will have no point or meaning, no way for those who engage in it to discern its purpose (as well as their own). Without wisdom, the cosmos and its memories simply float in space (wherever space *is*), drifting about without anchor, base, or demand. It's a picture of, as one writer put it, "nowhere." Remove wisdom, and the earth and its remembrances are orphaned, waifs without a home. They are there, but not, for where, really, is "there?" And what, apart from God's ordering and purpose, his hope and faithfulness and love in wisdom, does "there" mean? [350]

Wisdom ensures the existential integrity and material purpose of memory in the universe. It enables the possibility of meaningful recollection and recall, ours and God's. Without wisdom, memory would have no form or thought, no conduit or agency. Without wisdom's order, memory would mean nothing. As remembering can only occur in

---

[350] *View from Nowhere, op cit.,* and fifteenth century Catholic cardinal Nicholas Cusa's question, "But where is the world?" from his "On Learned Ignorance."

a universe whose fabric is ordered and predictable, one in which experience, communication, and exchange are possible and sensible, so is memory impossible without wisdom. In wisdom, in God's wisdom, we see the reality of memory and mnemonic purpose. Wisdom's fact and presence validates remembering in the universe.

When in the beginning of his *Divine Comedy* the medieval Italian writer Dante Alighieri enters *Inferno* (Hell) and looks at what is before him, Virgil, his guide and tutor, reminds him how essential wisdom is to the order of creation. In rather dark imagery, he says,

> "Through me you go into the city of grief, through me you go into the pain that is eternal, through me you go among people lost. Justice moved my exalted creator; the divine power made me, the supreme wisdom and the primal love. Before me all created things were eternal, and eternal I will last. Abandon every hope, you who enter here." [351]

Dante then realizes that God is far vaster than he could have ever imagined, and that his present life and the visible world are merely prelude to what is to come. He also recognizes that without God's wisdom, that which Virgil states made the "primal love" of the cosmos, he could not know God and God could not know him. God's memory of Dante would not exist if not for an ordered and purposeful universe, an ordered and purposeful universe that is the

[351] *Divine Comedy,* Canto III, 1-9.

result of the wisdom with which God endowed it. As Dante saw it, it is wisdom, the order of wisdom that, for us, ensures that we experience God and all that he is, memory, remembering, and all. Wisdom enables the fullness of God's mnemonic authority to express itself in the life and patterns of the cosmos.

Indeed, when the writer of Proverbs 8 personifies wisdom's presence at the beginning of creation, he presents wisdom as an integral part of the constructs of the universe, its frame, its ways, its memory:

> "From everlasting I [wisdom] was established, from the beginning, from the earliest times of the earth. When there were no depths I was brought forth, when there no springs abounding with water. Before the mountains settled, before the hills I was brought forth. While He had not yet made the earth and the fields, nor the first dust of the world. When He established the heavens, I was there." (Proverbs 8:22-27a)

Because wisdom is rooted in the very "stuff" (the *Urstoff*)[352] of the creation, its order choreographing and pervading everything that is made, we can remember. We can perceive, store, recollect, and recall. We can find meaning in how we remember the world, and meaning

352 *Urstoff* is a German word meaning roughly, "original substance."

in how it remembers us. Most importantly, we can find meaning in how God remembers us.[353]

A world filled with wisdom is a world filled with memory.

Conversely, wisdom enables God to remember the world. Wisdom's order means that God remembers the world, and that he remembers it—and all of us—fully and holistically. He remembers it in love, he remembers it in promise, he remembers it in hope. In this world, this world of his wisdom, God makes love and memory possible. He knows that when he loves and remembers, the planet will know it—and respond.

And it does. Consider Psalm 104:

> "There is the sea, great and broad, in which are swarms without number, animals both small and great. There the ships move along, and Leviathan, which You have formed to sport in it. They all wait for You to give them their food in due season. You give it to them, they gather it up; You open Your hand, they are satisfied with good." (Psalm 104:25-28).

---

[353] A fair question to ask here is, how does the world remember us? Although the material world cannot consciously remember us, as we pass through it in the course of our lives, the world learns to live with us. It reacts to us, it responds to us. It becomes part of us. See *Deep Ecology: Living as if Nature Mattered,* Bill Devall and George Sessions (Layton, Utah: Gibbs Smith, 2001); and Arne Naess's writings on his notion of deep ecology collected in *Ecology of Wisdom: Writings by Arne Naess* (Berkeley, California: Counterpart, 2009).

Because God made the world with wisdom, its inhabitants understand his love and memory for it. Although the world is marred by sin, it remains a good world. Despite its caprice, the world continues to exist with semblance and order. And God will continue to remember it. So does God promise Noah after the Flood that,

> "While the earth remains, seedtime and harvest, and cold and heat, and summer and winter, and day and night shall not cease." (Genesis 8:22)

As long as space and time remain, the rhythms of the universe, the rhythms of God's wisdom, his love, hope, and memory will continue. Enabled by wisdom's ordering presence, God's love, God's hope, and God's memory will endure. God's wisdom guarantees memory, the memory of God, his memory of all history, space, and time. It embodies the fact of his memory for us.

As we finish our look at God's wisdom and memory, we should also note that the God's wisdom in memory finds its truest and most visible appearance in the person of Jesus Christ. As Paul writes in his first letter to the Corinthian church,

> "But we preach Christ crucified, to Jews a stumbling block and to Gentiles foolishness, but to those who are the called, both Jews and Greeks, Christ the power of God and the wisdom of God." (1 Corinthians 1:24-25)

Not only is Jesus the highest vision of God's love for humankind, Jesus is God's most potent portrait of wisdom in the world. In Jesus, we see the greatest outcome of wisdom and, as a result, the deepest foundation of God's love, faithfulness, and hope in memory.

Jesus could not have happened apart from God's wisdom. God needed an ordered world to make himself known. If he were to step into space and time to commune with his creation, he needed to do so in a world rooted in a wisdom, a wisdom that ensures the meaningfulness of the present reality. We encounter God as Jesus because we live in a world of wisdom.

Memory as love, memory as hope, memory as faith; memory as trust: none can happen without wisdom. None can occur without wisdom's frame and order. Be it memory as the assertion of ultimate value; memory as the certain fulfillment of all longing; or memory as metaphysical confidence and faithfulness, it will not happen unless wisdom is present and working in the world. Value, completion, and confidence all require a cosmos governed by wisdom, a wisdom that ensures foundation, possibility, movement, and certainty. Patently seminal and inherently teleological, wisdom is that from which all of memory's love and hope and faithfulness flow and find meaning.

We have explored memory and love; memory and hope; memory and faith; memory and trust; and memory and wisdom. Buried in these is perhaps the most important of all the dimensions of God and memory: memory and being known.

Why? As we have noted, to be remembered is to be known. Whether it be by our fellow human beings, God, or both, when we are remembered, we are known. Moreover, in general, when we are known, we remember. We remember the one who knows us. To be known, in whatever way it happens or comes about and to whatever extent or degree it occurs, is the heart of memory. We cannot remember, and we cannot *be* remembered unless we know and are being known.

Understanding this in a human context is relatively easy. Think about anyone you know, regardless of how close you feel to that person. Now think about someone who knows *you*, irrespective of the extent to which she does. Next, think about a person you may know *about*, whether this person is an athlete, politician, "celebrity," or head of a prominent corporation. Knowing, being known, knowing about: in every case, knowing, along with remembering, on some level, is occurring. Yet which of these three relationships of knowing do you suppose has the most potential for genuine knowing to happen? If you picked the second, you would be most correct. While we can "know" or "know about" almost anyone, we do not really know this person until she knows us. Until that happens, although we may be in some way, broadly speaking, connected to that person, we do not really "know" her.

One of my colleagues in graduate school once told me this story. On the first day of one of his undergraduate classes, he and his fellow students sat in the chairs of the classroom, waiting for the professor to enter. Five minutes passed. After ten minutes, the professor walked into the room. Puffing on a large cigar, he strode to the lectern, and looked at the gathered students. After about a minute of silence, he said, "I know you, but you don't know me." Then he walked out of the room. Class was over for the day.

Granted, the professor didn't really "know" any of the students. Chances are, however, that at that juncture he knew more about them than they knew about him. He had read their files, checked their records, and discussed some of them with other professors. The students of course could have read his teacher reviews or discussed him with students who had had him before. Yet this would have been no substitute for knowing this professor as a person, his life story, his relationships, his hopes and dreams. These students did not have access to the details of this professor's life that he had of theirs. The "knowing" was not balanced.

Not until the students had spent time with this professor in the classroom could they say that they "knew" him, and even then they still would probably not know him as he is. Yet by reading and studying the students' written assignments and meditations, the professor could come to know a great deal about them. Even then, however, the professor could not claim that he really "knew" any of the students. In short, neither party would ever really "know" the other. Genuine knowing occurs only when all parties have equal stake and access to the other, when all parties agree to let their guard down and make themselves open and vulnerable to the other.

All hearts must be open, and all secrets must be known.

So it is with people and God. Because God is infinite and people are finite, however, the process works differently. As temporal beings, people cannot unilaterally connect intimately with God. No one can *ipso facto* enter into God's presence. God must come to them first. God must make himself known to them.

At two places in his letters, one to the church at Corinth, the other to the churches in Galatia, Paul speaks to this point aptly. He first tells his readers that yes, of course, they all know *about* God. Of course, he says, they all know that there is a divine person watching over them (1 Corinthians 8:3; Galatians 4:9). Indeed, nearly everyone in the Roman Empire could have said the same thing. Despite its moral and cultural debauchery, the Roman Empire remained a largely religious society.[354]

Now, however, things have changed. Now, "you," Paul reminds his readers, "are known *by* God." Why? Because God has made himself known to them. Not only do Paul's readers know and know about God, but now God, through Jesus, knows *them.* Knowing and remembering have become a two way street. Human *and* God are contributing to the relationship. Both sides are letting their guard down, both sides are opening themselves up to the other. Both sides are actively engaged in knowing the other. As John puts it in the first chapter of his gospel, those who have come to believe in Jesus have passed from being part of the family of the human creation to being part of God's chosen family within that creation. They are children of God. They enjoy a special relationship with their creator (John 1:12).

But the initiative was all God's.

Moreover, now that God has established this special relationship with those who believe in Jesus, he remembers them in a way that he does not remember other people. They

---

354 Indeed, as Paul's colleague James wrote several years before, even the demons, the Devil's denizens, believe in God (James 2:19)!

will remember God similarly. Do not most parents tend to remember their own more than they remember children of their friends? Do not most children remember and look to their own parents before they look to those of others? We and God are no different. If we know, really know each other, we will tend to remember each other more than we remember others. We will be inclined to remember our "own" first.

Does not God, however, know everyone? Do not God's eyes, as Judaism likes to say, "See everyone?" Sure. God knows everyone and everything on the planet. He knows everyone who has ever lived, everyone who is living, and everyone who will live in the thousands and millions of years to come. And he just doesn't know "about" everyone; he knows everyone intimately. He knows everyone's darkest secrets and deepest pretenses, everyone's richest desires and most intimate longings. God knows everyone inside and out.[355]

But this only makes God like Big Brother of George Orwell's *1984*. Big Brother knew everything about everyone, but Big Brother only did so for his own aggrandizement and gain. He didn't really care about those he watched; he only

[355] For an interesting look at the idea that the eyes of God are watching everyone, see Woody Allen's movie *Crimes and Misdemeanors*, Orion Pictures, 1989. See also Jeremiah 32:19, which reads, "[the Lord's] eyes are open to all the ways of humankind" and Hebrews 4:13, "And there is no creature hidden from His sight, but all things are open and laid bare to the eyes of Him with whom we have to do."

used them for his selfish purposes. And he certainly did not love them.[356]

Some may of course argue that God only uses most human beings, too, that he merely creates people to satisfy and serve his own purposes. At best, he's a benevolent tyrant; at worst, a conniving king. He knows human beings only to justify himself. After all, he is absolutely sovereign.[357]

Maybe, but all the evidence indicates that this is unlikely. As we have noted repeatedly, God loves people. He treasures human beings. God made people in his image and set them at the pinnacle of his creation (see Psalm 8). God views humans with a love and affection far more profound than that with which he loves the other animals. People are God's special joy.

God therefore thinks about people not to bully them, but to know and love them. Yes, he already knows everyone intimately, but he wants the pleasure of knowing that people are aware of him knowing them as such. He wants the joy

---

356 George Orwell, *1984* (New York: Signet, 1984). Consider also an episode of the television show *The Twilight Zone* titled "Obsolete Man." In this, a person who had been overseeing the extermination of people considered "useless" by the rulers of a dystopian world is one day himself determined to be "useless." Very quickly, he, too, is eliminated. (*Twilight Zone,* 1959-1964). See also Proverbs 16:4, which reads, "The Lord has made everything for its own purpose, even the wicked for the day of destruction." Is God making people only to destroy them? It's a difficult question to ponder.

357 See, for instance, Richard Dawkins, *The God Delusion* (New York: Houghton Mifflin, 2008); and Christopher Hitchens, *god is Not Great: How Religion Poisons Everything* (New York: Twelve, 2009).

of knowing that they consciously sense him living their lives with them. God wishes to go beyond merely knowing about peoples' lives; he wants to live their lives with them. He longs to walk through the days and years with them. In every way, God wants humans to know, to consciously know and believe, that he wants to be directly involved with their hopes, challenges, struggles, joys, and dreams. He wishes for people to find enduring comfort and peace in knowing that when everything else in their lives may fail, they are known and loved (and remembered) by an eternal God. God wants his human creation to know that they can always count on him.[358]

To be in the family of God and to be known by God is therefore to consciously experience God living with and within oneself. It is to be the particular object of God's focus, the special aim of his love and desire, the central goal of his desire and vision. When God knows and loves a person, he enmeshes himself fully into her. He fills her with the knowledge of his love for her. He makes her part of his highest intentions, a radically essential part of his eternal and loving prognostications, and invites her into the innermost layers of his hopes for human and cosmic destiny. This person becomes one with God and his purposes for the universe. As a valued member of God's family, the special community of human beings toward whom he extends the

---

[358] See John Piper, *God's Passion for His Glory: Living the Vision of Jonathan Edwards* (Wheaton: Crossway, 1998. In addition, consider Jesus' words to his disciples after his resurrection that, "I will be with you until the end of the age" (Matthew 28:20), and Paul's encouragement to the church at Philippi, words that we cited earlier, that, "He [God] who begins a good work in you will perfect it to the day of Christ Jesus" (Philippians 1:6).

fullest expression of his love and affection, this person lives and dies in a rich and perduring harmony with her creator.[359]

To be known by God is also to engage him with one's heart. It is to enter into a relationship of love with God, to step into an experience of divine care and longing that overwhelms and supersedes everything else. It is to know a love which, as Paul described it to the church at Ephesus (a passage at which we looked earlier), "surpasses knowledge" (Ephesians 3:19).

To know and be known by God is to know a love in memory whose meaning bursts all parameters of human knowledge. Those who know and are known by God experience the fullness of divine love, the divine love grounding the memory out of which the universe came, the love that birthed and, in the person of Jesus, died for the cosmos, the love that will one day revitalize and restore the universe to its original purity and being. To know and be known by God in memory is to know the love of a shepherd who, at all costs, looks after every one of his sheep, the love which, as Jesus puts it in the tenth chapter of John's gospel, "will never let one of my people fall out of my hand." It is to know the love of the father who, even after his prodigal son has spent, foolishly and frivolously, his entire share of his father's estate, nonetheless embraces and celebrates him when he returns home (see Luke 15). To be known by God is to know a love without boundaries, a love without limit. Loved and remembered, remembered and loved, those whom God knows intimately come to know and experience, day by

[359] On being filled with God, see Dallas Willard, *The Divine Conspiracy: Rediscovering Our Hidden Life in God* (New York: Harper, 1998.)

day, year by year, through remembrance, in memory, ever richer and more wondrous dimensions of God's eternal love and intention for them, his special children. It's a journey without end.[360]

God's memory as knowing also means that as he remembers, as he remembers his children now and forever, he is seeking constantly to ensure that they continue to learn, more and more fully every day, how much he wishes to be and do for them. In his letter to the church at Philippi, Paul writes,

> "That I may know him [Jesus] and the power of His resurrection and the fellowship of His sufferings, being conformed to His death . . . I press on to the goal for the prize of the upward call of God in Christ Jesus" (Philippians 3:10, 14).

Ensconced in God's love, his loving memory of knowing, we feel compelled to devote our every waking moment to responding to this love of memory, to digging ever more deeply into what it means in our lives. We seek to know God more and more with each passing day. We know that knowing and being known by God in this life are but foretastes of knowing him, the eternal and remembering creator, throughout eternity. We understand

---

[360] On this restoration, see Isaiah 64 and Revelation 21. On the prodigal son, see Tim Keller, *Prodigal God: Recovering the Heart of the Christian Faith* (New York: Penguin, 2011), and Henri J. M. Nouwen, *The Return of the Prodigal Son* (New York: Doubleday, 1994).

that our memory of being known is forever. We live being remembered and known by God, and we will die being remembered and known by God.

But death, however, is not the end. Indeed, it is the beginning. Ushered into a new life, a new life greater than what we can now imagine, we will live with God visibly and directly, experiencing being remembered, loved, and known by him in ways we could not have enjoyed during our sojourn on Earth. So does Paul remark in the first chapter of Philippians that, "To live is Christ; to die is gain" (Philippians 1:21).

To cite T. S. Eliot's *Four Quartets,*

> "And the end of all our exploring will be to arrive where we started and know the place for the first time."[361]

Or as naturalist and explorer Peter Anderson, quoting a homily from one of his most loved pastors, a person he called "the Padre," shares,

> "Death is nothing to worry about. Peter Pan had it right: it's out the window, second turn to the right, and straight ahead till morning."[362]

In being known by God in memory, we will find our truest home. We will be right where we ought to be. We will come into what, had sin not entered the world, we should have always

---

361 T. S. Eliot, *Four Quartets* (Orlando, Florida: Harcourt Brace, 1943), "The Dry Salvages".

362 Peter Anderson, *First Church of Higher Elevation: Mountains, Prayer, and Presence* (Golden, Colorado: Conundrum, 2015), 68.

been, the seminal picture and focus of God's vision for us. We will have found our permanent form, position, and place.

As we have noted time and time again, however, God is infinite and we are finite. How does he then know us? How does he enable us to know him? How does finitude enter into exchange with infinitude? How does temporality embrace eternity? How do people living in a material and "natural" reality apprehend the expressions of an immaterial and *supernatural* reality?

In short, how does God connect?

In the final verses in chapter thirteen of his first letter to the church at Corinth, Paul writes eloquently on this point. Here are the verses in full:

> "For we know in part and we prophesy in part; but when the perfect comes, the partial will be done away. When I was a child, I used to speak like a child, think like a child, reason like a child; when I became a man, I did away with childish things. For now we see as in a riddle, but then face to face; now I know in part, but then I will know fully just as I also have been fully known" (1 Corinthians 13:9-12).

What is Paul saying? We should note first that he is talking not just about the present, but the future as well. He's thinking about the things of today, yet he is also thinking about things that will come. And he is acknowledging that what is to come will in some way encompass, reflect, extend, and eclipse, in a singularly transforming way, what is going on now. Paul is saying that how we consider knowing in this life (its past, present, and future) is but prelude to an experience of knowing that will completely change the way in which we know and are known.

This is because the future to which Paul refers is not a future we will find in this life. It is a future that, as he sees it, we will experience in the life that follows this life, the life into which we will step when our earthly days are over. Paul is speaking of an experience of the afterlife. He is framing our present experience of knowing in the context of a future experience of knowing, the future to which we alluded earlier, a future whose center of weight will not be in our current reality. And he emphasizes that our present experience of knowing will pale in comparison to what we will know then. Now, as he puts it, we know in part. We know incompletely.

Paul understands the constraints of finitude well. He knows that however much we know things, including God, in this life, given that we are limited beings, it will never be everything we could know. Further, even if someone were somehow to know everything she possibly could about the content and meaning of this existence, she would still not know, fully, "knowing," God or anything else. She would still not know knowing's meaning, reason, essence, or purpose. She would strive in vain to construct a universal picture of knowing and existence, for she would not be able to grasp the totality of its scope and foundation.[363]

---

363 We think here about our earlier analogy of being in a box. When we are in a box, although we can see what is inside the box, we cannot see what is outside of it. We cannot "see" the box, and we cannot see where the box "is."

Paul also understands that we live our lives in the shadow of Ecclesiastes 3:11's observation (which we examined earlier) that, "God has put eternity into the human heart yet so that people will not find the beginning to the end." We will live, and know, as Paul poetically concludes, "as in a riddle" (what the Greek in this verse literally means). Life is a mystery, and our knowing in it will always be incomplete. In this present existence, we will not see life fully. Nor will we see God fully. We will not understand and know absolutely. Our purview will be painfully and, for every one of us, frustratingly limited.

Given this, Paul is encouraging us to look at knowing in a much broader context, a much more expansive ken. He's telling us that we are to look at knowing as more than a part and function of this life only. We need to look at knowing, he notes, as something we will only experience fully in eternity. We must realize, he suggests, that if we are to see our present life as one with genuine meaning, we must acknowledge that, in and of itself, it lacks any basis for claiming it has permanent point. It will not last. The way we know in this life, even the way in which we might know God, remains a thoroughly subjective experience. It will never be more than a collection and compendium of earthbound data and happenstance. Although we may find this data to be, in the moment, vastly important, and even if we know it to be connected to supernatural presence, we will not be able to visibly tie it to any larger purpose or point. We will see it come, we will see it go, but we will never know, in the big picture, what it meant. Why did we even live?

And why did we ever know? No, Paul is saying, we will only "know" knowing—and what we know—when "knowing" is known in turn. We are to see that we will only know what our knowing is when our knowing is known by God. We are to understand that, ultimately, our knowing is only as meaningful as we are open to what enables it.

In sum, we are to set our presently incomplete and disconnected experience of knowing in the compass of a "perfect" and completed knowing that is to come. We are to look at this life of knowing as prologue, prologue to something far greater still, to see our present existence as merely the beginning of knowing in full. We must see our knowing as inchoate and incipient, a mystery intriguing. Yes, by embracing the love and sacrifice of Jesus we come to know God as a member of his special family in this present life. And yes, through Jesus' work we come to know God as a God of memory, a God of memory as hope, faithfulness, trust, and love. And yes, it is in this that we come to know Jesus, the wisdom of God, as our pathway to God's remembering love in this existence, our journey to the heart of the memory of God. In Jesus, we come to know, come to know today, God's memory as hope, wisdom, love, and faithfulness.

But in this present life we experience Jesus in part. We remain creatures of finitude.

So we wait. We wait for the "perfect." We understand that there is more to come, and that how we experience knowing and memory in the present life is preparing us to experience it in its successor. Because we are now known and remembered by God in part, we know that, one day, because God is immutable, dynamic, and eternal, he will know and remember us in full. We know that one day we will wander in an epistemological blur no longer. Our sojourn will be over. We will know ourselves, we will know the world, we will know the universe and, most importantly, we will know God, fully and absolutely. We will know the source and point of existence, the beginning of all that is. And we will face inscrutabilities no more.[364]

In short, we will know the totality, the absolute totality of what it means to be known and remembered by God. We will stand at the apex of faith and hope in memory and being remembered and loved by God. We will know God's memory in its absolute and most complete expression. We will see, definitively and finally, memory and hope, memory and faith, and memory and love come together. Everything will have form, everything will flow, and everything will make sense.

Although while we were on the earth God knew, loved, and remembered us, he did so in our broken finitude and sinful inadequacy. He knew, loved, and remembered us as imperfect beings, as people who had not yet experienced the perfect. He didn't know and remember us as he most wanted to.

Now he will. And we will know God as he most is, too. Unlike Adam and Eve, caught in the Garden in untimely

---

364 It is well to note here that the root meaning of the Greek word being translated here as "perfect" is "to be complete." To know perfectly is therefore to know everything as it genuinely is. See "*telios*" in *TDNT,* Vol. VIII. In addition, we should say that however much we know and are known by God in this eternal condition, we will never grasp him fully. For ever and ever, though we will be God's treasured and beloved children, we will always be human beings—and God will always be God. Yes, Jesus will be the God-man for all eternity, but *all* who God is, well, that will always be beyond our grasp.

transgression, we will not stand before God in nakedness and alienation. While we at present walk before God as forgiven yet confused and bent physical beings, we will now present ourselves to him as whole people, complete and wholly purified *spiritual* beings. Every forgetting will vanish, every ignorance will be gone. Everything will be remembered, and everything will be known. It will all be present, like a book we read all at once, like a movie we see immediately and in full.

We will step into a communion of memory with our creator beyond our present reckoning, a communion in which memory will be as God intended for memory to be.

And after what may have been many, many decades of walking as "in a riddle," of tramping almost blindly through this present and bewildering existence, we will see. No longer will we live by faith, trusting in what we do not see, moment by moment and day by day clinging to what can often be the extremely raw nature of belief unseen. Now we will see in full. We will reach the goal, the supernaturally hidden goal we have pursued all our life. We will know, visibly and palpably know, that around which we have built everything in which we have placed our ultimate trust. We will see finish, we will see end. We will touch the truth of Emily Dickinson's words that, "This world is not conclusion." We will see the completion of the puzzle, the closure to the mystagogical shape of our earthly knowing. It will all be before us. In the flash of a moment—and for untold moments to come—we will see what is genuinely real, what is unaffectedly real about ourselves, life, and the memory of God.[365]

The universe will be before us. And God will be with us in a way which in this temporal life we cannot fully fathom. We will know him, the eternal God, as a fellow creature of eternity. We will know God as himself, as he really is. We will know the ultimate knowing (and knower and rememberer) of all. On this day, and for every day following, nothing will be hidden, nothing will be undone, and nothing will be unknown. We will know the fullness of truth, reality, and power, the fullness of God's fact and presence as the reality which defines and encompasses all things.[366]

Hence, although we are aware of, in our present finitude, our epistemological limitations acutely, and therefore wonder how we can possibly walk with an infinite God, we also know that through Jesus, we already are. We know that we are actively engaging with our future to come, that our present puzzlement is but prelude to clarity on the other side. In Jesus, the living wisdom and power of God, the Jesus with whom we live in the family of God, we already see glimpses of the vision to which our lives point; we understand that our present puzzlement simply foretells our imminent understanding. As writer Francis Schaeffer

---

[365] When we say the "raw nature" of belief, we are saying that, as many, many people of faith have realized, faith is one of the most demanding experiences of humanness. Finitude is rarely easy. See "Invisible Light" in *Thinking about God, op cit.* In addition, consult Julia Kristeva, *This Incredible Need to Believe* (New York: Columbia University, 2009).

[366] We use the term "day" loosely here. Eternity knows no conventional chronological demarcations.

observed, we live, "as though we had already died, been to heaven, and come back again as risen."

Our future is already here.[367]

But how will this happen? How will this experience of knowing come to be? How will this future, this greater future of knowing appear to us?

How will we remember when there is nothing left to remember?

We must die. As we must experience memory in time and space before experiencing in realms beyond them, so we must see death as the door that, though it closes this life, is also the door that opens the next one. Death is the gateway to ultimate knowing and memory. In dying, we leave this world, this world of spatial and chronological limit, and enter another world, a world in which time and space as we have understood them no longer apply. We enter the realm of the supernatural, the place of holiness, the presence of the eternal God. We are flesh and blood no more. We are spirit.[368]

Death is the only way that we will see God, as Paul puts it, "face to face." Only if we die will we see the full visage of God. Unlike the Irishman who told his wife, in the tale of the "Clockwinder," that he could "wind" her damaged

---

367 Francis A. Schaeffer, *True Spirituality* (Wheaton, Illinois: Tyndale House, 1971), 41. See also George Eldon Ladd, *The Presence of the Future* (Grand Rapids, Michigan: Wm B. Eerdmans, 1996), which argues that, per Jesus' words about the nearness of the kingdom of God in Mark 1:15, the long awaited arrival of God on earth has, in the person of Jesus, come. The future is upon us.

368 As Jesus in John 4 describes God as "spirit," so will we, as spirit, now share the medium and morphology of God. We will be creatures of earth no longer.

clock himself, we cannot, in ourselves, "wind" our way into the eternal presence of God.

We have to let go of earthly existence.[369]

Let's consider this a moment. As the Hebrew Bible frequently makes clear, no one sees the face of God. Not even Moses, Moses, the one whom Exodus describes as a person who "knew the Lord face to face," saw God's face as it really is (Exodus 34:10).[370]

Not even the mightiest of the other prophets saw God, either. Although Isaiah and Ezekiel write of seeing God, theirs is never a complete vision of who God is. It was never a full orbed view of God's face (see Isaiah 6 and Ezekiel 1). Similarly, although the patriarch Jacob remarked after spending all night wrestling with a person who eventually identifies himself as God that he "has seen God face to face and lived," he did not see God's face in its fullness. He saw it in earthly context (Genesis 32).

The psalmists are no different. Though they told God that, "Your face, O Lord, will I seek" (Psalm 27:8), they

---

[369] See "The German Clockwinder" (whose authorship is attributed to national tradition) in any collection of Irish poems and hymns.

[370] But Moses certainly tried. One day, as chapter 33 of Exodus describes it, Moses requested of God that he might see his face. But God said no. "No one," God replied, "may see my face and live." So, the account tells us, Moses saw God's "backside" instead. However, does God really have a backside as you and I do? No: the writer is using anthropomorphic language to describe God. As many writers have pointed out, in order to objectify and better grasp God, people have assigned various human appendages to his person. See, for one, David Tracy, *The Analogical Imagination: Christian Theology and the Culture of Pluralism* (New York: Crossroad, 1998).

readily acknowledged that only "the upright [the forever righteous] shall behold his face" (Psalm 11:7). Though people sought to see God's face (the "*peniel*" of God) in this life, they knew that they would not.

On the other side, freed of our earthly constraints, forever lodged in the love and memory and spirit of God, however, we will. We will see more than Moses and all the other prophets. We will see the face of God, the face of all life, presence, and truth.

We will seek and wish no longer.

And so it will be that, as we see God's face, as we openly witness and participate in his essence, we and God will begin to share the most profound commonality of form and communion and knowing and memory. No longer restricted to the world of land, sea, and sky, we will know and remember God as he really is. And God will remember us as we are most destined to be. Knowing and being known, and remembering and being remembered will come seamlessly together, fluently coalescing in a remarkable mix of earthly memory and heavenly vision. We will not use analogies, we will not use speculation, we will not use intimation. We will see and hear and remember God directly, and he us, for he will now be directly before us. Secrets are gone, guessing is over. Whatever we have thought or imagined about God, we need not think or imagine any longer: we *know.* The veil of mortality has been lifted, the curtain of finitude is gone. Life is earthly no longer. It is eternal. Everything is clear, everything is true. All questions will be answered, all mysteries will be resolved. Every twist of time will be untangled, and every blank space of being will be filled. Belief and knowing and memory will come full circle, woven into lasting truth. It's all before us.[371]

It all begins with death.[372]

---

[371] To enlarge on what we mentioned above, we note that those who most fully participate in this experience are people who are recipients of a process that, for some, began many years ago. We all begin life as infants, biological as well as spiritual. We do not know life, we do not know God. As we grow biologically, our awareness of existence steadily deepens. We also gradually became aware of ourselves as spiritual beings. We entertain the possibility of God. Although some of us reject this possibility, some of us embrace it. Those who embrace it, those who embrace it on the basis of belief in Jesus as Messiah and God, experience spiritual conversion. Spiritually speaking, they become new, totally new human beings. Subsequently, these people embark on a life path on which they come to know God more and more fully. They grow in their knowledge of God, not just knowledge as information about God, but knowledge as relationship and personal exchange with him. They live knowing that God is remembering them, and they die knowing that he is remembering them. They live tasting glimpses of what is to come: the perfect, the final perfection of memory, hope, and knowing.

[372] As Christianity, and many other religions, tell it, God will reveal and establish this new beginning at the end of the world, at the close of this present age. He will express it in a new and perfect world, complete and unbroken, a fully connected and wholly harmonious planet, which he has restored to his original intention for it. God will renew all things and make all things new. Earth will still be Earth, but everything about it, its essence, its expressions, and its manifestations will be radically and definitively new. As the Bible (and the *Qur'an)* tell it, it is Jesus, the Messiah (for the Christian) who will inaugurate this new age. At the end of all time, time as God has created it, time as God will now transform and render it moot, Jesus will return. He will descend from heaven and come to dwell visibly on this

Death is the universe's beginning, too. The verses before us are describing the end of the age, the close of space and time as we know it, and the appearance of the new heaven and earth (see, as a previous footnote mentioned, Isaiah 64 and Revelation 21). In this new age, the entire universe, not just the heights of heaven, will experience knowing God fully. The knowledge of God will palpably permeate the cosmos. No one will overlook it, nothing will miss it. As knowing has always been clear and full in the supernatural, now it will be clear and full everywhere else, too. Isaiah puts it well, saying that, "The earth will be full of the knowledge of the Lord, as the waters cover the sea" (Isaiah 11:9). The knowledge of God will be present, in fullness, in every corner of the creation. Everyone will understand.

And everyone will remember and be remembered. God's memory, his of us, and ours of him, will be indisputably clear and present.

Let's look at another passage, this one from the third chapter of the first letter of the apostle John. It reads,

> "Beloved, now we are children of God, and it has not appeared as yet what we will be. We know that when He appears, we will be like Him, because we will see Him just as He is" (1 John 3:2).

---

planet. One day, Jesus will consummate God's kingdom on earth. See Revelation 19-21. Also, consult Sigmund Mowinckel, *He That Cometh,* trans. G. W. Anderson (New York: Abingdon, 1951); and N. T. Wright, *The Resurrection of the Son of God* (Minneapolis: Fortress, 2003).

As did Paul, John indicates although those who are known and remembered by God are now his children, their present finitude prevents them from becoming and experiencing their final destiny. They are not whole beings, and they do not know fully. When Jesus ("He") appears, however, his children will be like God because, he adds, they "will see Him just as he is."

When will Jesus appear? As a previous footnote explains, one day, one day far into the future, a day when time and space have worn themselves out and God has definitively accomplished his intentions for the world and the cosmos through which it has traveled for many billions of years, Jesus will return to the planet he made. This day will be the day of days, a day on which human wonder and creational desire will be inseparably and forever fused, a day in which meaning itself will be undone and commenced anew. It will be, to borrow a phrase from the title of a volume of the *Lord of the Rings* trilogy, "the return of the king" (the king being Jesus) (Acts 1:11; Revelation 19:11-16). Predicted in many prophecies in the Hebrew Bible, usually in the numerous references to what is called the "Day of the Lord," this day will be the day on which God, at long last, exercises his final judgment on his creation and overturns all existing notions of reality. It is the day when memory comes indisputably home (Isaiah 13; Ezekiel 30; Amos 5; and Zephaniah 1, to name just a few).[373]

This day is also Paul's "perfect." As yet another previous footnote informed us, the Greek word which we translate into the English word "perfect" connotes "completeness," a

---

[373] To draw a line from the Newboys's song *Christ Our Savior*, "He reigns." Inpop Music, 2011. See also *The Lord of the Rings, op cit.*

"wholeness" that brings everything in a particular situation or circumstance together. It signifies a definitive resolution, a comprehensive summation. We can therefore look at Jesus' appearance, the "perfect," as the "completion" of God's work on Earth. Jesus' return will bring God's vision for the cosmos to its full weight and perfection, enable the final maturation of God's intentions for the planet. In it, all of God's children will be "fully known." And they will see God "face to face," "just as he is."[374]

One of the first statements Jesus made as he began his public ministry was, "Behold, the kingdom of God is at hand." (Mark 1:16). In making this pronouncement, Jesus was saying that the kingdom for which Israel had longed for centuries, the kingdom in which Israel had for so long invested all of its hopes and dreams, the kingdom that Israel believed would fulfill God's vision for them, had finally come to Earth. In Jesus, the kingdom of God had, literally and metaphorically, come. In Jesus, God's eternal reign is established on the earth.[375]

However, as numerous parables, particularly those in the thirteenth chapter of Matthew's gospel, make plain, although the kingdom is now established, it is not yet complete. It is not yet consummated on Earth. It is not yet whole; it is not yet "perfect." Until Jesus returns, until Jesus returns to set the entire planet free, God's kingdom will grow alongside the confusion, distortions, and sin of the world.

---

374 "*telios,*" *TDNT,* Vol VIII. Consider as well Jesus' words to be "perfect" (Matthew 5:48). Jesus knew quite well that no one could be morally perfect in this life. He was rather encouraging his audience to strive, as much as they can, for spiritual wholeness.

375 *The Presence of the Future, op cit.*

It will live with opposition and conflict, will battle daily the contusions of earthly limitation and human finitude. Because the world in which it lives and grows is at present wrapped and controlled by sin, the kingdom's perfect cannot yet fully come. Its fullness cannot yet happen.[376]

So it is for knowing and memory. In Jesus' return, when God completes and consummates his kingdom for all time and the "perfect" comes, God's children will be fully remembered and wholly known. Their memory, God's of theirs and theirs of God, will find its end. They will be remembered, definitively and completely, even as they are known, totally and fully.

In the kingdom's consummation, memory comes home.

And as John said, "we will be like God." Not only will we see God face to face, not only will we be fully known by God, and not only will we be remembered by God, we will become "like" him as well.

How is this? How can we human beings become like God? We will be like God, John adds, because "we will see him *as he is*." As creatures who are no longer flesh and blood but creatures of spirit, as creatures who are now experiencing the fullness of eternity, we will stand directly before God. No borders separate us, no fences keep us apart. We are fully before him, we are looking directly into his face.

We will see God as we have never seen him before. And God will see us similarly. God will see us as being "like" him.

As we have seen, regardless of his spiritual greatness, Moses remained a creature of flesh and blood. So long as he lived on Earth, he could not really see God. Likewise,

---

[376] *Ibid.* See also Matthew 13.

despite the remarkable relationship he enjoyed with God and the astonishing miracles he performed, Elijah, one of the two people who did not die an earthly death (the other is Enoch; see Genesis 5), could not see God as God is until he had been taken up to heaven in a chariot of fire (2 Kings 2:11). Although as we noted Isaiah and Ezekiel saw visions of God in his temple in heaven, they did so while they were in heaven, after God had transported them into his eternal realm. They could not see these things in their life on a planet of soil, fire, and water (Isaiah 6; Ezekiel 1). Similarly, Paul could not experience his vision of the "third heaven" without being "in" that heaven. He could not have had the vision while living on the physical earth (2 Corinthians 12).[377]

No one could see God without being "like" him.

The New Testament uses several words to denote "seeing." The first is *blepo. Blepo* describes the seeing of perception, a seeing of the five senses. *Blepo* expresses how we see when we look out our window in the morning. The other word is *orao. Orao* points to a seeing that is more akin to discerning. *Orao* is a seeing that sees between the lines, a seeing that looks into what it is seeing, a seeing of insight and wisdom. *Orao* is a seeing of thought, focused and concentrated thought.

When John writes in the passage before us, he uses *orao* to describe how we will see God. He is saying that we will see God as more than visual image. We will see God's

[377] Although Paul saw Jesus while he lived on earth (see the account of Paul's conversion in Acts 8), he saw him with earthly eyes as the risen God-man, not through the lens of heaven as the king of kings who sits by the side of the Father.

depths, his character, his essence. We will see the real person of God. We will be spirit.

Paul writes in similar fashion. When he states that in the present moment we see "as in a riddle," he uses *blepo.* He understands that our present seeing is, visually and metaphorically, wedded to the objects of this world. When Paul talks about seeing when we are "fully known," however, he uses *orao.* He knows that we will not see as *orao* until we are fully known by God on the other side.[378]

Hebrew is similar. In the nineteenth chapter of Job, Job cries,

> "Even after my flesh is destroyed, yet from my flesh I shall see God; whom I myself shall behold, and whom my eyes will see and not another." (Job 19:26-27).

The first time Job "sees," the text uses the verb *raah.* Like *blepo* in Greek, *raah* connotes the seeing of perception. It describes visual seeing, the seeing that, almost without thinking, we do every day. The second time Job "sees," however, the text employs *chazah.* Like *orao, chazah* is the seeing of insight and discernment, a seeing that ponders and looks into what it sees. In his flesh, Job saw God as visual image in his brain. On the other side, beyond death, Sheol, and doubt and uncertainty, he will see God as he actually is. He will be like him.[379]

---

378 *"Opaw" TDNT,* Vol V.

379 *"Ra'a"* in *TDOT,* Vol XIII. "Sheol" or "netherworld" is the general term for the Hebrew conception of the afterlife. Broadly speaking, although the Hebrew vision of the afterlife was rather murky and

As will we. When we *orao* God, when we *orao* and *chazah* God face to face, our knowing and memory will be complete. In the one remarkable moment, we will recollect and recall all that we knew and remembered in our earthly existence, every last vestige of what "has been," and set it into the lens of a robustly transforming "what is." The past happened, yes, and its memories remain, yet now everything about those memories becomes totally new. They linger, but they do not; they abide, but they change.

In short, no longer will we cling to the fleetingness of finitude past. No longer will we see what has been as simply a reflection of a life, for better or worse, lived on earth only. We will not see memories as manifestations of joyful temporality, occasions for regret or opportunities lost, wonderful yet impermanent points of splendor in a scattered and disconnected world. We will instead see them as windows and predictions and heralds of a much greater life to come, a life spent in the permanence of eternity, a

---

undefined, most of its expressions make Sheol its starting point. For some biblical writers, Sheol is a place of inactivity in which nothing happens and nothing changes: it is the end (Ecclesiastes 9). Some of the prophets, principally Isaiah, Daniel, and Hosea, however, underscore that, at the end of time, God will resurrect the righteous (Isaiah 26; Daniel 12; Hosea 6-9). See also *The Resurrection of the Son of God, op cit.* In addition, consider that for many modern Jews (Reconstructionist, Conservative, and Reformed), the afterlife is not important. What we do in this life is far more significant than what happens after we die. People experience heaven or, alternatively, hell, in this life through how they live and the effects of their deeds, but not necessarily in the next one—if there is one. Again, my thanks to Rabbi Jonathan Kohn of Chicago for his helpful insights.

finality of vision in which all things are grounded and find meaning. We will see our memory overwhelm the time and history from which it has come. We will see our memory connect with the fullness of the truth and knowing of existence. Our memory will be a beacon of life's wholeness, a harbinger of its future expansiveness. Nothing will be lost, but everything will have left; absence will reign no longer, yet earthly memory will be gone. Standing in the final vision of God, we will know our memory as we and it are fully and absolutely remembered and known. We will see our memory as creatures who have, in a way that we cannot now envisage, transcended it; creatures who are no longer earthly but heavenly; material creatures made in God's image but now spiritual creatures who are *like* God.[380]

Although our memory remains, it becomes entirely new.

So will memory and knowing come full circle. We will remember, remember as we have not been able to remember before, that we are remembered by God. Our hope will be met, our trust will be completed. We will know fully. And we will affirm, affirm in a way that we could not have previously, that without memory, without our knowing in memory, our remembering God and God remembering us, God, we, and life have no real point. We will realize, realize ever more convincingly, that apart from God's memory we have lived and died in a pointless reality.

---

380 Indeed, as Augustine writes in his *City of God*, history will be no more. See Augustine, *City of God* (New York: Image, 1958).

We will know what knowing and memory are to most be: we will bask in the visible and present remembrance of a personal and meaningful cosmos.[381]

In addition, we will see the fullness of the hope, the hope driven by faith and God's faithfulness, of memory. No longer will we walk without sight, no longer will we walk on paths invisible. We will see. We will see our hope, we will see our faith. We will see the reality of memory.

---

381 We will also see the redemption of seeing and knowing. If we look back at the very beginnings of humanity's exchanges with God, those of the Garden of Eden, we note that one observation God made about Adam and Eve after the Fall was that, "Now they are like us, knowing good and evil" (Genesis 3:16). While before the Fall Adam and Eve had not known evil, now they do. Good or bad, they "see" it. They know—too well—the dark side of the universe. The way they had seen and known previously is hopelessly gone. Now, like all of us in this present time, they see "as in a riddle," knowing and understanding imperfectly and incompletely. No longer is their desire for communion with God, but for communion with the perverse and violent undersides of creation.

As it now is, apart from stepping into the kingdom of God, for every human being. We live and die in the grip of misplaced longings and desires. When the perfect comes, and we see God as he is (because we are "like" him), knowing as we are fully known, however, this condition will prevail no longer. We will know evil no more, and we will never see "as in a riddle" again. Now we will see perfectly. We will see as God originally intended for us to see. We will know, know intimately and visibly, what is most true, that from which all knowing comes. We will know what is absolutely good and real. The cracks and fissures of the Garden will be gone, their undulations filled with the eternally transforming grace of God. The effects of Adam and Eve's deed will be vanquished and gone.

We will also see the final work of trust. Heretofore we had trusted in not knowing; heretofore we had trusted in not seeing. No longer. We will now see and know the object of our trust. We will touch that which our earthly life of disparate and incomplete memory could never physically conceive. We will come to rest completely in what the fact of being known, in memory, offers. We will take hold of the living impetus and reality of our trust, our hope. In every way, our lives will come together, definitively together, for all eternity. Everything, absolutely everything, will be perfect, and everything, absolutely everything, will be complete.

And wisdom, the wisdom that ensures the presence of memory, will reign.

To quote Isaiah, we will experience God's "name" and "memory" as the deepest desire of our soul (Isaiah 26:8).

So it will be that in knowing and memory, we will find the fulfillment of all the other dimensions of memory we have discussed: memory and love; memory and hope; memory and faith; memory and trust; and memory and wisdom. When we know and are known in full, when we are remember and are remembered absolutely, we will also experience, in equally absolute terms, the rich power of memory and love; the compelling desire of memory and hope; the dark wonder of memory and faith; the necessary ubiquity of memory and trust, and the sustaining fact of memory and wisdom.

In the knowing of memory, we will see it all.

Let's pause to review. After looking at God's memory in six different ways, memory and love; memory and hope; memory and faith; memory and trust; memory and wisdom; and memory and knowing, we see that to experience God in memory is to experience all that God can possibly be for the human being. It is to experience God's unconditional love; the hope found in this love; the joy of faith and trust in this love; the wisdom essential to enabling this activity of this love; and the knowing that inevitably attends this love. God and memory is a highly multi-dimensional phenomenon. In it, we come to know all things, and in it we come to know God. Apart from God and memory, we live and die never really being clear about why we are doing so.

So it is in love, hope, faith, trust, wisdom, and knowing that we participate in the memory of God, that we enter into exchange with the omniscience and sovereignty of our creator. We feel the weight of memory, we touch the freedom of being remembered. We know it all.

Now, however, we face a dilemma. If in the perfect our memory is totally transformed, and if in the perfect we will no longer experience hardship, sadness, and pain, what will happen to the memories which, unpleasant though they may be, have shaped us? What will happen to our memory of the people whom we loved and who enriched us but who are not sharing in our experience of the perfect? How we will remember them? How will we remember our memories? If everything we remember molds us into who we become, and everything we experience becomes part of us, what happens to these things? What becomes of them? As God tells Isaiah, there are things that we, and God, will no longer, on the other side, remember (Isaiah 65:17: "and the former things will not be remembered or come to mind"). And as he urges, earlier in Isaiah,

> "Do not call to mind the former things, or ponder things of the past. Behold I will do something new, now it will spring forth; will you not be aware of it?" (Isaiah 18-19)

How does this work? How can we avoid remembering the past that has taken us into the future, the good as well as the "bad" that "was always there"? And how can we fit what has been into what God indicates he will do, particularly when this is something of which we have no inkling? While for us to experience perfection and completion would seem that we would know everything, it also seems to mean that things which we did not find perfect in our earthly life we will no longer know or see. In addition, it seems that we will no longer even know these things, or at least not in the way we had known them before.[382]

In short, how, in a fully transformed beingness of love, hope, faith, trust, knowing, and memory, do we, and God, forget?

---

382 See Anita Shreve, *Testimony* (New York: Little, Brown and Company, 2008).

FORGETTING ABSENCE, ETERNAL PRESENCE

Although knowing perfectly and fully is to know that which is most true, the truest possible picture of reality, it is also to know that if God is eternally perfect, forever consistent and balanced in all his attributes, he will not cohabit with that which is antithetical to him. He will not live with things counter to his perfectly holy nature. That's why we will not see God until we are like him, and that's why we will not know fully until we are fully known by God as creatures of his eternal realm. It's also why when we see God face to face, we will be as complete and whole as we can possibly be. Like him, we will know only what is consistent with our transformed state, memory, life, and all. Does that mean, as we asked at the close of the last chapter, that when we are on the other side there will be things, people, experiences, and places we will no longer remember, things, people, experiences, and places that for one reason or another are not sufficiently blessed and whole to be part of God's eternal knowing?

That is, given the memories, good and bad, that filled our life and, in their unique and individual way, shaped and grew us, how will we then live in a place that, as the old hymn goes, there is "no sorrow that will not be healed?"[383]

The movie *Inside Out* presents a fascinating take on this issue. Briefly, it's about how five emotions—joy, sadness, disgust, fear, and anger—interact in the mind of a young girl named Riley. As Riley experiences difficulty, "Joy" wants to keep infusing Riley with happy thoughts and memories while keeping "Sadness" and "Anger" at bay. At the end of the movie, however, "Joy" and "Sadness" are forced to work together to help Riley deal with the trauma of her family's move from Minnesota to California. They realize that however much "Joy" may want Riley to be happy, and however much "Sadness" may wish for her to be morose and somber, Riley would not be Riley if she did not remember *all* her memories as she goes forward. Riley would not be Riley if she did not remember everything she had known and seen. As the five "emotions" came to understand, unless Riley experiences the *full* range of her emotions, she will not be a properly adjusted human being.[384]

We are like Riley. We know that memories build on themselves, and we know that what we remember today becomes the foundation of what we do and remember tomorrow. We know that we will carry all of our experiences, good and bad, as we move through life, and that they will never really leave us. We know that even if we do not consciously experience or recall them, we cannot eradicate them altogether. We may discipline ourselves to

---

[383] "Come, Ye Disconsolate," words by Samuel Moore (1779-1852).

[384] *Inside Out,* Walt Disney Pictures, 2015.

stop thinking about them; we may work to avoid becoming dependent on them; and we may strive to dismiss them as having any relevance to our lives today, but neuroscience, as we noted, tells us that they remain. They have made us what we are.[385]

If we then say that on the other side we will no longer remember what was painful and hard, we will no longer remember part of what brought us to this other side. If we say that what we do not wish to remember from this present life we will not recall in the next, what type of creatures will we be like? If we no longer remember what in our earthly existence, good and bad (and sometimes we cannot know, in the present moment, which will eventually be which) has brought us to this experience of fully knowing, will we not be deprived of a significant part of our being? Will we be like robots, programmed, with no part in how it's done, by another (God) to forget, to forget because it's allegedly "bad" for us? Will we be like onlookers in the movie *Men in Black* who, because the protagonists, Kay (played by Tommy Lee Jones) and Jay (played by Will Smith), did not wish for them to remember seeing aliens, would, with a push of a button, lose this memory completely? Will God simply eradicate everything we once were? How will this be?[386]

---

385 This thesis is of course fundamental to Sigmund Freud's vision of the human being. See *Introduction to Psychoanalysis, op cit.* It also underscores the immense difficulty that victims of, variously speaking, torture, sex trafficking, unjust imprisonment, and rape, to name just a few of the traumas that afflict the human race, face in overcoming the effects of those experiences and moving forward with optimism and hope.

386 *Men in Black,* Sony Pictures, 1997. In this movie, the protagonists, who devoted their lives to fighting aliens on the earth, did not,

Indeed: why *should* it be?

Consider Isaiah 65:17, which we mentioned in the previous section. In it, God says,

> "For behold, I create new heavens and a new earth; and the former things will not be remembered or come to mind [or heart: *leb*]." (Isaiah 65:17)

When we are on the other side, when God has ushered us into the permanence of eternity, we, God seems to be saying, will no longer remember what has been. We will no longer recall what we had or who we were. God, so he says, is making us, and everything else, new.

Moreover, as God promises in Isaiah 66, this new heaven and earth will endure eternally. Everything that had once been will be gone forever, thought of and imagined no more (Isaiah 66:22).

It all sounds great. Wouldn't we like to be rid of all our bad memories? Wouldn't we want our unhappy remembrances to be obliterated as supposedly happens to information that is pulled into a black hole?[387]

---

in the interest of public safety, wish for anyone else to be aware that aliens regularly roamed the planet. To ensure this would happen, they used a device that voided the memories of anyone else who saw such aliens. Consider also Aldous Huxley's vision of humans as totally programmable and, consequently, devoid of choice making capacity beings in his *Brave New World* (New York: Harper, 2006).

387 Although more recently, as a famous bet between cosmologists Stephen Hawking and Kip Thorne makes clear, perhaps the real story is not that, in a way that scientists are still

Perhaps. But is this really what we want? As Svetlana Alliluyeva, whom we have identified previously as Josef Stalin's daughter, remarked after she divorced Wesley Peters, her first American husband, that, "[Despite it all], I cannot get rid of the good memories I have [of him]." Given that so much of what we find to be good often occurs in the midst of what we find to be distasteful, sandwiched and mixed with seasons of downturn, we look at total mnemonic erasure with caution.[388]

In Revelation 21 (a chapter to which we referred a couple of times before), the writer (really, more an observer[389]), the apostle John, says that,

> "And he [God] will wipe away every tear from their eyes; and there will no longer be any death; there will no longer be any mourning, or crying, or pain; the first things have passed away. And He [God]

---

struggling to understand precisely, all information is lost but rather that it is dissembled and broken into incoherency. See http://physicsworld.com/cws/article/news/2004/jul/22/hawking-loses-black-hole-bet.

388 *Stalin's Daughter*, 429.

389 The book of Revelation, the final book of the Bible, presents John's recounting of a vision he had while in exile on the island of Patmos in the eastern Aegean Sea. It is a vision of how the world will come to an end, God's kingdom is consummated, and space and time are transformed into eternity. For intriguing perspectives on this scenario, see Elaine Pagels's *Revelations: Visions, Prophecy, and Politics in the Book of Revelation* (New York: Penguin, 2012).

> who sits on the throne said, 'Behold, I am making all things new.'"

In the next chapter, chapter twenty-two, John further writes,

> "They [the believers] will see His [God] face, and His name will be on their foreheads. And there will no longer be any night; and they will not have need of the light of a lamp nor the light of the sun, because the Lord God will illumine them; and they will reign forever and ever."

No longer, John says, will we worry about death, no longer will we cry or mourn, no longer will we experience pain. All these things will be gone. But what will we know, what will we remember when God makes everything—absolutely everything—new? What will we know and remember when God is our only light and night, visibly and metaphorically, is altogether gone? What will we know if what we knew, everything that made us who we are, is totally eradicated? What will we be like if we do not remember our journey, if, paradoxically enough, we do not remember our memory?

Many years ago, I heard a pastor talk about this passage in Isaiah. "I'm thankful," he said, "for these words. It means that when I am in heaven I will not remember the pain I've experienced in this life."

Not remembering pain is one thing. Not remembering how this pain may have shaped, guided, or illumined us, however, is another. Would we really wish to forget how our pain may have in fact brought us to the point where we believed in God and are now on the other side? Would we really wish to forget or give up the suffering that led us to insight and joy? Would we really want to not remember the contents of our life journey? Would we really wish to never know our life on earth again? In truth, even if we identify with Ecclesiastes' many moans about life's futility, most of us will also respond that life is, on balance, overwhelmingly good. Most of us do not believe that the person who, as Ecclesiastes says, "has never seen the evil activity that is done under the sun," is really "better" off than the person who has had opportunity to experience life in the fullness of its multiple joys and vexations. By and large, we are thankful we are here.[390]

Moreover, what if we do not remember those we have known, those who, for one reason or another, did not find the doorway to eternity with God? What if we do not know, much less remember those we loved who are not experiencing being fully known by God? What if we do not know or remember those who may have been most dear to us? How can we possibly enjoy eternity if we do not know and remember the people in our earthly life with whom we enjoyed its richest pleasures? Would we wish to spend

---

390 On this conundrum, see, among many others, C. S. Lewis, *A Grief Observed* (New York: HarperOne, 2015); William E. Marsh, *Imagining Eternity: A Journey Towards Meaning* (Indianapolis: Author House, 2007); and Thomas Merton, *The Seven Storey Mountain* (New York: Mariner, 2009). On Ecclesiastes, see Ecclesiastes 1:1, 1:11, and 4:3, to name just a few. Consider as well George Borrow's words about the joy of life which we cited earlier: given what most of us deem to be the alternative, we appreciate being alive and well on the earth.

eternity in "blissful" ignorance of those whom we held most joyfully in our previous existence? Would we be satisfied to live in "blessed" unawareness of whom in our life had been most wonderful to us?

Conversely, if we did remember these people, how would we do so? Would we *want* to remember them? Would we want to remember that they are not with us? Would we be sad that they are not with us? Will we despair for their eternal destiny, that they did not come to fully know and be fully known, when we are experiencing these in full? Will we remember them with grief? How would this be consistent with fully knowing and remembering in a perfect afterlife? How would this be consistent with living in the eternal love of God?

Would we want to see the many good times and wondrous stories we shared with these people in the course of our lives together become, as many Norwegians say, "glemmeboka," forever lost in the "Book of Forgetting"?[391]

These are exceedingly difficult questions. Few of us would like to forget those whom we loved. Few of us would like to live as though we had never known our friends and loved ones. We treasured our friends and loved ones in this life; why would we not wish to treasure them in the next? Each one contributed to the goodness and pleasure of our life on earth. In more ways than we can count, they've made us who we are. How could we forget them altogether? How could we enjoy knowing and being known in full while also knowing that those whom we loved most are not with us?

---

391 On the "Book of Forgetting," See *Welcome to the Goddamn Ice Cube* (New York: HarperCollins, 2016), Blair Braverman's memoir of her adventures in northern Norway.

Unfortunately, though from an intellectual standpoint we may be able to construct answers to these questions, emotionally we will likely be unable to do so. As one of my professors in graduate school, talking about the spiritual inclinations of his daughter, once told me, "Intellectually, I can accept that she may not be with me in heaven. Emotionally, however, it's a far different story."

In the end, we face paradox. We are looking at two things that are both true, yet two things which, when put together, we find nearly impossible to grasp. Indeed, we may even experience revulsion: why, our loving God, must this be?

On the one hand, as we have observed, the ultimate outcome of having faith in the hope and faithfulness of God's memory is fully knowing and being fully known and remembered by God. Enabled by the eternal memory of God, we and our memory will be perfected and complete. On the other hand, tragically, not everyone will choose to exercise faith and trust in the love, hope, and faithfulness of God's memory. Not everyone will decide to put her trust in the hope that God is actively remembering her, in this life as well as the next. Unfortunately, I know dozens of people who, unless they open their hearts to God, may fall into this category at their life's end. With enormous pain, I must conclude that theirs will be a knowing and remembering that will be far from complete, a knowing and remembering that will be rife with eternal doubt and uncertainty. They will never know God fully, they will never see him face to face. They will be lost for eternity. I'll never see them again. Ever.

As long as we live on this side of the afterlife, we live with tension and contradiction. We can speculate as to exactly what our memory will be like, we can wonder as to precisely how we will remember. We can ruminate on what it will mean to know fully or how it will be to be fully known. We can wonder what perfection of knowing and memory will be like. And we can ponder what the experience of those who do not will be like in turn. We can think about these things for the rest of our earthly lives. We can dwell in the pain they bring us until the day we die.

But we'll never know. We will never know the full picture. This side of eternity, we will never know, fully, how these things fit together. For now, we know only mystery, a profound and vexing mystery. Imperfect creatures that we are, we cannot now possibly be able to conceive, fully, what perfection is like, what it is to be perfect and complete, in memory as well as in all other things. As creatures who do not know or remember everything, we falter and stumble when we attempt to grasp what knowing or remembering in full actually means. We of temporality cannot take full hold of what it is not.

We only know this. In some unfathomable and presently unexplainable way, when we know fully and are fully known, we will experience memory in a way we could not have experienced it before. We will experience it not as creatures of proleptic flesh but as fully spiritual beings. We will remember as creatures of eternity.

But this solves nothing. We're simply shunting our dilemma into a facile acknowledgement of the impenetrability of "celestial" knowing. We've done no more than agree with Job who, as he drew his remarkable soliloquy to a close, realized that all he can know is that God knows and can do infinitely more than he can know and understand. That's it: nothing more, nothing less. As he says in chapter 42,

> "I know that You [God] can do all things, and that no purpose of Yours can be thwarted. 'Who is this who hides counsel without knowledge?' [Job is repeating what God said to him earlier] Therefore I have declared that which I do not understand, things too wonderful for me, which I did not know." (Job 42:3-4)

In the end, we're still prisoners of our finitude. We're still plagued by the puzzles of time and space, the exasperating conundrums of incomplete knowing. We're still befuddled by our insufficient grasp of the earthly contingencies of truth and reality.

We're still walking in the dark.

Let's shift gears. If the perfect has come and God knows us in full, knowing him means that we will know only what is holy and good. We will not know anything imperfect, we will not remember anything imperfect. We will remember what is good, in the truest sense, to remember. We will remember a perfect synthesis of past and present, an impeccably consistent collage of what has happened and what is happening now. Who we were and who we are will come together, in memory, flawlessly, holistically, and beautifully.

Yet because the planet on which we lived our earthly life was fractured and broken, structurally as well as spiritually, all of our memories of that life will be imperfect, too. From the most significant to the most trivial, the most memorable to the most forgettable, our remembrances will be imperfect. We had them in a life lived in a bent world, a world in bondage to the specter of impending death and certain sin. We had our memories in a life whose certitude of end we had carried from the day we became aware of it. However wonderful we may have found these memories to be, we must realize that they occurred in the midst of fallenness and finitude. They were fundamentally incomplete. However good they may have been, they were not commensurate with the full meaning of reality.

Yet this is simply using our present brokenness to justify the coming perfection which we expect to enjoy. It solves nothing. We are still left with tension, bravely but perhaps insincerely telling ourselves that what we have now will matter little in the light of what we will have next. We're still looking for relief.

What do we do? Consider the person of Jesus. As the New Testament tells us, even though he was God, Jesus took on human flesh and became a human being. He took on all the pain, vagaries, and hardships of being human. In addition, as a human, he died one of the most painful of deaths that humanity, in all of its perverted glory, had yet devised (2 Corinthians 5:21; Philippians 2:5-11; 1 Peter 2:23-24). As the writer of the letter to the Hebrews tells us, however, Jesus did so for "the joy set before him." He "endured the cross, despising its shame [so as to one day] sit down at the right hand of the throne of God" (Hebrews 12:2). Jesus willingly lived as a human being to fulfill the mission God had given him. He knew very well the joy of being known by God that awaited him (see also his words in John 17:24: "Father [God], I desire that they [the apostles] also, whom You have given Me, be with Me where I am, so that they may see My glory which You have given Me, for You loved Me before the foundation of the world.").[392]

We must therefore ask ourselves this: how does Jesus, safely settled on the other side, his life's directive fulfilled for all time, remember his suffering? How does he remember his pain? How does he remember being a human being?

More perhaps unanswerable questions. Nonetheless, let's look at the etymology of the Hebrew and Greek words for "new." Both the Hebrew (*chadesh*) and the Greek (*kainos*) words for new describe a "new" or state of newness that has no direct or morphological connection to what existed before it. It is a newness without antecedent, a newness that does not depend on existing materials to be what it is. It's totally different, wholly set apart. *Chadesh* and *kainos* point to a newness that, all things being equal, previous circumstance could not have possibly created, predicted, or explained. It is not the newness of a car, house, or birthday cake. These are ordinary and predictable points of pleasure, no more than recycled expressions of the furtive happiness of transience. *Chadesh and kainos* are not even the newness of a spring, the annual rebirth of a long slumbering land

---

392 On this, consider the Roman response to a slave revolt, led by Spartacus, of 73 B.C. As the historian Appian tells it, when he had finally suppressed the uprising, the Roman general Crassus proceeded to crucify not one, not two, but fully *6,000* of Spartacus's followers on the road between Rome and Capua (*Civil War,* 1:120).

which, for all its astonishment and brilliance, is in essence no different from its many predecessors.[393]

The newness of *chadesh* and *kainos* is a newness without precedent. It is unlike any newness we have known before. Before it, we will be dazzled and amazed. We will stand in awe before its unexpected strength and power. *Chadesh* and *kainos* portray a newness that has no visible precursor, a newness that, regardless of how carefully we work with what is before us, we will never, ever make. *Chadesh* and *kainos* present a newness that will trump all notions of cause and effect, all boundaries of space time linkage.[394]

And that's the point. We understand that, in Jesus' case, God made all things new. But we cannot understand,

---

393 In his *Anna Karenin,* Leo Tolstoy beautifully describes this spring as a time when, "the ice on the river began to crack and slide away, and the turbid, frothing torrents flowed more swiftly . . . the sun rose brilliant . . . and the warm air all around vibrated with the vapor given off by the awakening earth." But it is still spring, a spring that has come many, many times before. See Leo Tolstoy, *Anna Karenin,* trans. Rosemary Edmonds (New York: Penguin, 1954), Part II, chapter 13.

394 "*Kainos*" in *TDNT,* Vol. III; "*chadesh*" in *TDOT,* Vol. IV. See also 2 Corinthians 5:17, "Therefore, if any one is Christ, she is a new creation; the old things have passed away and all things have become new." One obvious example of this type of newness is spiritual rebirth. See William James's *Varieties of Religious Experience* (*op cit.)* for multiple vignettes of spiritual rebirth and change; Fyodor Dostoyevsky's account of spiritual conversion in his *Notes from the Underground* (New York: Watchmaker, 2010); and my *Imagining Eternity, op cit.* In addition, consider the concept of creation *ex nihlio,* the idea that God made the world, not from nothing and nothingness, but from nothing at all.

in this life, how he accomplished this. We cannot grasp the content of a newness wrought and effectuated by God alone. We falter when we try to comprehend a newness without connection to what we see. It's beyond our mortal capabilities. We cannot therefore understand how Jesus no longer remembers—but in fact "remembers" (for he lives eternally as the final mediator between humanity and God)—his pain. How could we? We are not God. All we know is that today Jesus sits in the active presence of God, totally shorn of his earthly existence yet always inhabiting it, forever and always the eternal fount of all life and meaning, in earth as well as in heaven. Yes, he will be the God-man for all eternity, and yes, the hosts of heaven will uphold him as the sacrificial Lamb of God without end, but how he experiences this and how God accomplished it, how God reached into Jesus and transformed him, this complex being of human and divine nature conjoining, we simply cannot know. Though we can certainly explain the theological framework of Jesus' labors, and though we can certainly know, in this life, its result and its benefits for us, we cannot now see the full frame of its inner intricacies and essence. And we certainly cannot grasp precisely how God, physically as well as spiritually, effected it.

Similarly, while we know that, as Paul writes, Jesus "became sin for us," and as the author of Hebrews states, "learned" from his pain (2 Corinthians 5:21; Hebrews 5:8), we cannot know precisely how all this happened. All we know is that as we have observed repeatedly, God is entirely able to make *all* things new. Somehow, some way, God is able to make Jesus' memory, the teeming caldron of all the time, space, and remembrance of his earthly existence, something fit for eternity, something so good, something so new, something so holy that its full reality is beyond our grasp.

God's newness of memory will be a newness of memory which we cannot now even come close to touching. It will be the culmination of a hiddenness which only the patterns of eternity will reveal, a picture of change heretofore wholly absent from even the outermost limits of our speculations. It will fracture and implode everything we have previously known.

And yet it is a reality imminently available to us. Though God is apophatic, mysteriously removed from yet entirely present in what we see, he can decisively bend all things mortal to the measure of his eternal realm. God is a being who is entirely able to do things utterly beyond us, a being whose power we cannot fully measure.[395] As he tells Isaiah, "I am God, and there is no other" (Isaiah 45:5) and, later, Jeremiah, "I am the Lord, is anything too difficult for me?" (Jeremiah 32:27).[396]

Yet even though, as Proverbs 19:21 observes, "the counsel [and intentions] of God will always stand," as it was for Jesus, so it will be for us. Jesus, the gospel writers tell us, struggled with his limited earthly picture of his destiny

---

395 See also Ephesians 3:20, which states that God "is able to do far more abundantly beyond all that we ask or think, according to the power that works within us."

396 See Hebrews 2:17-18: "Therefore, He [Jesus] had to be made like His brethren in all things, so that He might become a merciful and faithful high priest in things pertaining to God, to make propitiation for the sins of the people. For since He Himself was tempted in that which He has suffered, He is able to come to the aid of those who are tempted."

(see Matthew 26:39-44; Mark 14:35-39; Luke 22:21-22), and so will we. This side of death, we will never understand, fully, much less know, fully, how God will transform our memory. Although we may see it, in part, in the wonder of our own spiritual conversion, we do not see it in full. Like Job, like Paul, like countless other people throughout the pages of scripture, we see in this life, to use Paul's words once more, "in a riddle." We just don't know. And until we reach the end, we never will. All we know is that God promises to make all things new, things so remarkable and amazing that, as God says in the forty-eighth chapter of Isaiah, "have been hidden, which you [human beings] have not known" (Isaiah 48:6).

Until then, the "riddle remains."[397]

So does Paul write in the eleventh chapter of his letter to the church at Rome,

> "Oh, the depths of the riches both of the wisdom and knowledge of God! How unsearchable are his judgments and unfathomable his ways! For who has known the mind of the Lord, or who became His counselor? Or who has first given to Him

[397] See John 3:1-16, in which Jesus advised Nicodemus, a member of the Sanhedrin who came to him at night to ask a question about his ministry, "Do not be amazed that I said to you, 'You must be born again.' The wind blows where it wishes and you hear the sound of it, but do not know where it comes from and where it is going; so is everyone who is born of the Spirit'" (John 3:7-8).

> that it might be paid back to Him again?"
> (Romans 11:33-35)[398]

God's "understanding is inscrutable," Isaiah proclaims (Isaiah 40:28). Though this can be frustrating, it's fully true. This is why in the end, we will—indeed, we must—give into the heart of God.[399]

Of course, for those of us who pride themselves on obtaining precise knowledge of all things and who insist on having what they consider to be empirical evidence for all conclusions, this is confounding. Why should we accept something on the basis of incomplete knowledge or evidence? Why should we embrace something on the levers of its absence?

To this, we offer two counters. One, even science admits that there are things it may never understand, things that it will never be able to prove fully. Why do mathematical theorems always work? Why do we have these physical laws (electromagnetism, gravity, and the strong and weak nuclear

---

398 See also Deuteronomy 29:29a, which states that, "The secret things belong to the Lord our God."

399 This *contra* the words with which Stephen Hawking closed his *Brief History of Time,* that in solving the conundrums of life's origins, "We shall understand the mind of God." See *Brief History of Time, op cit.* In addition, we think of Paul's words in the second chapter of 1 Corinthians that, "We have the mind of Christ." Paul does not mean that we will understand everything that God does, but that as believers in him we will receive supernatural guidance and insight in our existential deliberations. We will see the world through God's eyes. Nonetheless, we will never see everything.

force, to name a few) and not others? What existed before the Big Bang? How do we verify "nothingness"?[400]

Two, we think of Ecclesiastes 3:11, which we mentioned twice before. Though we want desperately to know, we cannot. And we never will. We must therefore trust the God who does. We must trust the one who knows everything, even things we hope we never need to know.

As John Locke, whom we discussed earlier in our review of the history of memory, once noted,

> "What a darkness we are involved in, how little it is of Being, and the things that are, that we are capable to know," and that we must "sometimes be content to be very ignorant."[401]

Realizing that we do indeed walk in a kind of epistemological ignorance in this life, we therefore resolve

---

[400] See Karl Giberson, "Cosmos from Nothing?" in *The Christian Century*, June 10, 2015. Consult also the review of Thomas Nagel's *Mind and Cosmos: Why the Materialist Neo-Darwinian Conception of Nature is almost Certainly False*, in *The New Yorker*, July 16, 2013; and Noson S. Yanofsky's *The Outer Limits of Reason: What Science, Mathematics, and Logic Cannot Tell Us* (Cambridge, Massachusetts: MIT, 2015), which opens with a quote attributed to Albert Einstein, "As the circle of light increases, so does the circumference of darkness." In addition, consider Siddhartha Mukherjee's *The Gene: An Intimate History* (New York: Scribner, 2016), which leaves us wondering just how much weight we ought to give to what we had always thought was the key to our identity: our genes. We simply cannot know everything about ourselves or the world.

[401] *Essay Concerning Human Understanding,* Vol II, Book IV, III, 29.

to, yes, believe in what we see, but in addition purpose to believe in what we now cannot—for we acknowledge that it encompasses and explains what we now in part experience—the eternal counsel of God.[402]

In addition, we offer evangelist Billy Graham's observation on heaven:

> "Think of having complete fulfillment, knowing that our homecoming brings unspeakable joy to our wonderful Lord! So why do we prefer lingering here? Because we are not only earthbound in body; we are earthbound in our thinking. But when we leave this place, we will never dwell on it again. Our eyes and hearts will be fixed on Christ."[403]

Or as theologian Jason Byassee puts it,

> "And God has a future so remarkable we won't even remember Exodus, we won't even remember resurrection. We'll only remember God and all God's beloved children."[404]

---

402 As Stephen Hawking observes in his *A Brief History of Time, op cit.,* the universe is finite yet without boundary.

403 Billy Graham, *Where I Am: Heaven, Eternity, and Our Life Beyond* (New York: Thomas Nelson, 2015).

404 "Between a Rock and Arising," Jason Byassee, *Sojourners,* March 2016.

As troubling as it may be from an emotional standpoint to contemplate not seeing a loved one in heaven, we must recognize the facts: more than likely, when we stand in God's unique and wholly "new" newness, we will no longer think about what has now forever passed away.

How this will happen, however, we cannot now know.

Yet if God is omniscient, and if God somehow makes our memories seminally new, we see another problem. Does God forget? Outwardly, it seems as if God, the eternally omniscient being, would not be able to forget anything. It seems as if he would remember everything for all time. But he doesn't. Consider that, as a previous footnote stated, the Bible repeatedly tells us that when we come into a saving relationship with God, he "forgets" our sins. When we genuinely know God, when we are truly known and remembered by God, we come to understand that, in a way we find difficult to grasp fully, he no longer has any memory of our sins.

Describing the new covenant (a covenant with which Jesus, on the eve of his death, identified himself (Luke 22:20)) in Jeremiah 31, God says, "I will remember their [Israel's] sins no more." Everything is forgiven, everything is forgotten. "As far as the East is from the West," God says in Psalm 103, "so far have I pushed away their [Israel's] sins." In the eyes of God, come the new age, Israel's sins are gone, gone completely. He's forgotten them, totally. Their sins happened, yes, but God will not let them in any way affect or color the way he sees his chosen people. He loves them unconditionally, and fully intends to carry them in his arms through this life and safely into the next.

As God will do for everyone else who comes to trust in his memory, love, and presence. As the writer of Hebrews says in the final chapter of his letter, God, "will never ever, no never [the literal meaning of the Greek] abandon or forsake" his beloved (Hebrews 13:5).[405]

How can this be?[406]

We do best to look at this question metaphorically. So magnanimous is God's holiness, so transforming is his righteousness that although God remains well aware that those who put their trust in him remain sinners and continue to transgress and violate his ways, the mysterious and, to us, hidden confluence of his person and attributes enables him to "forget" these things in light of that which his righteousness has accomplished in the sacrifice of Christ. As God in his righteousness has forgiven sin, so he in his love "forgets" the sins of those who accept his offer of absolution and forgiveness. The essence of his eternality is such that, for

---

[405] This works both ways. When after God told the prophet Jonah to preach about him to the Assyrian capital Nineveh, universally acknowledged as the center of the most feared empire of its day, Jonah fled the country. He boarded a ship, and after a storm hit it, asked to be thrown overboard (he knew the storm was God's way of telling him to fulfill his mission), saying that this would stop the storm. It did. For better or worse, God didn't forget Jonah (Jonah 1–4). Nor regardless of our ups or downs will he forget us. Yet consider Ezekiel 25, in which God tells the prophet that he will ensure that, "the sons of Ammon will not be remembered among the nations." In addition, consult Psalm 139 as well as two passages we discussed earlier, John 10:27-28, and Romans 8:38-39. Somehow, God remembers forever as much as he also forgets, forever. How, we cannot know.

[406] We think here of Charles Wesley's hymn which we cited earlier, "And Can It Be That I Should Gain?"

God, although he is the absolute judge of the universe and is therefore perfectly aware of his children's flaws, God no longer sees his children as lost and forsaken sinners. He sees them as part of his family. And he will never stop working in them (again: Philippians 1:6).

As Paul tells the churches of Galatia, "In the fullness of time," God intervened in human affairs to create a way that he, the holy God, could undo, on behalf of his human creation, the effects of its sin. God, not humanity, solved humanity's dilemma of angst, alienation, and guilt. Finite and sinful as it was, humanity could never have undone or unraveled its sin. Only God could do that. And he did. In Jesus Christ, God did it all. In Jesus' sacrifice on the cross, God reconciled humanity to himself and made himself able to forgive its sins (2 Corinthians 5:19).[407]

So Paul writes in his second letter to the church at Corinth, a passage to which we referred earlier,

> "He [God] made Him [Jesus] who knew no sin to be sin on our behalf, so that we might become the righteousness of God in Him." (2 Corinthians 5:21)

As the only one who could take on ("become") sin to conquer it, God really can "forget" the sins of those who appropriate the fruits of God's victory. As an eternal and infinite being, God lives (exists) in a continuous present, an

---

[407] For more on this, see Wolfhart Pannenberg, *Jesus: God and Man*, trans. Lewis L. Wilkens and Duane A. Priebe (Philadelphia: Westminster, 1968); and Oliver Crisp, *God Incarnate: Explorations in Christology* (New York: Bloomsbury Academic, 2009).

eternal endlessness that subsists and inhabits beyond space and time. As he is, so he does, and as he does, so he is. God is holy and just and loving and forgetting all at once, all the time. What he has been, he always will be. Out of all creation, God is the only being who can fully forget sin even while he is fully loving those who turn to him.[408]

Is God's forgetting, however, merely metaphorical, an analogical twist to help us understand what Jesus has done? Clearly, if God's forgetting is to have any real effect, it must be more than metaphorical. It must be fact. And it is: God really does forget. As do we. We forget according to who we are and how we are made, and so does God. However, God's forgetting accrues to our benefit, whereas ours does not always do so for ours. Does God's forgetting contribute to his benefit? If God loves humanity and wishes for each member of it to be known by him and see him face to face, then, yes, God's forgetting does indeed contribute to his pleasure and benefit. It is good for us, we frail and sinful beings, that God forgets. Conversely, it is not as good for us, broken as we are, that we forget, be it things in this world or, much worse, God.[409]

This, however, raises a very troubling and dark question. It is this: does God ever forget human beings? If God created everyone, does God forget those who once lived in "the land of the living" (Psalm 27) in which he placed them?

---

[408] Earlier, we mentioned the English writer C. S. Lewis. For an intriguing, somewhat magical take on this process, consider reading Lewis's *The Lion, the Witch, and the Wardrobe,* one of the volumes in his *Chronicles of Narnia,* which we mentioned earlier. Those who love fantasy will find it particularly good.

[409] On analogy, us, and God, see *Analogical Imagination, op cit.*

Does God remember those who do not remember—those who forget—him? Or as the psalmist asks, "Will Your wonders [Lord] be made known in the darkness? And Your righteousness in the land of forgetfulness?" (Psalm 88:12). How will God remember in the darkness, the darkness that Jude chillingly describes as "the black darkness [literally, "blackness of darkness"] [that is] forever" (Jude 13)?

How will God remember people who did not know and remember him and who, upon death, are forever gone from his presence?

According to the twentieth chapter of Revelation, at the Great White Throne Judgment, God will resurrect and acknowledge and make known everything about everyone who ever lived. God will look back on all of history and all that filled and comprised it, and reflect on and judge it. He will assess every human being and his or her life. He will acknowledge whether a particular person will join her family for eternity or, conversely, whether this particular person will not. God will do so because he remembers. Although he has "forgotten" the sins of some, he has not forgotten the sins of others, those who did not avail themselves of his salvific work. He will, tragically for them, remember their sins forever (Revelation 20:11-15; see also Matthew 25).

Is God's memory therefore selective? Not really: it simply reflects who he, in the entirety of his essence, is. As we noted, all at once and all the time, God is holy, loving, righteous, mnemonic, and just. So we must ask our question again. Once these individuals are no longer in God's presence, will God continue to remember them? Will he continue to remember them as creatures made in his image? Will he continue to remember them as beings who came into, lived, and died in the world he made? Even if they are existing in a realm utterly apart from him, forever and irretrievably removed from his presence, will he, their creator and maker, remember them?

This are insuperably painful questions. Let's think again about the person of God and the tension that we humans daily encounter in trying to interpret and understand it. If God is holiness, righteousness, and love continuously and all at once, then somehow, in ways we cannot fully grasp, he will remember these unfortunates for all eternity, forever and ever and ever and ever, even if he never has contact with them again. His holiness, righteousness, and love demand and, regrettably for these people, ensure it.

Will this make God sad? Will this spoil his eternity with those who love him? Though it seems as if it would, it also seems as if it would not. God will remember in his love, yet he will remember in his righteousness. He will remember in his benevolence, yet he will remember in his holiness. Only God knows how he will balance everything in this regard. And he will balance it perfectly.

But what's "perfectly"? Sadly, we cannot know.[410]

This is sound and true theology. Emotionally, however, it feels as raw as the roughest sandpaper. Because in this life darkness, spiritual, physical, and otherwise, is all too real, we have great difficulty thinking beyond it, even in eternity. Questioned as to whether he planned to be anywhere near the prison in Terre Haute, Indiana, when his son, Oklahoma bomber Timothy McVeigh, was executed, McVeigh's father, Bill, responded, "Would you want to watch your son die?"

---

[410] So does the psalmist say, "God's understanding is infinite (or innumerable)" (Psalm 147:5).

Though Mr. McVeigh made clear that he loved his son Timothy, he also understood the severity of his son's crime and had resigned himself to the penalty the jury assigned to it. But he didn't want to watch it carried out.

Will he, however, ever stop thinking about it? It's very unlikely. His darkness will remain with him to the day he dies.[411]

On the other hand, God *can* stop thinking about darkness. God *can* forget. As one who perfectly balances holiness, righteousness, memory, and love, God understands and forgets, simultaneously and forever. And this applies even if, as we observed, in some mysterious and unfathomable way, he, as the omniscient God, does not.

Consider the etymology of forgetting. The Latin roots of "forgetting" picture it as the opposite of remembering, a sort of "anti-remembering." While to "get" is to acquire, receive, or remember something, to "forget" is to lose or cease to remember that something. What we once had, we have no longer. It's gone.

The Greek roots of forgetting further illuminate this picture. The Greek word for "forget" is *lethos* (so was the Greek god of forgetting called Lethe). The Greek word for truth is *alethia.* What we see is that *lethos* is a part of *altheia.* Hence, to forget is to, as it were, "lose" or "fall away" from the truth. It is a sort of "untruth." When we forget, when we overlook a fact of our experience or reality in general, we are, in a way, "forgetting" what is (or has been) true. To forget is to miss or fail to any longer realize what is true or correct about a particular dimension of our experience of

---

411 See http://www.nytimes.com/2001/04/29/us/a-father-feels-the-weight-of-his-son-s-sins.html

reality. We no longer "have" what we did before. It is now "untruth" to us.[412]

In addition, we should note that buried in *alethia's* picture of truth is the idea of discovering what has been hidden, to uncover and unpack what a fact might reveal. To invest in truth is to find something that one had not found before, something which is fully congruent with reality and the nature of existence but which one has not to this point seen. To see truth is to see the disclosure of another aspect of what has always been true about life and living, but which until now we did not know. It is to see what we had not experienced before yet which we now realize corresponds to what's genuinely real. If as we live we seek truth, we are therefore seeking to discover the essential facts, the true and genuine nature of this peculiar experience of being conscious and sentient beings.

Consequently, when we forget, we are failing to see what is real or true about life and existence. We miss the point. Oddly, forgetting and truth are inseparable.

Knowing this, we can set the idea of God's forgetting in a larger framework, one invested in the notion of truth. What's truth? Though this is a highly complicated question, we will say that, without going into a great deal of intricate philosophical detail, truth is,

> "Generally and roughly speaking, that which corresponds to reality, that which lines up with what we believe, on our best and worst of days, is an accurate picture of our reality. If something is truth, it will

---

412 "*aletheia*" in *TDNT,* Vol. I.

> agree with reality, not necessarily reality as we know, perceive, and experience it, but reality as it really is. Truth is something that faithfully represents, reflects, and explains reality as it is."[413]

In other words, truth is what is most real, in the broadest possible sense.

As the Bible makes clear, God is truth (Psalm 119:160; John 1:17; John 14:6). God is the ultimate arbiter and definer of reality and that which corresponds to it in the cosmos. When God "forgets" something, when something has become a sort of "untruth" to him, it has therefore ceased to have any genuine reality. It has become something inconsistent with what "somethingness" is. It is neither created nor creator. It has no presence at all.

---

413 *It's All in a Word, op cit.*, 73. Also, see Gerald Vision, *Veritas: The Correspondence Theory and Its Critics* (Cambridge, Massachusetts: MIT, 2004) as well as "The Semantic Conception of Truth" by Albert Tarski in *Truth*, edited by Simon Blackburn and Keith Simmons (Oxford: Oxford University, 1999). In addition, consult Eric Dodson, "Heidegger in Twelve Minutes," https://www.youtube.com/watch?v=A04RhtR0imY&app=desktop.

This in turn invites another question: what is reality? Again, without getting lost in metaphysical muddles, let's describe reality as the total breadth of our experience. Here, however, we encounter a roadblock. Some of us will argue that reality is limited to what we can see, hear, and taste with our present senses, that whatever we learn through our senses is the sum of reality. Anything we cannot see or hear is therefore not reality. As we have noted repeatedly, however, reality must be physical *and* metaphysical, the latter encompassing and enabling the former.

Devoid of all connection to what is real, it becomes something of which truth cannot possibly know or conceive. It has neither content nor meaning.

Yet in a metaphysical universe guided by an eternal and sovereign God, the absence of physical presence does not void presence altogether. As in a meaningful universe all things have purpose and point, so does the absence of such things have purpose and point, too. Even though those whom God does not remember will one day be forever apart from his presence, their inherent meaningfulness ensures that they will not one day cease to exist altogether. "Untruth" to God but nonetheless part of the truth of eternity, space, and time, these poor souls nonetheless remain, forever present, yet forever abandoned and set aside by that which has given them life, presence, and point. Ever here, but ever not, they are caught in an endless and unlockable vise of eternal death, existing, sensing, and lasting, but in the darkest possible sense.

Or as the "mad" professor Frankenstein says in the movie of the same name about the "being" he has made, "This creature has never lived." The monster had neither been born nor had it died. But it is here.[414]

Similarly, talking about Judas Iscariot at the Last Supper, the night before he was crucified, Jesus remarked, "It would been good for that man if he had not been born." Though Judas is "here," and always, in some form, will be, he really is not here. He is forever apart from the presence of all that could possibly be "here," all that is real and true. Most importantly, he is forever apart from God (Matthew 26:24).

---

414 *Frankenstein,* Universal Pictures, 1931.

It would have indeed been better if Judas had never been born.

So we ought to think, with pain and trepidation, about those who did not choose to remember God and whom God did not remember in turn. Because God is not remembering them, they have become, as it were, "untruth" to him. They are no longer part of his world, no longer present in his experience of existence. They are no longer in the compass of his presence. They cannot be: they are "untruth." These people are inconsistent with what is true, incompatible with what ought to be. Although given the purposefulness of the cosmos, they exist, somewhere, yet as far as God is concerned, they no longer exist as existence is. They are somewhere, but in fact they are nowhere. No longer do they inhabit God's world, no longer do they move in his reality, his total reality of absolute truth and presence. Indeed, they *cannot.*

As C. S. Lewis observes in his *The Great Divorce,*

> "Evil can be undone, but it cannot 'develop' into good. Time does not heal it. The spell must be unwound, bit by bit, 'with backward mutters of dissevering power'—or else not. It is still 'either/or.' If we insist on keeping Hell (or even earth) we shall not see Heaven: if we accept Heaven we shall not be able to retain even the smallest and most intimate souvenirs of Hell."[415]

---

415 C. S. Lewis, *The Great Divorce* (New York: Simon & Schuster, 1946), 10.

God cannot remember that which is not part of who he is. That is the nature of perfection. If perfection evinced any loss or degradation, it would no longer be perfect.

Nonetheless, the question remains: does God remember those whom he "forgets"? Only as he remembers all things continuously and forever. He is remembering them, as difficult as this is for us to understand, as entities that are really no longer, in his view of the universe, "real" or "true."

Yet God grieves. He so desperately wants for this to be otherwise. He so very much desires that all whom he created be with him for eternity. As one writer suggests,

> "God remembers, even cherishes, all our attempts to work with God at banishing the one thing even God cannot abide—being alone, unknown, and forgotten."[416]

And as the apostle Peter observes,

> "The Lord is not slow about his promise, as some count slowness, but is patient toward you, not wishing for any to perish but for all to come to repentance." (2 Peter 3:9)

But if people do not work with God, he cannot work with them. So with immense sadness, holiness, righteousness, and regret, God forgets. He lets these people go. He abandons them to their destiny. For those to whom this happens, this will be a very, very lonely existence. They

[416] Frederick A. Niedner, "The Mystery of Marriage" in *The Christian Century*, July 8, 2015.

will be alone, utterly, utterly alone forever and forever. For now and all time and eternity, they will see no one, absolutely no one, ever again, eternally existing in a bitter and endless consciousness of abject and unyielding isolation and darkness.

This is surely a frightening thought, a thought that, try as we might, we will never completely understand. After all, eternity or not, we're created creatures. We live to commune with each other, to communicate, reach out, and love those whose paths we cross. We live to be a human being in the company of other human beings. We cannot fully comprehend how it will be to exist being aware of our need to commune yet never being able to engage in it, to exist as humans yet to do so as humans who can no longer be human.

This side of eternity, we cannot imagine what it will be like to *not* be, as the prophet Zechariah puts it, sitting, known and remembered, content and at peace, under our "vine and fig tree" in the coming eschaton (new kingdom) of God (Zechariah 3:10).

We also wonder, given that those whom God forgets are not with him in eternity, and given that picturing a "place" absent of God is frustratingly beyond our frail human capacities, "where" will these people be; where will they really be if, as Proust sees it, even memory, sweet, bitter, God, and all, will evaporate "in time"?[417]

In short, if, as orthodox theology holds, God is, in some way, everywhere, where is "where" he is not?[418]

---

417 *In Search of Lost Time, op cit.*

418 A difficulty illustrated poignantly in *The Giver, op cit.,* when the two primary protagonists, Jonas and "The Giver," discuss how,

As one who once lived as a human being, Jesus knows this all too well. In the midst of his agony on the cross, he cried out,

> "My God, my God! Why have you forsaken me?" (Matthew 27:46; Mark 15:34. See also the first verse of Psalm 22, from which Jesus drew these words.)

At one awful point in history, God even forgot his son. In the crucible of Jesus' suffering, he was the loneliest person who has ever lived, as alone as anyone could possibly be, irredeemably apart from even whom he humanly—and divinely—was. For three horrific hours, Jesus, the God-man, became less than God and man, stripped of his humanness, wrenched from his divinity, cruelly pushed and pressed into the darkest corners of an inhuman and divinely necessitated darkness, a hell from which there was absolutely no return.[419]

---

if "love" is the ultimate memory, it would be singularly terrible to experience such "love" in the pain of absolute loneliness (195).

[419] We use the word "irredeemably" carefully here. Clearly, God redeemed Jesus in the end. Yet he first had to make him "irredeemable." Otherwise, he could not have accomplished his salvific purposes. On the one dimension of the theological complexity of this circumstance, consider how, at the Council of Chalcedon in 451, the Christian church decided that Jesus had two natures, one human, the other divine, with no admixture between the two. While we do not dispute this, we realize this leaves us with more questions than answers: who was really suffering on the cross. Nonetheless, the verse's truth remains: God deliberately and purposefully abandoned his son. See Peter Frankopan, *The Silk Roads* (New York: Albert A. Knopf, 2016).

Yet God had to forget. He had no choice. Otherwise, Jesus would not have been able to accomplish his mission. Otherwise, Jesus could not have suffered for humanity's sins. In his holiness and righteousness and, significantly, love, God had to let his son go.

So will we realize that if we have loved ones who are not with us on the other side of existence, loved ones who are not participating in our eternity, our endless experience of transformed knowing, remembrance, and remembering, it will be because they will be to us, as awful as this sounds, "untruth." The effects of them and their lives upon us will have been gathered up and subsumed into a greater picture of truth, a picture that will in no way be dependent upon what is no longer present or true, a picture that will not be contingent upon or intimately connected to earthly pasts. The meaning they have exercised in our lives will now be part of a larger truth, one that is, in a way we cannot in this life fully grasp, seminally and absolutely (think of *chadesh* and *kainos*) new.

The past as we have known it will be gone forever.

There will not be room for "untruth" in eternity. What was good will continue to be good forever. What was true will continue to be true forever. And what has been real will continue to be real forever. Everything else will be gone.

As the Reverend John Ames puts it in *Gilead,*

> "We fly forgotten as a dream, certainly, leaving the forgetful world behind us to

> trample and mar and misplace everything
> we have ever cared for."[420]

Once we're in truth, what is not truth will leave us and, in a singularly horrible way, we will forget it. For what is not true will be, in an achingly penetrating and conclusive way, no more.[421]

As we have seen, however, even if such observations make sense intellectually, they are highly jarring, and unbearably painful emotionally. It is highly depressing to think about people whom we loved not being with us for eternity. It is a thought that should tug at the deepest fabric of our hearts. It should tear us up. It should cause us to weep uncontrollably.

Worse, however, is that we do not yet know exactly how all this, this eternal mix of divine will and human destiny, will be. We are not fully in its context. We are not fully embedded in its vision. Etymology and theology notwithstanding, we therefore have, in this life, nowhere to turn for clarity, nowhere to turn for full understanding. So we look to the only thing we can. We look to the deepest driver of memory, the act of unreserved surrender that fuels the heart of our remembering: faith. We step into our faith, our faith in the love, goodness, hope, and faithfulness of God. We trust in God, we hope in his light (so 1 John 1:5:

---

420 Marilynne Robinson, *Gilead* (New York: Farrar, Straus and Giroux, 2004), 218.

421 This outcome runs decidedly counter to how much of popular literature of film portrays the worlds of heaven and hell. For instance, in *What Dreams May Come* (Polygram, 1998), those in heaven are very much aware of those in hell and, conversely, those in hell are aware of those who are not.

"God is light, and in him there is no darkness at all"). We trust in the light, the light of God that, as the psalmist described it, enables us "to see light" (Psalm 36:9).

Maybe one day we will know how God has orchestrated and executed all of these outcomes, but then again maybe we will not. In this life we find God's ways to be, at best, enigmatic, and at worst, outrageous. In the next life, however, because we will see God as he is, we will understand him as he is. We will be like him. We will see, we will know. And we will see and know God. God will remember us, and we will remember him, palpably and visibly, forever and ever.

So for now, we trust. We trust in the ever present, immutable, and incomprehensible counsel and memory of God.

Is this easy? On the one hand, yes: we fall into the arms of the ultimate truth, the ultimate source of life, love, and being. On the other hand, no: we still do not have all the answers we would like to have. We still struggle. We will struggle with uncertainty and incomplete knowing until the day we die.[422]

---

[422] Such thoughts find horrific compounding in James Hogg's words in his *The Private Memoirs and Confessions of a Justified Sinner* (New York: Hogg, 2013 (originally published in 1824)): "Seeing that God had from all eternity decided the fate of every individual that was to be born of woman, how vain was it in man to endeavor to save those whom their Maker had, by an unchangeable decree, doomed to destruction . . . it made the economy of the Christian world appear to me as an absolute contradiction." We think also of John Calvin, who in his *Institutes of the Christian Religion*, asserted, "As Scripture, then, clearly shows, we say that God once established by his eternal and unchangeable plan those whom he long before determined

What can we do? We remember. We remember life, we remember death. Above all, however, we remember God.

So did we earlier hear the writer of Ecclesiastes say, "Remember your creator" (12:1). And so did we previously witness Moses telling the Hebrews in the forty years they traveled through the wilderness of Sinai after eluding the pharaoh of Egypt by crossing the Red Sea, "Remember your God" (Deuteronomy 28:30). We understand that to remember God, to remember our creator is to recognize the true framework and impetus of the cosmos, the genuinely primal centering energy of who we are. It is to step into the originating power of space and time, to participate in the most fundamental vision for the universe, to enter into intimate relationship with where we and everything else are ultimately going. To remember God is to affirm that we one day will see it all, the final picture of life, the complete fullness of the hope, meaning, and memory which empower all things. It is to cast ourselves into God's all-encompassing vision of reality and truth, and daily underscore the supernal fact of the trust we hold, the trust that ensures we and our lives are not without a point. When we remember God and abide in his memory of us, we know that one day, one day unfathomably distant from the present one, we will see validation of all our desire, form, question, and intention.

---

once for all to receive into salvation, and those whom, on the other hand, he would devote to destruction." In other words, Calvin is endorsing double predestination, insisting that God freely chooses who will be saved and who will not. *Institutes of the Christian Religion,* Book Three, Chapter XXI. See also Proverbs 16:4, which we mentioned earlier, that "God has made everything for its own purpose, even the wicked for the day of destruction." How can we really know what anything means?

We will see the creation and all that has ever passed through it rendered eternally worthwhile and whole.

We also know that in remembering God we will one day see ourselves rendered worthwhile, too. As part of God's family, we will finally see our part in God's intention and plan. We will finally see how deeply we have been loved, included, and remembered. We will revel in the intimacy of God, the counsel of his ways, the affections of our creator (Psalm 25:14).

Moreover, we know that in remembering God in the present moment we one day will know, definitively know the heart of God's love. As we have seen repeatedly, in its fullest and deepest manifestation, though memory is about hope, faith, trust, wisdom, and knowing, memory is ultimately about love, our love for each other, our love for God and, most importantly, God's love for us. As love, God's eternal and undying love, memory ignites, displays, and enables enjoyment of the core principle of the cosmos, the goal of all being: to be at home with God.[423]

So does Paul say in his first letter to the Corinthians,

> "But now faith, hope, and love, abide these three; but the greatest of these is love." (1 Corinthians 13:13)

[423] And this is a home to which we do not merely "return" in the way that Edith, the protagonist of Anita Brookner's *Hotel Du Lac,* who, after rejecting a man whom she had earlier agreed to marry, wrote a telegram to a friend to say that she was "returning." It is a home to which we are coming for the very first time. Although we had been aware of it, and although we had ideas of what it might be like, we had never seen it before. It's totally new. Anita Brookner, *Hotel Du Lac* (New York: E. P. Dutton, 1984), 184.

Love, God's love, God's love in memory, the memory of divine essence, material point, and existential meaning, overcomes all.

So it is that in love, the love in which memory's hope, faith, trust, and knowing are perfectly meshed together, we come to the end of our journey. After traveling, accompanied by Beatrice, through Hell (*Inferno*) (an experience to which we referred previously) and Purgatory (*Purgatorio*) and describing everything he has seen, Dante enters the most glorious part of his trip: Heaven (*Paradiso*). Here he comes to what he believes to be the cumulative experience of existence, what we might call the beatific vision. It is here that he comes face to face with God. As he puts it so marvelously,

> "O grace abounding and allowing me to dare to fix my gaze on the Eternal Light, so deep my vision was consumed in It! I saw how it contains within its depth all things bound in a single book by love of which creation is the scattered leaves: how substance, accident, and their relation were fused in such a way that what I now describe is but a glimmer of that Light. I know I saw the universal form, the fusion of all things, for I can feel, while speaking now, my heart leapt up in joy."[424]

Dante tells us that he sees "the Eternal Light," the endless illumination which contains and "consumes" all

---

[424] *Divine Comedy,* Canto XXXIII.

things. Everything is before him. Indeed, so perfectly does he see that he now witnesses, as he puts it, the "universal form, the fusion of all things." Dante stands face to face with the person of God, the eternal light, face, and ground of all things. He witnesses the celestial expression of the earthly face of Jesus Christ. In a way he has never been able to do before, he touches the substance and being of his creator. As a result, as he says in the final lines of this canto, he experiences the "Love which moves the sun and other stars"[425] Dante touches the love out of which all has come, the love of history, the love of space and time, the love of all living and inanimate things, the love in which all memory is encountered, framed, and set free. He sees the love embodied in the heart of God, the love that is, as theologian Karl Barth often voiced it, the "Yes" of God. Dante sees, definitively, that God is saying, yes, he loves us, and that, yes, he remembers us, and that, yes he wants to enjoy us for eternity. God's "yes," God's love and memory, Dante understands, now understands fully and completely, are forever.[426]

So does Jonathan Edwards state,

> "They [the blessed] shall see every thing in God that gratifies love. They shall see in him all that love desires . . . So the saints in glory shall see God's transcendent love to them; God will make ineffable manifestations of his love to them. They shall see as much

[425] *Ibid.,* Canto 33.

[426] Karl Barth, *Church Dogmatics*, ed. G. W. Bromiley and T. F. Torrance; trans. G. W. Bromiley *et al* (London: T&T Clark, 2004).

> love in God towards them as they desire; they neither will nor can crave any more . . . when they see the boundless ocean of God's goodness and grace, they shall see it to be all theirs."[427]

Or to quote Tennyson in his "In Memoriam," after often many earthly decades of not doing so, the beloved will finally see, "The far-off divine event toward which the whole creation moves." They will see the reality of God.[428]

When God remembers us, now and in eternity, the life we live in the world today, tomorrow, and every day to its end, we live in a "yes" world, the "yes" of the memory of God.

---

427 As quoted in Carol Zaleski and Philip Zaleski, *The Book of Heaven* (Oxford: University of Oxford, 2000), 174-175. See also the closing scenes of J. R. R. Tolkien's *Lord of the Rings* trilogy, which we mentioned earlier as being indicative of the ancient penchant for placing the afterlife in the West. As the story draws to a close, Frodo, having successfully completed his mission to destroy the Ring, is escorted onto a boat which will take him to the golden land in the West. There, he will enjoy perfect and endless bliss and peace, knowing and being known forever. *Lord of the Rings, op cit.*

428 Lord Alfred Tennyson, "In Memoriam A.H.H." in *Poets of the English Language, op cit.*

ENDINGS

As we ponder where we have been in the course of this meditation, as we reflect on what we have found, we see that memory is the work of a unique nexus of phenomena and conditions. Out of memory, the memory of God, the memory of God the eternal and everlasting creator, comes the universe and everyone and everything in it. In this work of memory, this enduring work of memory and desire that births and animates the cosmos, God's love manifests itself, communicating his unending longing to love, know, and remember, and to be loved, known, and remembered in turn. Speaking out of the wisdom with which he has endowed the world, the wisdom that enables meaningful creation, life, and being, God makes his heart known. He promises intimacy, he promises fulfillment. In love, in memory, God makes hope and faith and knowing possible and complete.[429]

In this memory, this work of memory, we trust. We trust unreservedly and fearlessly in the memory of God.

[429] So it is that, as we observed much earlier, Paul calls Jesus, God's Messiah, the "wisdom of God" (1 Corinthians 1:30).

We trust that his memory of creation, love, and wisdom are forever. We trust that God's eternal memory upholds all things, all points of meaning, all paths of insight and discovery. We trust that God's memory expresses, contains, orders, and explains the full weight of reality, the full burden of the purpose of all existence and destiny.

We trust that we see everything we need to see.

We also understand the futility of memory apart from God. A song by a long ago band called Cream (featuring Eric Clapton, Jack Bruce, and Ginger Baker) tells a tale about people living in a world of pain, a world without remorse, care, or pity. In language reminiscent of the opening of the prophet Jeremiah's lament over Jerusalem in the wake of its destruction at the hands of the Babylonian king Nebuchadnezzar in 586 BCE (the exile to which we referred earlier), the song mourns a lost civilization. Its lyrics bewail the fate of a land, a land that although it was once grand, one of the great epochs of history, is now a land that is irrecoverably gone, a kingdom that will never return. Its demise is permanent. All who lived in it mean nothing.[430]

No one will ever know this world again.

Cormac McCarthy's *The Road* tells the story of a boy and his father who wander through a land devastated by what appears to be some form of nuclear holocaust. It is a barbarous land, one torn by disorder and lawlessness, a world

---

[430] Cream, "World of Pain," 1967. As Jeremiah voices the words, "How lonely sits the city that was full of people! She has become like a widow who as once great among the nations! She who was a princess among the provinces has become a forced laborer. She weeps bitterly in the night and her tears on her cheeks; she has none to comfort her among all her lovers" (Lamentations 1:1-2).

with no rules, structure, forgiveness, or commiseration. It is every person for him or herself. No one cares about anyone else. Vigilantes and gangs control the roads, dealing brutally and harshly with anyone who dares use them, and killing and abuse are reduced to triviality and banality. All human glory is gone. Any memory of the world which has been lost is gone, too. It's no more than a nuance of the cortex.[431]

It is a world which God never knew.

Although we can still remember without God, though we can still construct meaningful lives without remembering our creator, we will remember things as the memory of the world of *The Road.* While we may hold our memories for weeks, months, years, even our entire lives, once we leave this world, we will never see them again. We will never again know their warmth, meaning, and vitality. We will cherish them, we will love them, yet in the end we will lose them.

We'll lose ourselves, too. Everything will go dark. All neurons will shut down, every synapse will stop. Forever.

And we will wonder why.

In God's memory, in the eternal love of God's memory, its knowing, faithfulness, and hope, however, we see that even our most distant memories will one day be present again. We will not forget them. Nor will they forget us. If they are good memories, they will last forever, enhanced and glorified; if they are bad memories, they will be gone, rendered in some mysterious way a part of something far more wondrous. Their pain is over, their trouble is gone. If they have contributed to human good, they will be retained, glorified and, in a way difficult to understand, made new. If they have not, they will vanish, forever buried in the eternal

---

[431] Cormac McCarthy, *The Road* (New York: Vintage, 2007).

newness of the memory, the memory of the love, hope, knowledge, and wisdom of God.

Think again about space and time. As we observed, time and space, working together to encapsulate and express existence, are essential for memory. Without them, memory could not be. For memory to be, things must be born, and things must die. Space must shift, energy must be expended, and time must move. Life must happen, and life must not. But life must continue, too.[432]

Now think about who we are, who we are in ourselves, and who we are in God. Think about our creation in the image of God, think about our being spiritual creatures, and think about how our lives will end. Think about memory in a fallen world. Think about a loving God and endless darkness. Can we put all of these, space, time, life, love, and darkness in perfect balance? No, we cannot. But we see that memory, God's memory, is essential to enabling us to live through their connections with realism, purpose, and hope. We see that not only does God's memory hold everything about life together, but that it is God's memory that gives life its definitive point. It is God's memory that enables life's significance. It is God's memory that captures and grants meaning to the angst, subjectivity, and joy of physical

---

[432] In *The Vital Question: Energy, Evolution, and the Origins of the Complex Life* (New York: W.W. Norton & Co., 2015), author Nick Lane suggests that life began when hot water from the ocean floor "spewed" through the enormous rocks that dotted the bottom of the sea. It was the interaction of the water with the elements in these rocks that produced the molecules necessary to birth life. In other words, though once life did not "happen," now it did. Yet as the world continued to evolve, this "life" eventually ebbed into a new form. Life goes on, but it does not.

existence. Baffling and frustrating though we may find life to be, we see that God's memory, the memory of which Paul, John, and countless other prophets and sages speak so powerfully, provides its ultimate and lasting resolution. God's memory holds all.

Now think about love. Realize that memory is ultimately about love. Without love, does memory have a point? We remember because we love, and we love because we remember. Without love, although we will still exercise practical memory, coping with life as best we can, we will not know life's essence. We will not know life's fullest meaning. Why? Without love, God's remembering love that washes across every point of the cosmos, everything that we remember, everything that we nourish and treasure, and everything that we recollect and appreciate about this earthly existence means little. It is as meaningless as the world out of which it comes. Now wonderful enough, one day, one day not, in the big picture, so very far away, it will vanish. One day, memory will vanish, lost in an abyss of impenetrable nothingness beyond comprehension. Its glory, magnificent in its place, but *only* in its place, will be gone.

If God's love is not present, if God's love is not coursing through the fabric of the cosmos, memory loses all point. And so do we.

Finally, think about trust. Think about trusting in memory, trusting in the loving memory of God. Realize that although we still do not have answers to some extremely difficult questions about memory, we can forgo them, at least for now. We can set our reservations aside and trust in the goodness of the memory of God. We can trust in who God is. We can trust in God's love, we can trust in God's wisdom, we can trust in God's hope and faithfulness. We can trust that he has made himself known, that we can know him, and that he can know us. We can trust that we are remembered.

As a result, we can trust that our present memory of God and his of us is sufficient for us to make sense of this existence, sufficient to bring meaning to some of the patently awful and wholly immeasurable bedevilments we face each and every day. We can trust in the promise of the coming perfect, we can trust in the fact of our impending union with God. We can trust in that day when we will "know fully" just as we are "fully known," that day when we will see God "just as he is." We can trust that, for now, the promise and certainty of an eternal future of memory, an eternal future of memory that will forever eclipse the present moment, are enough.

In this is our walk of memory. In this is our walk of mnemonic trust. Because we believe in memory, God's memory, because we believe that God loves us, knows us, and remembers us, we have faith. We have faith in our memory of God today, we have faith in our memory of God tomorrow. We have faith in our memory of God beyond the grave. We believe that memory, God's memory, is forever. We believe that without God's memory, we would not be. We believe that in God's memory, we will be forever.

We believe that in God's memory we will never be unknown.

ABOUT THE AUTHOR

William E. Marsh has taught theology, philosophy, and world history to high school, college, and graduate students for over thirty years. Memory as Life, Life as Memory: The Mystery of Memory is his fifth book.

Printed in the United States
By Bookmasters